Medieval Naval Warfare, 1000–1500

How were medieval navies organised, and how did powerful rulers use them? *Medieval Naval Warfare, 1000–1500* provides a wealth of information about the strategy and tactics of these early fleets and the extent to which the possibilities of sea power were understood and exploited.

This fascinating account brings vividly to life the dangers and difficulties of medieval seafaring. In particular, it reveals the exploits of the Italian city states, England and France, and examines:

- why fighting occurred at sea
- how battles were fought
- the logistical back up needed to maintain a fleet
- naval battles from the Mediterranean to the North Sea.

With accompanying maps and illustrations, this much needed account will appeal to students of military history, medievalists and the general reader alike.

Susan Rose is Senior Lecturer in the Department of History at University at Roehampton Surrey. She is also author of *The Navy of the Lancastrian Kings* (1982).

Warfare and History
General Editor
Jeremy Black
Professor of History, University of Exeter

Medieval Naval Warfare
1000–1500

Susan Rose

London and New York

First published in 2002
by Routledge
2 Park Square, Milton Park, Abingdon, Oxon, OX14 4RN

Simultaneously published in the USA and Canada
by Routledge
270 Madision Ave, New York, NY 10016

Routledge is an imprint of the Taylor & Francis Group

© 2002 Susan Rose

Typeset in Bembo by HWA Text and Data Management, Tunbridge Wells

British Library Cataloguing in Publication Data
A catalogue record for this book is available from the British Library

Library of Congress Cataloging in Publication Data
Rose, Susan, 1938–
    Medieval naval warfare, 1000–1500 / Susan Rose.
       p. cm. – (Warfare and History)
    Includes bibliographical references and index
       1. Naval art and science–History–To 1500.   2. Naval history.   3. Europe–History,
    Naval.   I. Title.   II. Series

V43.R66 2001
359´.0094´0902–dc21   2001041987

ISBN 0–415–23976–1 (hbk)
ISBN 0–415–23977–X (pbk)

For David, Bernard, Philip and Dinah

Contents

List of illustrations

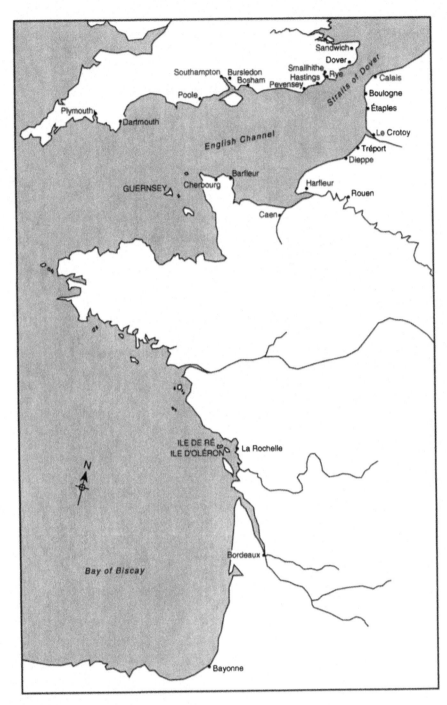

Map 1 The English Channel and Western approaches

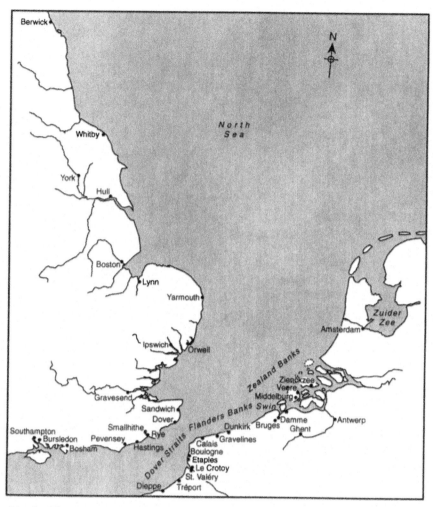

Map 2   The English Channel and the North Sea

Map 3 The Mediterranean Sea

Preface

In the period with which this book deals, 1000–1500 AD, the peoples of Western Europe had little if any contact with those of both the Far East and the Americas. As every schoolboy used to know, Columbus did not sail the 'ocean blue' until 1492 while da Gama did not reach India and the port of Calicut by the Cape route until 1498. On the east coast of the Americas there were no indigenous craft capable of a long sea voyage and the use of watercraft in warfare was confined to the transport of warriors from one island to the next on raiding expeditions. In the East, there were large and highly successful ships in the service of the Emperor of China but no interactions between Chinese and western sailors. Even the mainly Arab trading vessels of the Persian Gulf, Red Sea and Indian Ocean were little known to Mediterranean seafarers from the Christian states. The infamous Crusader Baron Raymond de Chatillon in the late twelfth century is one of the few medieval Europeans who certainly attempted to use ships on the Red Sea. It therefore seems justifiable for this work to concentrate on events in the Mediterranean, the Black Sea, the so-called Western approaches and the North Sea. To most European sailors, even at the end of our period, the maritime world of which they had knowledge, was that shown on Ptolemy's world map from his *Cosmographia* with no hint of the existence of the Pacific Ocean or the Americas and a landlocked Indian Ocean. The routes which they travelled, the ports where they sought shelter, the enemies whom they feared, were all to be found in the familiar waters of the seas stretching from Iceland in the North to the coasts of North Africa in the South. Stories of the East were avidly read but it is doubtful if the fantastic voyages of Sir John Mandeville were clearly differentiated from the more soundly based stories of Marco Polo.[1]

Any discussion of naval warfare must necessarily take some account of the construction and design of the ships in use at the time. This book, however, is not primarily concerned with this aspect of maritime history. Both the documentary and archaeological evidence for the details of the design of medieval ships in Western Europe can be found in the works of, among others Ian Friel, Gillian Hutchinson and Sean McGrail.[2] Our chief concern here is the way in which ships and mariners were drawn into the service of rulers, to serve their ends in war. This involves an attempt not only to investigate the strategy and tactics used in any battle but also to try and understand the degree to which the possibilities of seapower were understood and exploited. This concern has also been informed by an attempt to bear in mind the limitations imposed on mariners by the nature of the element in which they operate. Ships at sea, even in coastal waters, are always subject to the forces of wind, tide and current. These forces may limit the way in which ships can operate quite as much as their design.

I have in the course of writing this book received much help and encouragement both from fellow historians and from the staff in libraries and archives. I would like to thank particularly my former supervisor Dr Alwyn Ruddock, who first suggested that I should work on Henry V's navy, and Professor Nicholas Rodger who has been an inspiration to all writers on naval history. Professor Jeremy Black sowed the seed which resulted in this book by suggesting a topic for a paper read to the Anglo-American conference in 1997. My colleagues at the University of Surrey Roehampton have been a source of intellectual stimulation and encouragement and also most generously allowed me a semester's study leave in which to write and pursue research in Venice. The staff in the Reading Rooms in the old Public Record Office in Chancery Lane were a great source of encouragement and help in the early stages of my research, as also at a later stage were the staff of the British Library, the Biblioteca Marciana and the Archivio di Stato in Venice. I also owe a great deal to all those who have sailed with me on expeditions to the Western Isles, in the Channel and in the Mediterranean thus allowing me to understand much more about the possibilities and difficulties faced by those who 'go down to the sea in ships'. Lastly my husband and my children have offered endless support and encouragement without which this project would never have been finished.

Susan Rose, London, 2001

Notes

1 The extent of Marco Polo's travels has been disputed but it is generally accepted that his writing contains much genuine information about the East.

2 I. Friel, *The Good Ship: Ships, Shipbuilding and Technology in England 1200–1500*, London, British Museum Press, 1995. G. Hutchinson, *Medieval Ships and Shipping*, London, Leicester University Press, 1994. S. McGrail, *Ancient Boats in North-West Europe: The Archaeology of Water Transport to AD 1500*, London and New York, Longman, second edition, 1998.

Introduction

To modern historians, the phrase 'naval warfare' conjures up a picture of a fleet action or of patrols, and blockades. We may think of ships of the line in the days of Nelson, sailing majestically out of harbour or bearing down on the enemy at Trafalgar, or in more recent times, of minesweepers in the Channel on a raw January day, or of vessels bristling with aerials and missile launchers. Despite their evident differences all these vessels are part of an organised service with clear lines of command, dedicated personnel and the support of offices, dockyards, and the government of the day. The distinction between naval vessels and the merchant marine is clear. No modern trading vessel, even if requisitioned as a transport, in any way resembles a warship. None of these assumptions hold good for the period with which we are concerned, c.1000–c.1500. For the greater part of our period there was little if any structural difference between ships primarily engaged in warlike activities and those engaged in trade.[1] Individual ships could and did perform both functions at various times during their career, while if we consider ship types in general, it is hard to isolate any features that belonged exclusively to one category or the other. In the same way the commanders and crews of ships would seldom have been able to describe themselves as members of an organised service and the support from dockyards and administrators would often be at best haphazard and intermittent. It is even perhaps unsafe to say that ships engaged in aggressive activities were always clearly acting with the knowledge of a ruler. The distinction between outright piracy and the actions of privateers, conveniently described by the phrase *'guerre de course'* was blurred and might change according to circumstances.[2] Certainly the same individual might be a respected renowned naval leader at one point in his career and the leader of at least quasi-piratical raids at another.

The major concern here, therefore, is activity at sea which seems to have as its primary purpose the promotion of the interests of a state or a ruler and which usually involved some kind of conflict between ships. Not all of these actions included vessels in the ownership or acting under the orders of a ruler but all had some element of the public interest as that was understood at the time. A major difficulty for all states in our period is that while an army could be conjured from the resources of the community with relatively little preparation this was not the case for armed ships. Even a band of peasants armed with no more than the hatchets and sickles used in their normal occupations could give some sort of an account of themselves in a fight. A ship cannot put to sea, let alone fight, without at least the basis of a skilled crew and sufficient supplies. Moreover wooden ships cannot be stored until required whether in or out of the water. They need continual maintenance and repairs, while canvas sails and hemp cordage and other supplies deteriorate whether used or not. All this implies not only the expenditure of money but also the existence of some sort of permanent office or bureaucracy. Neither of these was easy for medieval states to supply on a regular basis, although they were not unaware of these difficulties. Sir John Fortescue, a fifteenth century English judge and writer on politics, pointed out that ideally 'the king always keeps some great and mighty vessels for the defeat of an army when any shall be made against him upon the sea; for then it shall be too late to have such vessels made'.[3] The relative success with which medieval rulers tackled the problems of naval logistics will therefore be discussed. The aim will be to look at how states coped with the problems of having ships of war ready to go to sea. The details of ship design and construction which have been the subject of specialist works will not be discussed.

It is also necessary to keep in mind the problems that face all seafarers at any period; the problems of navigation, ship-handling and seamanship. Tides and currents affected all ships and we should also not forget the constraints imposed especially on a ship powered by sails by the vagaries of the wind and on a ship powered by oars by the limits of human strength and endurance. At least as important is also the configuration of the coastline, straits and islands, sandbanks and shallows, all of which had great strategic importance and considerable influence on the location and even the outcome, on occasion, of battles fought at sea. Even if part of the common experience of much of medieval mankind, warfare brought danger and at times disaster. At sea, where the natural dangers were so much greater, a battle was an even more hazardous undertaking. An unknown poet graphically described a storm and shipwreck:

> ...the sky grew dark, the wind blew loud,
> And angry grew the sea.

> The anchor broke, the topmast split,
> Twas such a deadly storm.
> The waves came over the broken ship
> Till all her sides were torn.[4]

It is as well to remember these possibilities when reading the often laconic accounts in chronicles such as, 'then when our men rowed on past Askelon to investigate whatever they might find, they discovered ten other ships ... coming towards them. They took those ships together with much war equipment ...'.[5] Boarding and taking another vessel at sea was never wholly without danger either to the crews or to the ships involved. Casualties were often very high and there is at least some evidence to suggest that battle might be declined if the odds seemed too great.[6] In the same way possession of the weather gauge (that is being the windward ship), or a favourable wind, a 'good wind' is the phrase used by medieval chroniclers, could be the decisive factor in an action, especially in northern waters.

The evidence for the tactics pursued in sea battles in the medieval period is, however, not always easy to assess. Most comes from chronicles, the great majority of which were written by men with little experience of the sea or nautical affairs. There is often a somewhat suspicious similarity in the detail of incidents recorded as occurring at quite different times and in different circumstances. There is for example the incident in which a heroic individual brings down the sails of an enemy ship with one mighty blow to the halyard. This is described as happening at the battle of Dover in 1217 and during the battle of Winchelsea in 1352.[7] Does this reflect reality or is it an example of a standardised, conventional sea battle event? In many cases, chronicles whether semi-official or kept by clerics, content themselves with a bald statement of the outcome of a battle, often stating only the number of ships 'taken' conveying no idea of how this was achieved. Less formal records, letters or eye witness accounts, come only from the end of our period.[8] More informative than most seem to be records kept by Venetians, whether the newsletters sent by the factors in Bruges to their head offices in the Republic,[9] or the accounts of galley commanders like Domenico Malipiero.[10] Official documents from royal and state archives can provide details of the repair or building of ships and of the associated costs, of the gathering of fleets, of the musters of crews. English archives relating to such matters are relatively copious from the middle of the fourteenth century to the middle of the fifteenth century. They then become more dispersed and scanty until the accession of Henry VII.[11] In France, there are some good records for the *Clos des Galées* but these cease in 1418 when the yard and galley sheds were burnt when the English took Rouen.[12] There are accounts relating to the building or repair of galleys in the archives of Aragon and in those of the house of Anjou[13] which are dispersed in both Italy and France. The records of Genoa and Venice contain a great deal of material on maritime matters but in neither city are what we would call 'naval' matters separated from those concerned with trading ships and voyages at this period. None of these records has much if anything to say directly about the course of an action, though the preoccupations of commanders are often there by implication.

The evidence from pictures and illustrations is similarly often hard to interpret. Specialists in ship construction have long wrestled to make sense of the features they discern in the representations in MS illuminations, paintings, carvings and sculptures, and coins and seals.[14] Those which show battles in progress can be of great beauty, as for example those in an illustrated version of Froissart's Chronicle in the *Bibliothèque Nationale* in Paris, but convey little about the nature of war at sea.[15] Archaeological evidence mostly from underwater sites is now much more copious than in the recent past but while it can provide highly useful details of ship construction, it is less illuminating on ship use.[16]

Despite these difficulties, an attempt will be made here to bring together the consideration of the evidence that does exist with the unchanging requirements of seafaring in order to provide a plausible account of naval warfare in medieval days in the west both in the Mediterranean and in northern waters.

Notes

1 The same point is made strongly by N.A.M. Rodger, *The Safeguard of the Sea: A Naval History of Great Britain, Vol. 1, 660–1649*, London, HarperCollins, 1997, p. xxv.

2 J.F. Guilmartin, *Gunpowder and Galleys: Changing Technology and Mediterranean Warfare at Sea in the Sixteenth Century*, Cambridge, Cambridge University Press, 1974, p. 23, feels this was also true in the sixteenth century.

3 Sir J. Fortescue, *The Governance of England* (ed. S. Lockwood), Cambridge, Cambridge University Press, 1997, p. 97.

4 *Collins Albatross Book of Verse* (ed. L. Untermeyer), London and Glasgow, Collins, 1933, p. 36.

5 *A History of the Expedition to Jerusalem 1095–1127* (trans. F.R. Ryan), Knoxville, University of Tennessee Press, 1969, p. 244–5.

6 See below p. 91; the Duke of Exeter refused to close with the Earl of Warwick in 1460.

7 J.B. Hattendorf *et al.*, *British Naval Documents 1204–1960*, London, Scolar Press for the Navy Records Society, 1982, 9, p. 19 and 15, p. 24–5. The accounts come from the chronicles of Matthew Paris and Froissart respectively.

8 Some naval incidents are described in letters in the Paston Collection. The battle of Zonchio in 1499 is also described by a participant, Domenico Malipiero.

9 The chronicle of Antonio Morosini contains much material from these reports.

10 *Dannali Veneti dal anno 1457 al 1500 del Senatore Domenico Malipiero* (ed. F. Longo), Florence, 1843, vol. I, pp. 50 et seq.

11 The English accounts relating to shipbuilding and repairs by the Crown are found at first in the Pipe Rolls; after 1344 under a separate heading, 'the King's ships'. From 1377–1452, the accounts of the Keeper of the King's ships are found on the Lord Treasurer's Remembrancer's Rolls of Foreign Accounts. Records relating to the use of ships can also be found widely dispersed in the Patent and Close Rolls. See Chapter 1, p. 17.

12 These have been published by A. Merlin-Chazelas, *Documents Rélatifs au Clos des Galées de Rouen et aux Armées de Mer du Roi de France de 1293 à 1418*, Collection de documents inédits sur l'histoire de France; serie in. 8, vols 11 and 12, section de philologie et d'histoire jusqu'á 1610, Paris, Bibliothèque Nationale, 1977–8.

13 The whereabouts of the Angevin archives are discussed in J. Mazzolini, 'Les archives des Angevins de Naples', in I. Bonnot *et al.*, *Marseille et ses Rois*, Aix en Provence, 1989. An account for building a galley in 1273 can be found in N.M.H. Fourquin, 'A medieval shipbuilding estimate (c.1273)', *The Mariner's Mirror*, 85, 1999, pp. 20–9. Accounts for the building of galleys by order of Charles of Anjou can also be found in G. del Giudice (ed.) *Alcuni Documenti Inediti di Carlo I d'Angoio in Materia Marinara*, Naples, 1871, p. 25, and in R. Filangieri (ed.) *I*

registri della cancelleria angoina, Naples, 1950–81, vol. 12, pp. 126–9. Aragonese galley accounts have been published in D.P. de Bofarull y Mascaró, *Coleccion de documentos ineditos del archivo general de la corona de Aragon,* Barcelona, 1850, vol. VI, pp. 320–40

14 I. Friel in *The Good Ship: Ships, Shipbuilding and Technology in England 1200–1520*, London, British Museum Press, 1995, makes much use of illustrations from such sources all through his very thorough survey of these topics.

15 Bibliothèque Nationale, Paris, MS Français 2643, one illustration from this MS is reproduced in colour in J.R. Hill (ed.) *The Oxford Illustrated History of the Royal Navy*, Oxford, Oxford University Press, 1995, facing p. 32.

16 Important underwater and landbased excavations include those undertaken at Roskilde, (the Skudelev ships), in the Hamble river (Henry V's *Gracedieu*), and on various sites after the draining of the Zuider Zee.

CHAPTER ONE

Dockyards and administration: the logistics of medieval fleets

Wooden ships are graceful, beautiful objects. The first sight of the Viking ships preserved in the Oslo museum is breathtaking. The little fifteenth century *ex-voto* model from Portugal, now in the Prins Hendrik museum in Rotterdam, may be slightly battered but even so the form of the hull is full and satisfying. Wooden ships, however, are also complex to build, requiring many skilled craftsmen, and are highly perishable especially when afloat. No fleet, no vessel could stay long in a seaworthy condition in our period without the support of some form of repair slip or dock. To build ships required not only access to the necessary raw materials, suitable timber, hemp for cordage and sails, iron for nails and other fittings, but also a pool of workmen with experience in the craft of the shipwright. Beyond this there was also a need for ancillary supplies and tradesmen. Galleys sometimes with crews of well over 100 men needed large quantities of food and drink especially *biscotti*, a form of hard baked bread which supplied many of the calories needed by men expected to row for long periods. Any ship, but especially one preparing for war at sea, needed arms for its protection and for attack. How did medieval states deal with these problems? Did rulers largely depend on the resources established by the maritime trading community or did something approaching the modern concept of a naval dockyard emerge by the end of our period?

The Mediterranean

Since the Mediterranean had known extensive seaborne commerce and naval warfare on a fairly large scale both in ancient times and in the period before AD 1000, it is not surprising that the idea of a centrally provided facility for the building and maintenance of ships mainly intended for war, was well accepted during our period. The derivation of the term 'arsenal', (usually in this region meaning shipyard rather than munitions or arms store) from the Arabic *dar al-sina'a* meaning 'house of work' is widely accepted. It is also often suggested that the earliest dockyards originated in the areas conquered

6

by the Arabs in the seventh century. More probably the Byzantine facilities at Clysma and Alexandria were taken over by their Arab conquerors but the term they used spread throughout the area because of the power of their navy at this period. Certainly in papyrus letters from this date and into the ninth century there are many references to some sort of docking facilities available to ships in many ports on the Egyptian and Syrian coasts. Damietta was fortified and the anchorages at Acre and Tyre were protected by chains.[1]

There were also, of course, dockyards or ship building and repair facilities in the later Byzantine Empire particularly in the immediate vicinity of Constantinople itself. Very little is known about their organisation or their working methods. Chroniclers are not usually interested in this kind of administrative information and more mundane institutional sources have not survived. By the late eleventh century the Byzantine authorities seem to have relied largely on the Venetians to provide the naval element in their forces. Lewis and Runyan attribute much of the later failure of the Greeks to maintain their hold on the Empire in the face of the expanding power of the Latin West to their reliance on Italian mercenary ships and crews.[2] We should, however, be careful of overstating the extent of the decline of Greek seafaring skills. Michael Paleologus rebuilt and fortified the dockyard at Kondoskalion after the restoration of the Greek Empire. Even if the navy of the Empire was of little strategic importance compared with its land forces in the period before the fall of Constantinople, the shipyards and the shipwrights in the neighbourhood of the city were subsequently of great value to the victorious Ottomans. It is these yards and these skilled workmen who are usually credited with providing the expertise which allowed the emergence of the Sultan as a major player in war at sea by the 1470s. Bayazid I had, however, begun the building of dockyard facilities for the Ottoman fleet at Gallipoli in 1390, which by 1397 could provide a safe anchorage for about 60 ships with adjoining storehouses. After the fall of Constantinople, Mahomet II probably took over the former Genoese galley repair yard on the Golden Horn which was developed in the sixteenth century into the major Ottoman naval base.[3] The only important shipbuilding facility established by a Muslim ruler in the period of the Crusades is that built in the early thirteenth century by Ala al-Din Kayqubad in Alanya on the south-west coast of Anatolia. This seems to have had facilities for at least five galleys with ship-sheds and a fortified entrance.[4]

We are on much firmer ground if we consider the way in which the Italian city states, particularly Venice, dealt with these problems. In the early fourteenth century Dante had used a vivid picture of shipwrights working in the Arsenale of Venice, as the official base of the Venetian State fleet was known, as a simile for the crowded lower depths of Hell.[5] By the seventeenth century it was one of the best known and most admired industrial enterprises in Europe exciting the wonder of visitors and the envy of rulers, described as 'the most worthy [of] notice of all that is in Venice,' by an English observer in 1620.[6] Its precise origins are obscure; a date as early as 1104 has been rejected by Concina.[7] Martino da Canal, in his chronicle written between 1262–75, links the first intervention by the Venetian state in shipbuilding with the contract concluded by the republic with would-be crusaders in 1204. Concina found mention of an *'arsana'* at Venice in 1206 but it is clear that for much of the thirteenth century the building of all types of ships took place in many small yards all over the city. The building of galleys in particular was not confined to a state-run yard. By the end of the century, however, when Venice was engaged in a bitter naval war with Genoa, the need to build and equip large numbers of vessels suitable for use in war was urgent. There were also difficulties in ensuring adequate supplies of timber of the right type and quality, hemp for cordage and sailcloth. In 1302 the Arsenale was placed on a much firmer footing by the Doge and Council with a monopoly of the building of galleys. It was closely associated with the neighbouring Tana, a ropewalk dedicated to supplying the needs of the galleys built in the Arsenale. A 'house of canvas' a sail loft where canvas was also made followed between 1304–7. At this date it was not, of course, the complex organisation that so impressed its later visitors but it had a dedicated skilled workforce the *Arsenalotti*, who lived in the area immediately surrounding the Arsenale itself and thus formed a distinct elite group among the artisans of Venice. In the early fourteenth century c.1325, the original basin of the *Darsena Arsenale Vecchio* was linked to the much more extensive, newly built *Darsena Arsenale Nuovo*. This could accommodate a large number of galleys either being built or refitted. It was planned that at least 25 should be kept ready to put to sea. In the immediate aftermath of the loss of Negroponte in 1470, when the Venetians were very alarmed by the number of ships that the Turks could put to sea, the Arsenale was again enlarged. The *Darsena Nuovissima* was built with a full range of covered berths and auxiliary buildings.[8] These included armouries, foundries and powder mills for explosives. The whole complex was surrounded by walls while the entrance from the Bacino di San Marco along the Rio dell Arsenale, was guarded and adorned by two towers bearing the Lion of St Mark built in 1460 in the latest Renaissance style.[9] The Tana was outside the walls, as were the *Forni Pubblici* where the essential *biscotti* were baked, but the whole quarter of the *Arsenalotti* was almost, by the end of the fifteenth century, a city of its own. On the plan of Venice engraved by Jacopo Barbari in 1500, the Arsenale is a prominent and unmistakable feature.

As well as controlling the building of galleys, whether intended for war or for trade, as a state monopoly, the *Serenissima* as the Venetian republic was known, was also aware of the need to ensure constant supplies of the raw materials needed in the shipyards. Timber had always come for both the communal and private boatyards from the so-called 'imperial' (communal) forests in Istria and Dalmatia. In 1464 the Senate set up the *Provveditori sopra le legne e boschi* whose duty was to ensure the supply of timber, especially oak, for the Arsenale. Certain forests were reserved for its use especially near Trevigno. Later on in the sixteenth century this was further developed with the specialist cultivation of trees to produce knees, the shaped curved timbers needed for the frames to support deck timbers. In the same way, at the end of the fifteenth century, the government of Venice intervened to control the supply of hemp for the Tana. This had largely been grown around Bologna but in 1476 Michele di Budrio was lured from Bologna to teach the inhabitants of Montagnana on the Venetian *terra firma* the best way to grow the crop. The bulk of this, once the cultivation was established, was then destined for the workshops of the Tana.[10]

Apart from the extensive facilities in Venice itself the republic also established repair yards, supply depots and even shipbuilding yards in its colonies in the Adriatic and eastern Mediterranean. All were generally known as 'arsenale' even if on a much smaller scale. The most important was that at Candia which was capable of building galleys from scratch and which had increasing importance in the fifteenth century in the face of the growing threat of Turkish seapower. The others including those at Corfu, Zante, Zara and Retimo held supplies and could perform repairs but little is known of the detail of their organisation. In the same way there are references to facilities known by some variant of 'arsenal', (*arsene, drassanes, tarsianatus, tersana*) in many other Mediterranean ports. In some the area formerly occupied by the arsenal is known and there are occasionally some surviving remains of the buildings. Accounts relating to the building of galleys and other ships, usually for the ruler concerned, can also be found. It is, however, very hard to get any clear picture of the operation of these shipyards over a period of time or the nature of their workforce. It is probably the case that, given the perishable nature of wooden ships, most ports of any size had facilities of some sort for the repair and even the building of ships. War fleets often benefited from these facilities or rulers established state dockyards in much the same part of the port. There were certainly yards of this kind in Sicily, at Palermo and Messina. That at Messina which may have had as many as ten galley sheds, was used by Charles of Anjou in the later thirteenth century when he pursued an active policy of galley building both here and at Marseille.[11] In the western Mediterranean both Pisa and Genoa, great rivals for the domination of the trade routes of the area, also had shipyards described as arsenals. In Pisa some sort of communal facility seems to have existed. The earliest mention of a '*tersana*' dates from 1200 with officials from the *Opera della Tersana* in charge of the yard and the building of galleys. Later in the same century a wall was built around the yard with a tower and a chapel, but by 1325 when Pisa had not only been decisively defeated by the Genoese at the battle of Meloria (1284) but had also lost its position in Sardinia, their naval power (and the arsenal) was in decline. The survival of some fragments of the wall is probably due to the use made of Pisan naval expertise by the Florentines in the fifteenth century.[12] The galley sheds drawn in 1685 by

Edward Dummer, an English visitor to the newly-renamed Grand Duchy of Tuscany, give some idea of the extent of these later facilities.[13]

More is known about the situation in Genoa. As Lane has pointed out, however, the attitudes of the two most important maritime states, Venice and Genoa, to the operation of galleys were fundamentally different. In Genoa the galleys were owned 'by the managers of their mercantile voyages' and hired by the government when needed for naval expeditions, while in Venice the galleys were owned by the state and 'rented for mercantile uses when they were not needed for war'.[14] The same differences seem to have applied to the operation of a state run arsenal or dockyard. We have already seen the degree to which the Venetian authorities saw it as their duty to set up and manage the building and supply of galleys and the supply of the necessary raw materials. In Genoa there are early references to shipbuilding at Sarzano outside the first city walls[15] and by Caffaro to 'scarii' on the shore of the bay. These may have been slips for building ships or even wharves for landing goods. These were, however, private activities with the comune being involved only in the building of the Molo to provide more shelter for ships at the eastern end of the bay. Near the Molo the comune also built the Loggia Sancti Marci where all galley arrivals were recorded. Within the arm of the Molo the darsena davanti S. Marco was set up around 1276, but this was a small enclosed anchorage not a shipyard nor did it have any association with war galleys. Shortly afterwards, at the other end of the bay at Porta dei Vacca another darsena was established largely for the use of wine ships. Adjacent to this, by the end of the fifteenth century, was an area known as the Arsenale which did include storehouses for marine stores and which by the end of the sixteenth century had moved on to build galleys for the state. It is this darsena which can be seen protected by a wall and towers on the view of Genoa drawn by Dummer who, as we have seen, had earlier visited Pisa.[16] At our period, however, in the opinion of Luciana Gatti the Arsenale was 'a mere physical space not an organisation'.[17] Ships were built in Genoa and all along the Ligurian coast especially at Savona, Sestri Levante and Sampierdarena but by private individuals not by the state.

In the territories of Aragon, Catalonia and Majorca, the earliest mention of an arsenal dates from 1149 found in a charter of Tortosa. In Majorca some sort of shipyard existed from Moorish times, as was also the case in many of the ports on the Andalusian coast.[18] In 1348, the governor of the island proposed to Peter III the building of a shipyard with covered berths for twenty galleys but lack of funds ensured that no progress was made with this plan.[19] The centre of naval and maritime activity in our period was undoubtedly the city of Barcelona. The arsenal there first appears in a document in 1243. In 1328 the custom dues from trade with the Mamluks of Egypt were assigned to the support of this facility. This implies a degree of support by the crown but later references give the impression that the shipyard was a joint enterprise between the crown and the city authorities. It is certainly the case that it had no monopoly over ship construction. Galleys and other vessels, which might be used for war, were built all along the coast wherever there was a suitable harbour at places like Blanes and San Feliu. The fifteenth century archives of the crown of Aragon contain three volumes of galley inventories from 1421–71 which give full details of the value and nature of the vessels and their equipment. These galleys were valued when on loan by the *General de Cathalunya* to various citizens of Barcelona. It was not unusual for state owned vessels to be hired to merchants at this period but the process does imply that there was also a continuing state involvement in some form of galley base where these vessels could be prepared to go to sea and where supplies could be stored.[20]

From Valencia there is some evidence of co-operation between the royal and civic authorities in the provision of port and dockyard facilities for ships used in a war-like manner. An arsenal had first been established outside the town walls at Villanova del Grau in 1284 but no permanent squadron of royal ships was based there. Galleys prepared for war were sought in time of need, usually being merchant galleys with increased numbers of armed men on board. These galleys were financed by the city and the *generalidad* acting in concert.[21] This method of providing for the defence of the city and its commerce, most often from the activities of corsairs and pirates changed somewhat in the fifteenth century. The *bailo* granted licences to shipmasters from Valencia and nearby ports to pursue pirates but between 1456–60 the city owned a galley of its own for the same purposes.[22] We must suppose that this galley was kept in repair and supplied with the necessary munitions and other stores at the public expense. This would not require, however, separate facilities from those used by trading ships and galleys.

It seems therefore that while the term arsenal, in its various linguistic variations, was widely used in the Mediterranean during the period 1000–1500 it did not always signify the same kind of establishment. Its use in Venice for the state shipyards and all their ancillary functions has perhaps created the impression that other maritime powers in the same region possessed similar facilities albeit on a smaller scale. It is clear that some rulers, whether of city states or kingdoms, usually at times of particular need, did undertake shipbuilding and organise supply and repair bases. None of these bases, however, before the sixteenth century can be shown to have had a long separate existence. If an enclosed fortified anchorage was created it was often used as much by merchant ships as state warships. The repair slips and chandlery storehouses which any port needed at this time could be pressed into the service of warships with little difficulty. The degree of control exercised by the *Serenissima* over the building and supply of its galley fleets was perhaps more extraordinary before 1500 than in the sixteenth and seventeenth centuries.

The Channel and Atlantic waters

In more northern waters the evidence for royal dockyards which lasted for more than brief periods is also patchy and often unsatisfactory. If we consider the main maritime states of this region, England and France, it is clear that their rulers did at various periods control quite large groups of ships. It is not, however, always equally plain how these ships were built, or came into royal ownership, in the first place and were then maintained and supplied with war *matériel* and victuals. More is known about the details of administration, the names of officials and mechanisms of payment than about the organisation of dockyards.[23]

In England, Henry II probably owned at least one ship sometimes described as an *esnecca*, and certainly employed a certain Alan Trenchemer as the commander of ships in the royal service on more than one occasion. The payments listed in the Pipe Rolls do not, however, hint at the existence of any one base for royal ships or storehouse for supplies.[24] His son, Richard I, whose fame as a Crusader has a considerable maritime element,[25] is, perhaps, responsible for the first beginnings of something worthy of the name of a royal dockyard in England. Gillingham has associated the granting of a royal charter to Portsmouth in May 1194 with the establishment of the town as a base for military operations across the Channel. The town (only forfeited to the Crown earlier in the same year) soon included not only a palace for the king but also a storehouse for military and naval supplies and some facilities for ships.[26] Much more is known about the considerable development of these facilities under John. In May 1212 the sheriff of Hampshire was ordered by the king to build a good strong wall around what is called an *esclusa* to protect the royal vessels at Portsmouth. It is not at all clear what is meant by this. The word itself is normally used of a dam or sluice raising the possibility that there was at Portsmouth an enclosed dock with a lock gate controlling the entry and exit of the ships (mainly galleys in this case). Not only is it very early for the building of this type of wet dock but it is not clear why such a facility was necessary at Portsmouth where there is deep water in the anchorage at all states of the tide. The relevant order goes on to describe how penthouses should be built against the wall to store the galleys' gear and that the work should be completed before the onset of winter storms. The enclosure could, therefore, have been no more than a yard in the ordinary sense with secure storage and slipways for the galleys.[27] Certainly during John's reign officials with special responsibilities for royal ships are named in the records, usually described as *custos galliarum* or *custos portuum*, the most prominent being William de Wrotham who was also Archdeacon of Taunton. His financial transactions for the royal ships can be traced from the Pipe Rolls. In 1212 he handled as much as £6,912 8s 10d. A list on the dorse of the Close Roll for 1205 includes 50 vessels in three groups based at ports from Lynn to Gloucester with five in Ireland[28] and the numbers had probably not greatly declined by 1212. There are also frequent references to his being commissioned to arrest merchant vessels for action in company with royal ships and to the mustering of fleets for projected missions overseas. No such precision is possible on the question of the management and location of the repair and maintenance of king John's galleys. Winchelsea may have been used as much as Portsmouth. The base at the latter port was certainly still in use till c.1230 [29] but in 1243 an order from Henry III refers to the need to extend the galleyhouse at Rye so that it will hold seven ships with space for their equipment.[30] By the end of the century, however, it seems clear that dockyard facilities in royal control for royal ships no longer existed. The enclosure at Portsmouth and the ship-shed at Rye do not feature in any records of this date and we can only presume that they had fallen completely out of use. What remained of course was what had existed all along: the boatyards, slips and chandlers stores which were normally found in any reasonably prosperous seaport and which could be relatively easily adapted for use with royal ships or those impressed for war.

In France, England's traditional opponent at sea as on land, naval developments followed a somewhat different course. Until the last half of the nineteenth century, historians tended to assume that France had little direct royal involvement in the logistics of war at sea before the reign of Francis I. This was shown to be erroneous by the study and analysis of documents from the late thirteenth century which plausibly granted to Philip IV *le Bel*, the title of the founder of the French navy.[31] Before the final decade of the thirteenth century, the French monarchy had had some involvement in the provision of facilities for ships for war in the Mediterranean, when Louis IX had founded Aigues Mortes as the embarkation port for his expedition against the Mamluks in 1248. Philip's cousins, Charles I and Charles II of Anjou were also of course involved in a prolonged and bitter naval war with Aragon and had ordered the building of galleys at Marseilles and elsewhere in their dominions.[32] In northern waters, however, the French crown had, to this point, shown little interest in naval matters. Between 1293, when a document mentions the presence of Genoese shipwrights in France and 1295 when land at Rouen was purchased by the crown for the purpose of setting up a galley building yard a definite decision seems to have been taken to establish a squadron of royal ships and a royal shipyard.[33] The French king also concluded an agreement to hire Genoese galleys under the command of Benedetto Zaccaria, granted the title of admiral general of France, shortly before 1296.[34] The influence of Mediterranean models of naval warfare, probably stemming from knowledge of the activities of his Angevin cousins, is unmistakable.

The shipyard itself was established on the left bank of the Seine at Richebourg. Although Rouen itself was some distance from the sea, the river was still tidal at this point and ships had been built there from at least the beginning of the century. The galley yard at first was quite modest, consisting of an area on land enclosed with ditches and a palisade and a basin with sluices to control the level of water in the ditches as well as the entry and exit of vessels from the river to the yard. By the end of the fourteenth century, there were some quite elaborate buildings within the enclosure including stores for victuals, an armoury, workshops and houses for the workmen and for the master of the yard.[35] The master's house not only possessed a garden and a chapel but was also quite well furnished including a walnut chest specially made with double locks for the safekeeping of money received from the crown.[36] The windows of the chapel and the hall were fully glazed and had borders of coloured glass and coats of arms. In 1411 John Myffray, a glazier, repaired these windows and cleaned and reset others in the yard for a total of 25 sous.[37] His work would have been destroyed along with all other buildings when the victorious English fired the *clos des galées* when Rouen fell to them in 1417.

It is hard, however to estimate how important this yard was in relation to the maritime exploits of the French monarchy in northern waters in the fourteenth century. The surviving accounts and other documents provide a fairly clear picture of French naval administration as a whole, but do not provide anything like a continuous account of activities at the *clos* itself. In the opinion of their editor there is some indication that this establishment was more a 'winter shelter for war ships and an arms workshop' than a state shipyard. In her view, the French crown had no intention of maintaining a fleet 'always ready to go to sea'. It was much easier and less expensive to hire ships from the Doria or Grimaldi families from Genoa with their long experience of warfare in the Mediterranean, or to arrest merchant ships in the French Channel ports. Merlin-Chazelas also points out that the vessels of the *clos des galées* had no permanent crews and that the money provided by the crown (which tended to dry up in times of peace or when a truce was in operation) was sufficient only to pay the master of the yard, his men and repairs to the buildings. Their aim, she feels, was often to prevent rain dripping through holes in the roof or from damaged gutters adding to the decay caused in wooden ships by the mere passage of time.[38] The purpose of the tiny flotilla maintained and built in the yard was to stiffen the large fleets of arrested merchant ships by leading the attack. The yard may have only had a few dozen workmen who built small vessels ('*des coques de noix*') of less than a hundred tuns but even so it was an object of fear to the English for a century.[39]

An overall view of French naval expenditure is provided by an account of 1346. Total receipts were as much as 97,000 *livres tournois*, nearly 150,000 *florences* and 1000 *chaieres d'or*. Among other things, money was spent on the wages of officers engaged in the campaigns (this was the year of Crecy and the siege of Calais by the English), including the admiral Floton de Revel and on the expenses and fees of Carlo Grimaldi of Genoa who had contributed 32 galleys to the French forces. This included payments to pilots who guided the galleys along the Channel coast. Further moneys went to the masters of arrested ships from Leure (13), Honfleur (2), Harfleur (1), Chef de Caux (1), Dieppe (8), Tréport (1), St Valery (3) Crotoy (2), Abbeville (3), Boulogne (7) Berc (3), Wissant (1), Calais (1). Payments are also recorded to nearly 50 small victuallers taking supplies into Calais itself. There is no specific mention of the *clos* at Rouen nor of royal ships except the wages of Thomas Peverel, a cleric, based at Abbeville who was charged with the safekeeping of the royal galleys and their equipment under the supervision of Gilbert Poolin, and the expenses of the *St Marie de Morticle (qui est du roy)* in early 1346.[40]

Much more closely focussed on the activities of the *clos des galées* is the account of Jean Champenois for 1382–4, a period of financial stringency for the government of Charles VI.[41] It does not reveal a happy state of affairs in Rouen. Champenois received only just over 1800 *livres tournois*, including 90 *l.t.* from the sale of a mast of the *Saint-Jehan*, said to be in danger of rotting in the dock.[42] Payments were made to mariners bailing out this vessel and for building a cradle for her in the galley sheds. The mast sold out of the ship was replaced with another which apparently came from a cog wrecked off Leure.[43] The main expenditure, however, was not on the ships at Rouen but on the provision, fitting out and repair of cannon and other weapons and equipment for what is called the *armee de la mer* at Harfleur. This included no fewer than four dozen banners with the arms of the king and the admiral, 160 stone cannon balls and large quantities of cross bow bolts.[44] Including his own salary for two years Champenois was owed £457 11s 10d *tournois* by the crown at the end of the accounting period.[45]

The inventory section of the account also makes depressing reading. Three galleys, the *St Agnes*, the *St Croix* and the *St Vitor*, were on the stocks in the galley sheds but were at least partially equipped and could probably be made ready for sea fairly quickly after the necessary pitching and caulking. Two, the *Magdelaine* and the *Berenguier Vidal* are described as being beyond repair although again on the stocks. The *Saint-Jehan*, here described as a *huissier* as well as a galley, is said to have been on the stocks for 26 years even if repairable, a situation which also applied to two further *huissiers*, one painted with the arms of the dauphin and the other with the arms of M. de Valois. Four barges are said to be under construction with named master shipwrights in charge but the account gives a long list of work still remaining to be done on each. There is no sign of any money being available to do this. The storehouses in the yard contained a large amount of ships-stores of all kinds and arms too but again much is said to be old or in poor repair; a small amount of similar stuff was also kept at Harfleur.[46]

Some idea of the role of the premises at Rouen as a victualling store can be gained from documents from 1355 and 1385. In 1355 the *vicomte* de Rouen (*not* the keeper of the *clos des galées*) was ordered to provide provisions for 10 royal galleys, five barges and three *bargots*. The galleys were to be victualled for 200 men for a month. This involved the supply of eating, cooking and drinking utensils, biscuit, water or other beverage, oil, barley, candles and dressings for wounds. The officers and the crossbowmen also received beef, pork, wine, and salted or dried fish, dried peas and beans, salt, onions and garlic.[47] In 1385 the yard provided biscuit generally at the rate of one or two barrels per vessel for 21 ships from Harfleur, one from St Valery and 32 Spanish ships. None of these are said to be in royal ownership and they are described variously as barges, *bargots*, balingers or *nefs*.[48] Some idea of ship-building procedures in the yard can similarly be derived from accounts. In May 1388 work was underway on two galleys and a galiot for the king. The wood came from the forest of Rommare and the master shipwright was Antoine Blegier who was assisted by a master caulker, Constance de Rodes, described as a foreigner along with his 16 assistants. All these workmen were probably from Italy or the eastern Mediterranean; two certainly came from Venice and one from Naples. Blegier's assistants are described as Normans. Ironwork, including large numbers of nails was bought in; there is no trace of a forge operating in the *clos* itself.[49] In the following year, the same two master craftsmen were working on three galleys, one galiot and one *lin*. It is not clear whether this was a completely new order or an expansion of that of the previous year. The same mix of local and foreign workers was employed though a master oarsmaker with three assistants is also mentioned.[50] The total amount spent on this work is not clear nor in fact whether the vessels were ever finished.

The overall impression created is that the fortunes of this naval facility belonging to the French crown varied, depending on the energy and skills of the keeper and the drive of the monarch concerned. It was at times of great benefit to the French *armée de la mer* but it was not this yard up the Seine which frightened the English but the fleets led by the fighting galleys of the experienced Genoese and the bold Castilians. Vessels, whether galleys or round ships, in royal ownership, were never more than a small proportion of these fleets nor were they all as a matter of course maintained or built at the *clos des galées*. However overall French naval forces could be highly effective. It is also clear that French ports could be very well defended against attack from the sea. The *Gesta Henrici Quinti* describes the impression that Harfleur made on the invading English in 1415. The harbour had walls, 'higher than the town walls'. At the harbour mouth there were 'two fine towers', with 'chains stretching from one to the other'. The enemy had also 'prudently fortified in advance with piles and large tree trunks thicker than a man's thigh' the anchorage so that an attacking force would either be forced to withdraw, 'or if perhaps the piles were covered by the tide they would be suddenly dashed against them and most likely wrecked'.[51]

In England during the fourteenth century there was no organisation similar to the *clos des galées* nor was the same reliance placed on vessels hired from more experienced captains. Various expedients were used including vessels built for the Crown by port towns, arrested ships and the development of a squadron of ships wholly owned by the Crown. The administration needed to raise, organise, pay and equip varied groups of ships of diverse origins gradually became more standardised and, it is to be hoped, more efficient. The leading official was known as the Clerk of the king's Ships. His title is significant: the ships were his concern, not any particular location and the surviving documents make plain that work for royal ships was carried out in many different places, in differing circumstances.

The enrolled accounts of this officer can be found from 1344 on the Pipe Rolls; and from the first year of Richard II on the rolls of Foreign Accounts of the Exchequer. Of the early clerks, William Clewer held office for the longest period from early 1344 till c.1363. The surviving particulars of his accounts for the years 1344–1360 to be found in a small leather bag in the Public Record Office allow a more detailed look at his activities than that available from the more formal rolls.[52] Clewer was unusual compared with other clerks of the king's ships. He was neither a cleric nor a career 'civil servant' to use the modern term but had first come to the attention of the king as the clerk (a post akin to a modern purser) of the *Cog Thomas*, the vessel Edward III preferred for his own use. During his period in office he was responsible for from 20 to as many as 31[53] ships but, although these were often based in London between voyages, there is little mention of specific royal facilities for their upkeep. The suffix, 'of the Tower', was often used in royal ships' names in this period and has been connected with their anchorage in the vicinity of the Tower of London. It is certainly the case that the Tower was the storehouse for the royal ordnance[54] but Ratcliff was more prominent as a centre for maintenance. Here the *Cog Thomas* and the *Cog Edward* both underwent repairs, the first in 1352, the second in 1350. There may have been difficulties in finding sufficient skilled labour on the Thames as mariners were brought from all the Sussex ports including Winchelsea, Shoreham, and Pevensey to work on the *Cog Thomas*.[55] In 1352, a roll of expenses for shipkeeping, reveals that of 19 named royal ships, 10 were said to be at London (this probably implies that they were anchored in the Pool); one was at Wapping *wose* and another at Rotherhithe also on the mudflats, another in 'Seintkatereneflete',[56] two at Ratcliff and two down the estuary at Cliffe in Kent and one at the unidentified 'La Ramdesburn'.[57] By 1357 however, 14 of the 21 vessels in his care were based at Sandwich; only two were in London, the *Isabell* and the *Welfare*, while the remainder were scattered at Cliffe, Yarmouth, Southampton, Small Hythe and Dartmouth.[58] This pattern of dispersal can be related to the varying needs of the campaigns against France in these years but it also makes clear that the notion of a royal dockyard as a specialist facility for the king's ships did not really exist.

It can, in fact be argued that this remained the case until the reign of Henry VII. Both Richard II and Henry IV had possessed a small squadron of royal ships but these were used more for the sea crossings of royalty or even as a means of display than as fighting ships.[59] Their normal base was in the Thames near Deptford and Greenwich but there was little in the way of dedicated facilities for them. Under Henry V royal interest in the provision of ships increased rapidly as the renewal of the war with France became the centre of crown attention. The clerk of the king's ships from 1413 was William Catton who was responsible for a growing number of vessels, ranging from 11 in 1413 to 36 in 1419.[60] Although Catton himself seems to have been based on the Thames, (his most important commission was the rebuilding of the *Trinity Royal* at Greenwich in 1413), work on new ships for the king also took place at Winchelsea and Small Hythe. The *Jesus* was built at the first in 1416 and the *George*, a balinger, on the Rother between 1416 and 1420. A great deal of shipbuilding and ship repair work also took place on the Solent, most of it at Southampton but some at Bursledon on the Hamble. In general charge of this work was William Soper, a Southampton merchant who would follow Catton as Clerk in 1420 but who earlier held commissions to repair or build royal ships in his home town. Soper's activities were so extensive, (he built the *Holyghost de la Tour*, and the *Ane*, extensively remodelled the *Gabriel de la Tour* and was in overall charge of the building of the *Gracedieu*, the *Valentine* and the *Falcon*), that it is tempting to assume that a royal dockyard must have been created in Southampton.[61] It is clear, however, that, while Soper built a forge and storehouse for the work on the ships, it is very difficult if not impossible to identify any site within the town or its outskirts, which was exclusively for the use of royal ships. The storehouse, a substantial stone building costing some £120, seems to have been near Soper's own business premises in the Watergate of Southampton.[62] The *Gracedieu* was a clinker-built vessel of 1400 tons, something unprecedented at the time and for some considerable time later. On the stocks she must have been an imposing sight and launching her must have been a tricky operation but there is no indication of precisely where this took place in the town or its environs. Later in her career she and the other large ships belonging to the king, often collectively know as the king's Great Ships, were moored in the Hamble river. Some protection was provided to begin with by a small garrison based in a wooden 'bulwerk' also built on Soper's orders. Clearly Southampton could be called the base for the royal ships but nothing like the arsenals of the Mediterranean or even the *Clos des galées* at Rouen existed. This is perhaps emphasised by the fact that in 1418 when the slipways of Southampton Water must have been largely occupied by the king's ships Soper sent his confidential servant, David Savage to Deptford to supervise repairs to the *Thomas*. On the death of Henry V, according to the terms of his will, most of the royal ships and their equipment were to be sold to the highest bidder. This somewhat melancholy task, combined with the care of the Great Ships, soon laid up to rot away on the mudflats, was, from 1423, more or less the sole function of Soper and Richard Clyvedon his successor as clerk. Clyvedon's last account for 1452 disclosed a profit to the crown of £56 19s 6½d from the sale of old stores. Despite the increasingly threatening situation in the Channel the Crown had turned decisively away from the ownership and maintenance of ships on its own behalf, a situation which did not begin to change materially until the accession of Henry VII. His son, Henry VIII has sometimes been seen as the true founder of the Royal Navy who managed to create 'an adminstrative and logistical structure … capable of maintaining a permanent navy'.[63] It was his father, however, who took the decisive step of ordering the construction of 'a dock for the king's ships' at Portsmouth. This construction, an echo perhaps of that commissioned nearly three hundred years earlier by king John, marked the establishment of a true dockyard for English royal ships. This was no mud slip dug out on the shore and protected by a furze hedge, the kind of 'dock' made by Soper, but a substantial affair. Although the work was spread over 46 weeks in all, the major construction work occupied 24 weeks and employed from 60–21 men a week. The total cost was £124 2s 3½d. Later in April 1496 the gates were put in position and in July the head of the dock was strengthened.[64] Its exact form is not entirely clear and Rodger has strenuously denied that it can be rightly called the first dry dock. This is so but it is equally clear that it was an advance on anything seen in the earlier years of the fifteenth century,[65] and that its location at Portsmouth was to mark the reinstatement of the town as the foremost base for royal ships. As well as the dock there was a store called the Blockhouse and provision for the protection of the anchorage. These facilities were already available when in Henry VIII's reign naval administration was greatly expanded and put on a more permanent footing, both at Portsmouth and along the Thames from Deptford to Erith.[66]

Ships were of course built in other northern states as well. Lubeck and Danzig had flourishing shipyards in the fourteenth and fifteenth centuries. It is hard, however, to describe these activities as being undertaken by the government or for the express purpose of producing warships. The land on which the yards stood was often *lastadie* or belonging to the municipality but the yards were private businesses. There is no evidence for ships specially designed for war belonging to the Hanse towns. Piracy was so prevalent in the area that all vessels were prepared to defend themselves but, on the other hand, there are few if any accounts of more large scale engagements.[67]

Victualling

As well as the building and repair of ships, governments attempting to send a squadron of vessels to sea also had, of course, to take into account the victuals needed by the crews. Most voyages might not be of very long duration but there was no guarantee that sufficient food to replenish the stores of several ships could be found in a port unprepared for their arrival. This is particularly the case with regard to galleys with their large crews and, as is discussed below, the supply of *biscotti* was a continual worry for the Venetian authorities in time of war, especially when the fleets were operating at some distance from the city itself. From surviving accounts and ration scales drawn up by commanders, however, we have a clear idea of the diet provided for seamen at least in the fourteenth and fifteenth centuries.

The French authorities at the *clos des galées*, perhaps because this institution was originally largely staffed by Genoese concentrated very much on the provision of *biscuit*. In Jean d'Hopital's account for 1346–7 this makes up most of the food provided, although wine is also mentioned and, on one occasion 50 small cheeses.[68] In 1355 the procuring of a supply of wheat and other grain for baking biscuit is included in the list of the duties of the newly appointed master of the *clos*, Etienne Brandis.[69] In 1385 biscuit, usually at the rate of two casks per vessel, was distributed to the masters of 53 ships at Sluys by the quarter-master of the fleet.[70] At the beginning of the sixteenth century Phillipe de Cleves advised that a more elaborate scale of rations should be provided. A thousand people for one month should receive as well as the ubiquitous biscuit large quantities of cider and wine, 4 lbs of beef per person per week, 8 lbs of bacon per person every 18 days, 4 lbs of cheese for fast days (12 in this case) and also butter on a similar scale. Dried peas and beans should also be provided along with 500 lbs of rice to make soup. Salt fish, (herrings, 'mollue', and shrimps) would be needed for fast days as well as quantities of salt, vinegar, mustard, onions, and garlic. The list finishes with the note that sheep, capons, pullets and other foodstuffs can also be provided by the crew themselves either for their own consumption or for the sick and injured.[71]

Victualling on this scale was never attempted either by the Venetians or by English shipmasters. The ration scale for galleymen in 1428, said to have been in existence 'ab anticho' was 18 ounces of *biscotti* or 24 ounces of fresh bread per day. The other victuals provided were wine, cheese and beans.[72] English ships in the king's service in the early fifteenth century were victualled with bread and flour, beef, mutton and salt meat, salt and fresh fish, beer and wine[73]. In 1440, Thomas Gylle, from Dartmouth, who was commissioned by the king to undertake a voyage to Gascony in his ship the *Christopher* accounted to the Crown for the purchase of flour, beer (54 pipes for a crew of 93), 27 beef carcasses, salt fish including ling, hake and 'chelyng' some extra salt and four bushels of oatmeal.[74] Even if these provisions would provide only a very monotonous and not very nutritious diet, assembling them for a large fleet could be a great strain on the food supply in the vicinity of a port. The possibility of a naval expedition feeding itself 'off the country' in the manner of an invading army clearly did not often exist, something which added to the expense and difficulty of conducting war at sea.

Looking at maritime states on the coasts of both the southern and the northern seas over this period, it is clear that the larger kingdoms had at best an intermittent and variable engagement with the problem of the provision of naval forces. It was usually easier and cheaper, and not necessarily less efficient, to rely on arrested merchant shipping or mercenary fleets than to incur the expense of acquiring and maintaining royal ships. The states which did pursue much more consistent policies were those merchant cities of Northern Italy, Genoa and Venice, which could plausibly claim that their very existence depended on their prowess at sea. Unger has argued in an article first published in *Technology and Culture* that it was the 'advances in ship design' between c.1000 and 1500 which were 'the principal force in dictating the pattern of development in naval administration'.[75] The key factor was the increasing extent to which warships could be clearly differentiated from merchant ships, something associated with the placing of heavy 'ship-killing' guns on board warships. This can certainly not be disregarded but we also need to consider developments in the tactics of naval warfare itself and the higher level of specialised skills demanded of successful commanders of warships. These factors will become evident when we turn in succeeding chapters to the actions fought at sea in this period.

Notes

1 A.M. Fahmy, *Muslim Sea Power in the Eastern Mediterranean from the Seventh to the Tenth Centuries*, London, Tipografia Don Bosco, 1950, pp. 27–31.

2 A.R. Lewis and T.J. Runyan, *European Naval and Maritime History 300–1500*, Bloomington, Indiana University Press, 1985, pp. 37–9.

3 R. Mantran, 'Istanbul' in E. Concina (ed.), *Arsenale e Citta nell Occidente Europeo*, Rome, NIS, 1987, pp. 97–9.

4 C. Hillenbrand, *The Crusades: Islamic Perspectives*, Edinburgh, Edinburgh University Press, 1999, pp. 566–7. Hillenbrand also includes a plan of the arsenal at Alanya in this work.

5 'As in the Arsenal of the Venetians ... / one hammers at the prow, one at the stern / this one makes oars and that one cordage twists / another mends the mainsail and the mizzen.' From lines 7–15 of canto 21 of *Inferno*, in F.C. Lane *Venice: A Maritime Republic*, Baltimore and London, Johns Hopkins University Press, 1973, p. 163.

6 R.C. Davis, *Shipbuilders of the Venetian Arsenal: Workers and Workplace in the Pre-industrial City*, Baltimore and London, Johns Hopkins University Press, 1991, p. 3. Similar comments were made by John Evelyn and other travellers including the story of the galley built by the *arsenelotti* while the French king Henry III ate his dinner. *Loc. cit.*, pp. 2–4.

7 E. Concina, *L'Arsenale dell Republica di Venezia*, Milan, Electa, 1984.

8 A plan for the enlargement of the Arsenale to accommodate 80 galleys exists in the Venetian State Archives. ASV, Misc. Mappe 1391.

9 A contemporary described it as having a magnificent wall and towers, able to contain 70 galleys besides those in the *Arsenal vecchio*, ... making or providing all the armaments needed by galleys ... and many other things needed for war. In *Storia di Venezia: Temi: Il Mare* (ed. A. Tenenti and U. Tucci), Rome, Istituto della Enciclopedia Italiana, 1991, p.151.

10 F.C. Lane, 'The rope factory and the hemp trade in the fifteenth and sixteenth centuries,' *Venice and History: The Collected Papers of F.C. Lane* (ed. by a committee of his colleagues), Baltimore and London, Johns Hopkins University Press, 1966.

11 Accounts for the building of galleys by order of Charles of Anjou can be found in G. del Giudice (ed.), *Alcuni Documenti Inediti di Carlo I d'Angoio in Materia Marinara*, Naples 1871, p. 25, in R. Filangieri (ed.) *I registri della cancelleria angoina*, Naples, 1950–81, vol. 12, pp. 126–9 and in N. Fourquin, 'A medieval shipbuilding estimate (c.1273)' *The Mariner's Mirror*, 84, 1999, pp. 20–9.

12 E. Concina (ed.), *Arsenale e Citta nell Occidente Europeo*, Rome, NIS, 1987, pp. 51–6.

13 Plan and view of the grand-ducal arsenal at Pisa. E. Dummer, *A Voyage into the Mediterranean Seas*, London, British Library, 1685, King's MSS, 40, f.45v.

14 F.C. Lane, *Venice and History*, p. 226.

15 F. Podesta, *Il Porta di Genova*, Genoa, E. Spiotti Ed., 1913, p. 2.

16 Drawing by Dummer reproduced in L.C. Bianchi and E. Poleggi, *Una Citta Portuale del Medioevio: Genova nei Secoli X-XVI*, Genoa, SAGEP Ed., 1980, Tavole V, pp. 94–5 and VI, pp. 124–5, and illustration p.103.

17 L. Gatti, *L'Arsenale e le Galee: Pratiche di Costruzione Tecnico a Genova tra Medioevo ed Eta Moderna*, Genoa, Quaderno del Centro di Studio sulla Storia della Tecnica sel Consiglio Nazionale delle Ricerche, 1990, pp. 15–24.

18 C. Picard, *La Mer et les Musulmans d'Occident au Moyen Age VIII-XIII siècles*, Paris, Presses Universitaires de France, 1997, p. 68.

19 A.G. Sanz, *Historia de la Marina Catalana*, Barcelona, Editorial Aedos, 1977, p. 76–81.

20 A.M.U. Abello, 'Los costes de las galeras en el siglo XV: La Galera *Sant Narcis* destinada a las comunicaciones con Italia', *Anuario d'estudios medievales*, 10, 1980, pp. 733–9.

21 A.G. Sanz, *Historia de la Marina Catalana*, *loc. cit.*

22 J. Guiral-Hadziiossif, *Valence, Port Mediterranéen au XV Siècle (1410–1525)*, Paris, Publications de la Sorbonne, 1986, pp. 131–7.

23 According to the OED, the term 'arsenal' meaning dockyard is not found in English until 1506 and by 1579 the word was most frequently used to mean an arms store.

24 F.W. Brooks, *The English Naval Forces 1199–1272*, London, A. Brown and Sons, n.d., pp. 133–4.

25 See below, Chapter 3, p. 41.

26 J. Gillingham, 'Richard I, galley warfare and Portsmouth: the beginnings of a royal navy' in M. Prestwich, R.H. Britnell and R. Frame (eds) *Thirteenth-Century England VI*, Proceedings of the Durham Conference 1995, Woodbridge, Boydell Press, 1997, p. 14.

27 The Portsmouth dockyard is discussed by Rodger, *The Safeguard of the Sea*, p. 53. The order to the sheriff of Hampshire, from the Close Rolls, is printed in translation in J.B.Hattendorf *et al.*, *British Navy Documents 1204–1960*, London, Scolar Press for the Naval Records Society, 1993, p. 42.

28 F.W. Brooks, *The English Naval Forces*, p. 138. He argues forcefully that the ships listed are not impressed vessels but the king's own.

29 There are frequent references to the payment of the wages of mariners at Portsmouth in the Close Rolls for this period. F.W. Brooks, *The English Naval Forces*, pp. 185–6.

30 Hattendorf *et al.*, *British Naval Documents*, p. 43.

31 C. Jourdain, 'Les commencements de la Marine Militaire sous Philippe le Bel', *Revue des Questions Historiques*, 28, 1880, p. 398.

32 See below p. 44 et seq.

33 A. Merlin-Chazelas, *Documents Rélatifs au Clos des Galées de Rouen*, 2 vols, Paris, Bibliothèque Nationale, 1977–8, vol. I, pp. 27–8.

34 Baron de Rostaing, ' La marine militaire de la France sous Philippe le Bel 1294–1304', *Revue Maritime et Coloniale*, 62, 1879, p. 88.

35 A. Merlin-Chazelas, *op. cit.*, pp. 29–30.

36 C. Bréard (ed.), 'Le Compte des Clos des Galées de Rouen au XIV siècle 1382–84', in *Melanges Documents; Deuxième Serie*, Rouen, Société de la Histoire de Normandie, 1893, p.66.

37 A. Merlin-Chazelas, *op. cit.*, vol. II, p. 205.

38 A. Merlin-Chazalas, *op. cit.*, vol. I, p. 103.

39 A. Merlin-Chazelas, *op. cit.*, vol.I, p. 104.

40 A. Merlin-Chazelas, *op. cit.*, vol. II, texte no. xxxii, pp. 71–142.

41 C. Bréard, *op. cit.*, pp. 51–154.

42 C. Bréard, *op. cit.*, p. 65.

43 C. Bréard, *loc. cit.*

44 C. Bréard, *op. cit.*, pp. 68, 71, 75–6

45 C. Bréard, *op. cit.*, p. 90.

46 C. Bréard, *op. cit.*, pp. 90–154.

47 A. Merlin-Chazelas, *op. cit.*, vol. II, XXXVII, pp. 144–5.

48 A. Merlin-Chazelas, *op. cit.*, vol II, LXXII, pp. 176–8.

49 A. Merlin-Chazelas, *op. cit.*, vol II, LXXVII, pp. 182–8.

50 A. Merlin-Chazelas, *op. cit.*, vol II, LXXX, pp. 188–92.
51 F. Taylor and J.S. Roskell, *Gesta Henrici Quinti or the Deeds of Henry V*, Oxford, Clarendon Press, 1975, pp. 30–1.
52 Public Record Office, E101/24/14
53 Thirty-one ships said to be 'of the king' are listed in P.R.O. E372/209, Clewer's enrolled account for 1344–52. The expenses for keeping 31 ships are listed in 1345.
54 N.A.M. Rodger, *The Safeguard of the Seas: A Naval History of Great Britain, Vol. 1, 660–1649*, London, HarperCollins, 1997, p. 129.
55 P.R.O. E101/24/1.
56 This can cautiously be identified with the area beside the Tower where the later St Katherine's dock was built.
57 P.R.O. E101/24/5.
58 P.R.O. E101/24/10.
59 Richard II used the Trinity for his voyage to Ireland in 1398: the biggest item of expenditure in the clerk's account for 1399–1406 was the cost of the Queen's voyage to England in 1402. Henry IV's ships were elaborately painted in bright colours and included a ceremonial river barge painted red and gold with carved leopards, at least one with a golden collar, on the prow. S. Rose (ed.), *The Navy of the Lancastrian Kings: Accounts and Inventories of William Soper, Keeper of the King's Ships, 1422–27*, London, Navy Records Society, 1982, p. 31.
60 P.R.O. E 364/54 and 59. Catton's accounts as Clerk.,
61 Soper's enrolled accounts are P.R.O. E 364/ 61, 65, 69, 73, 76. His work as Clerk of the King's Ships is also discussed in S. Rose (ed.), *The Navy of the Lancastrian Kings*, pp. 28–56.
62 This location depends on the storehouse being identical with the Long House in Southampton. S. Rose (ed.), *Southampton and the Navy in the Age of Henry V*, Hampshire Papers 14, Winchester, Hampshire County Council, 1998, p. 11.
63 N.A.M. Rodger, *The Safeguard of the Sea*, p. 221.
64 M. Oppenheim (ed.), *Naval Accounts and Inventories of the Reign of Henry VII 1485–8 and 1495–7*, London, Navy Records Society, 1896, pp. xxxvii–xxxix and 143–160.
65 The dock for the *Gracedieu*, dug at Bursledon in 1434 cost 28s 6d and 30 men were employed in all. P.R.O. E101/53/5.
66 N.A.M. Rodger, *The Safeguard of the Sea*, vol. I, p. 223.
67 A. d'Haenens, *Europe of the North Sea and the Baltic: The World of the Hanse*, Antwerp, Fonds Mercator, 1984, p. 152.
68 A. Merlin-Chazelas, *Documents Rélatifs au clos des Galées de Rouen*, 2 vols, Paris, Bibliothèque Nationale, 1977–8, vol. II, p. 77.
69 A. Merlin-Chazelas, *op. cit.*, p. 158.
70 A. Merlin-Chazelas, *op. cit.*, pp. 176–8.
71 P. de Cleves, *L'Instruction de Toutes Manières de Guerroyer sur Mer*, J.Paviot (ed.), Paris, Libraries Honoré Champion,1997, pp. 66–7.
72 L. Greco (ed.), *Quaderno di bordo di Giovanni Manzini prete-notaio e cancelliere 1471–1484*, Venice, Il Comitiato Editore, 1997, p. 96.
73 S. Rose, *op. cit.*, *The Navy of the Lancastrian Kings* p. 47.
74 H. Kleineke, 'English shipping to Guyenne in the mid-fifteenth century: Edward Hull's Gascon voyage of 1441'. *Mariner's Mirror*, 85, 1999, p. 475.
75 R. Unger, 'Admiralties and warships of Europe and the Mediterranean, 1000–1500', in *Ships and Shipping in the North Sea and Atlantic, 1400–1800*, (reprinted from *Technology and Culture*, 22, 1981, p. 36), Aldershot, Ashgate Variorum Press, 1997.

CHAPTER TWO

Invaders and settlers: operations in the Channel and the North Sea c.1000–c.1250

The image of the Viking is one of the most potent to remain from the Middle Ages in Northern Europe. The Orkney Saga contains an arresting picture of Swein and his men returning from a voyage during which they had plundered English ships of their cargoes near Dublin; 'when they sailed into the Orkneys they sewed cloth onto the forepart of their sails so that it looked in that wise as though the sails were made altogether of broadcloth'.[1] Anglo-Saxon literature also provides some notable accounts of battles by the shore. Describing the battle of Brunanburh in 937, when Athelstan defeated a mixed Scots and Scandinavian host, the chronicler quotes a poem:

> There the prince
> of Norsemen, compelled by necessity,
> Was forced to flee to the prow of his ship
> With a handful of men. In haste the ship
> Was launched, and the king fled hence,
> Over the waters grey, to save his life.[2]

What, however, was the nature of warfare at sea in this period? Was it no more than confused scuffling at the water's edge or in shallow bays and estuaries? Early medieval naval encounters were, in the opinion of most commentators predominantly boarding actions. The dramatic descriptions of the encounters between the forces of Magnus of Norway and Earl Svein Ulfson in 1044 and between Harald Hardraada and Svein in 1062 from the *Heimskringla* bear this out to some extent. The first was clearly decided by boarding. Magnus, we are told, led his men forward 'and rushed along the ship, shouting loudly and egging on his men and he went right forward to the bow to the hand-to-hand fight'. Eventually he 'cleared the ship (Svein's) and so he did one ship after the other'. However the opening phase of the battle was fought with missiles, a mixture apparently of 'of barbed spears or gavelocks or darts'.[3]

24

The second battle was on a larger scale with the opposing fleets engaged in quite complex manoeuvres. Once, however battle was joined the first feature seized upon by the bard was the flights of arrows and the hurling of stones. He also makes clear that before the battle began 'both sides roped their ships together in the midmost parts of their fleets. But because the armies were so big there was a great number of ships which went loose'. He seems to be implying here that the forces in the centre of the two fleets, of Harald on the one hand and of Svein on the other, linked themselves together so that the enemy was faced with a solid mass of ships. Round the edges of these groups were numbers of unattached or 'loose' ships. These 'loose' ships, especially those under the command of Hacon the *jarl* seem to have had a decisive influence on the outcome of the battle, 'wherever he came nothing could withstand him'. In the end, however Harald and his men went 'up on king Swein's ship and it was so thoroughly cleared that every man fell except those who leapt into the sea'.[4] Both these battles took place in the sheltered waters of fjords on the east coast of Denmark but are more complex encounters than might be thought. Battles in the open sea were certainly hardly a realistic possibility given the design of the vessels in use and the difficulties of finding the enemy. Many so-called naval battles at this date were really amphibious engagements, combined operations, when the role of seafarers was to transport warriors with silent speed to unexpected landfalls.[5] If the landing was opposed, or if an opposing sea patrol lit, almost always by accident, on the incoming ships, fighting would take place. This would usually end in boarding or involve beached vessels or end with them driven onshore. Before this, however, a furious exchange of missiles might take place combined with attempts by both sides to manoeuvre their vessels into the most advantageous position. This might include an attempt to come up on the beam of an opponent breaking his oars or an attempt to drive the enemy aground. An invading force, however, was far more likely to be defeated on land than at sea.

There is very little in the history of events during the eleventh and twelfth centuries in the Channel and Western Approaches which seems to contradict this belief. Despite the ability of Saxon kings to assemble fleets by using the obligation to provide vessels for national defence which seems to have rested on territorial units sometimes called ship-sokes,[6] the invaders from the North, the Danes and their kings Swein Forkbeard and Cnut the Great had little trouble getting their forces on shore. In Ireland the Norse trading towns were well established with their Viking rulers, on occasion hiring their fleets to Gaelic lords.[7] French chronicles betray little interest in maritime affairs. Almost the sole exception to this general indifference to naval affairs are the events of 1066, the conquest of England by the Normans. There has been quite a considerable amount of discussion of the forces deployed by each side; the precise numbers built or otherwise obtained by William I; the exact sequence of the steps taken by Harold to guard his Southern coastline; the rationale for the course sailed by the Norman ships particularly their decision to leave Dives and sail for St Valery before making the Channel crossing.[8] Much of this makes some valuable points concerning, among other things, the design of William's ships or the need to consider wind and tide and the configuration of the coastline as well as the words of chroniclers. It does not, however, alter the basic fact that, given the experience of other invaders, albeit operating on a somewhat smaller scale, William had every right to hope to get ashore unopposed. The crucial battle would be on land; it was there that the issue would be settled.

The campaigns of Tostig, Harold's brother, and Harold Hardraada bear this out. According to the Anglo-Saxon Chronicle, Tostig had sailed from Flanders to the Isle of Wight in the early summer of 1066 to attack his brother's lands. Harold then collected a fleet to oppose him and also the looming threat from William. Tostig hastily left Sandwich when he learned that his brother was under way from London and continued up the East coast, burning and looting as he went. Undoubtedly these raids were locally disturbing and in fact Edwin and Morcar, the Northern earls, managed to drive Tostig north to Scotland away from their provinces but the situation demanded the presence of Harold himself when Tostig and his ally Harold Hardraada of Norway got ashore near York. Ships had allowed the invaders the mobility they needed but did not affect the eventual outcome, Harold's triumph at Stamford Bridge.[9]

In the same way William's fleet, however numerous and however assembled, fulfilled its purpose in bringing the army to the battlefield. The *Carmina de Hastingae Proelio* may well be the most accurate account of William's Channel crossing, with its description of the east wind, 'foul weather and ceaseless rain' which trapped the fleet at Dives and William's intense anxiety at St Valery before he was able to set sail for England.[10] The decisive moment was, however, the victory at Hastings. In particular circumstances well-led and well-armed naval forces could be a crucial factor in a military operation, for example the siege of a coastal city or fortress but, in 1066, this was not the case.[11]

Once the Norman invaders had established themselves as rulers of England, however, it was clear that the conditions governing possible naval strategies in northern waters had changed radically. Both sides of the Channel were largely ruled by the same family; disputes occurred between individuals who wished to make good their rival claims to the throne of England but the resulting fighting had more the character of civil wars or rebellions than international conflict. The French kings had, in fact, until the early thirteenth century no portion of the Channel coast directly under their control. The rulers of the Scandinavian realms were also involved in complex internecine disputes. It has been claimed that until the fourteenth century, England was 'the principal naval and maritime power in the northern seas'.[12] If this claim is to be made good, it is as well to consider the physical world in which mariners in the northern seas operated. Was England particularly well placed to dominate the seas which surrounded her?

Pryor has very effectively drawn attention to certain features of the geography of the Mediterranean, winds, currents, and coastal configuration which ensured the use of certain sea routes whether for trade or for war. He has also pointed to the fact that states on the northern littoral of the sea were in a better position to profit from these factors than those to the south.[13] In northern waters it is hard to make a similar case with regard to the winds and the tides which are a major navigational factor in this area. Winds are much less predictable than in the south; the prevailing winds are westerly but periods of east winds may occur at any season of the year. The dominating factor in wind direction is the presence of Atlantic depressions and the weather fronts associated with them. Tides can, of course be calculated in advance (and such knowledge was part of the necessary skill of a medieval mariner) but while locally of great importance no one state could claim to be favoured by them. Position and coastal configuration are perhaps of more importance. The east and south coasts of the British Isles as a whole are well placed to have access to, and potentially control sea routes along the Channel and through the North Sea. The Straits of Dover offer similar opportunities but the advantage rests as much with France and Flanders to the south as England to the north. To the west in the Irish Sea possession of the Isle of Man can be shown to have strategic advantages. In general, sea conditions are more difficult than in the Mediterranean with more complex navigation and more days of storm.

The clearest effect of this is seen in the type of ships preferred in the makeup of war fleets from at least the early thirteenth century. This applies with particular force to the use of oared fighting ships. In the Mediterranean the predominant form of fighting ship from classical times until as late as the sixteenth century was the galley. Though known, at different periods, by a variety of names and with a variety of ways of arranging the banks of oars and the rowers' benches, the general type of vessel is remarkably similar, a vessel long in comparison with its beam with a shallow hull and a low freeboard. It might have, (and by the end of the period always had) a mast or masts often rigged with lateen sails to provide an alternative means of propulsion. It was an effective and feared weapon of war with a long record of successful use. The design of Northern ships, whether those of the Vikings or of other peoples, in about AD 1000 was not essentially different from this. Although the hulls were constructed in a different manner and square sails were raised on the single mast, these were long ships in name and in nature. The details of the design and construction of such ships is well known from those that survive, whether the Viking ships in the Oslo museum (from Gokstad, c.850–900, and Oseberg, c.800) or those excavated at Skuldelev in Roskilde fjord in Denmark (eleventh century).[14] The records of both English and French monarchs record them as owning and building vessels called galleys from the early thirteenth till the early fifteenth centuries. It is, however, clear that by at least the fourteenth century if not before, in northern waters, round ships (cogs or similar types) were much more effective in naval warfare. What had led to this change? Why were the vessels which had served the Norsemen so well no longer the core of any fleet? Unger has linked this change to the development of trade in the area. Longships, even those designed for trading voyages, were less efficient as carriers of goods than cogs with their deep roomy hulls and low length to breadth ratio. The sailing abilities of cogs had been much improved by the addition of a keel and they could deal better with heavy seas and high winds. In a sea fight the high freeboard of the cog also made it 'an excellent platform for hurling missiles down on an enemy'.[15] In an era when the bulk of any war fleet would consist of arrested shipping, it is not surprising that the merchant's favoured vessel soon became that of kings too.

Why then did galleys maintain a place at all in northern fleets? To some extent this can be argued to be the result of the influence of mariners from the South with their experience of galley warfare and their reputation as experienced naval commanders. It is also the case that there were situations even in northern waters when galleys could be very valuable weapons. These were, of course, those situations in which the Norsemen had used similar ships; coastal raids especially with an approach up a shallow river or estuary where winds were fluky and erratic and attacks, again in coastal waters, depending on surprise and speed when rapid mobility was essential. It is, however, hard to argue that any one of the maritime states of northern Europe had any decisive natural advantage over its rivals or any great technological superiority. Change occurred gradually over the whole region with the advantage at sea going to the realm with the strongest leadership with the clearest view of its aims at sea.

This becomes clear in the reign of king John whose loss of Normandy in 1205-6 had ensured the geographical separation of his territories in England and France and placed the southern coast of the Channel in the hostile hands of Philip Augustus, king of France. We have already noted the beginnings of a form of dedicated naval administration in England at this time.[16] John has also been linked with the growth of the idea that a fleet could be used in war as something more than a means of transport; in particular with the notion that 'a naval offensive is the best and surest defence against a threat of invasion'.[17] In 1213 France faced him with such a threat and, as well as using the diplomatic tactic of submitting to the Pope in order to remove Philip's justification for his actions, John dispatched a fleet under William Longsword, Earl of Salisbury to Flanders. Both John and Philip had been actively seeking the support of Flemish lords in their quarrels and at this point Philip had invaded Flanders furious at the suggestion that the Count of Flanders had made a compact with John.[18] He had also ordered the fleet which he had assembled in the mouth of the Seine to sail instead to the Zwyn, the area of the estuary of the Scheldt adjacent to the town of Damme. The English fleet also sailed to the Zwyn and from the tone of the chronicle it would seem that the commanders had no idea that they would find the French fleet already there. Despite their surprise they sent out scouts who confirmed that this was indeed the French fleet and also that it was virtually unguarded, most of the crews and the men at arms being on shore sacking the town and the surrounding countryside. The Zwyn at Damme was already a very shallow anchorage (the town is nowadays some distance from the sea) and it seems that some of the French ships were beached. Those at anchor were boarded, the few defenders overwhelmed, and the ships sailed back to England with their valuable cargoes of victuals and arms. Those on the mudflats were burnt once the spoils had been removed.[19] Philip and his army on discovering this disaster were left with no option but to withdraw and to abandon the idea of invading England. In the context of the whole campaign, however, this English victory had no strategic importance; the final outcome, as in 1066, was decided by a land battle, the battle of Bouvines in 1214, a triumph for Philip.

Despite Brooks' grand claims for a change in the perception of naval warfare, the nature of the engagement and the tactics used seem very traditional.[20] The battle of Dover, however, which occurred in 1217 substantiates the theory of a new view of the possibilities of war at sea. When civil war broke out in England between John and the barons, the king should have been able to use his control of a relatively large group of ships to his own advantage. He failed, however to ensure the loyalty of the Cinque Ports. This made it possible for the rebellious barons, convinced that John had no intention of keeping the promises enshrined in Magna Carta, to receive help from the dauphin to whom they went so far as to offer the crown. French forces got ashore at Sandwich in May 1215. By the time of the king's death in 1216 they controlled more than half the country.[21] The lords ruling in the name of the child king Henry III needed to prevent their reinforcement and subsequently ensure their eviction from England. Strong personalities were involved on both sides. In France the wife of the dauphin Louis, Blanche of Castile (who was also Henry II's granddaughter) was energetically raising fresh troops for his cause. Eustace the Monk commanded the fleet needed to bring them to England. This seafarer called a *viro flagitiosissimo* (a real pain) by Matthew Paris was almost a legendary figure to his countrymen.[22] He came from near Boulogne and may have had some early connection with the religious life. He gave it up, however, when his brother died without male heirs and by c.1205 was in the service of king John. He seems to have conducted raids in the Channel and as far as the Channel Islands with a squadron of ships based on Winchelsea. By 1211 he was forced to flee from England and took service with the dauphin and was of great use to him in his English campaigns. The ballad written of his exploits includes many dramatic and unlikely stories involving magic and phantom ships among other things but it is clear enough that he was a skilled and experienced seaman.[23] Louis himself, although his position had worsened since John's death, was a determined leader. The English forces were in the capable hands of William Marshall and Hubert de Burgh. The main source for the battle itself is Matthew Paris who was himself told the story long after the event by de Burgh. Before the main engagement on 24 August, there had been brief encounters between the naval forces of each side with no clear advantage to either. On the 24 August itself the French put to sea and made a quick crossing driven on by a strong southerly wind. Paris then describes the dramatic scene of de Burgh with the Marshall, the Bishop of Winchester and other lords, standing on Dover cliffs and watching the French fleet draw nearer. De Burgh clearly fully understood the gravity of the situation and, despite the reluctance of his companions to join him in a seafight, went on board the best ship and set sail.[24] We can presume that by this time the French were not far off shore. Paris then relates how the English apparently set a course which would take them to Calais, (Eustace thought it was their intention to seize the town while its main defenders were absent), but as the wind fell and then shifted they changed course came up on the rear of their opponents and grappled with them. This was clearly a battle between vessels under sail on the high seas in which ship-handling skills had a material effect on the outcome, a development of great importance in naval warfare.

Once de Burgh's ship had grappled with a great ship clearly marked as that of nobles from the number of banners it was flying, Paris's account of the battle becomes more conventional. He mentions the tactic of cutting the haliards and shrouds so that the sails fell to the deck trapping the defenders and also the use of crossbowmen and longbowmen. He then goes on to describe the English as possessing galleys with iron rams which holed and sank the enemy and as using quicklime thrown onto the French ships to blind the crew. The final triumph was the discovery of Eustace, ('a traitor to the king of England and a most wicked pirate'[25]) hiding in the bilges. He was dragged out, taken before the lords and beheaded without more ado.[26] From the accounts of the building of galleys in both England and France, which make no mention of anything in the nature of an iron, or any other kind of ram, we can be sure that when mentioning this, Paris is following classical models; to him this is how a seabattle should be fought. The use of quicklime quite often features in chronicle accounts but again it cannot be found in the lists of purchases for English ships preparing for war.[27] The use of archers, whatever kind of bow they were using, is in a different category; this does seem to reflect general practice. Virtually all chronicle accounts from this period describe sea fights as beginning with the throwing or firing of missiles of some kind, whether stones, lances or arrows. Only after the crew of an opposing ship had been thrown into confusion and had taken casualties did grappling and boarding take place.

When the English seamen reached Dover, towing the captured French ships behind them, they were greeted as heroes who had won a miraculous victory. On this occasion there was no doubt that the outcome of a naval battle had had great strategic importance. Matthew Paris undoubtedly expressed his own views in the words he put into de Burgh's mouth before the battle began but he was right when he claimed that, 'if those attacking forces enter England without loss, we shall all be disinherited, the kingdom lost and the king confounded'.[28] On this occasion it can be rightly asserted that this was 'one of the most decisive medieval naval battles in northern waters'.[29] Neither William the Marshal nor de Burgh were at this point confident that the young king's supporters would be victorious in a land battle against the re-supplied forces of the rebel barons and the dauphin.

The long reign of Henry III did not see, however, any further advances in naval tactics. The area of greatest interest shifted away from the Channel to the seaways off the west coast of France. Here the king attempted to re-assert English rule over the territories lost by his father particularly in Poitou and Gascony. His most determined campaign was, perhaps that of 1242. The naval aspects of this have aroused some interest especially because he is seen as having organised a blockade of the port of La Rochelle. The purpose of this, it is surmised, was to keep the French forces confined so that English ships could have a safer passage to Bordeaux. There is certainly evidence that the king ordered vessels, mostly galleys, from Bayonne, Bordeaux and Oléron, to cruise in the vicinity of the Ile de Ré from around July 1242 and that money was being directed to the ships' masters as late as December in the same year. But can this activity really be called a blockade? Galleys cannot remain at sea for long periods because of the need for constant access to large supplies of food and water. They are very vulnerable to stormy weather. Supply fleets from England, as Henry in fact discovered, could be attacked at many other points of their long journey from England. This fleet may have brought him some local and temporary advantage but the campaign as a whole ended in a truce with France.[30] More important than any so-called blockade may have been the widening of the area in which the English and the French might expect to pursue their rivalry on the sea. This was no longer confined to the Channel and the southern North Sea but included the Western Approaches, the coasts of Brittany and the Atlantic coast of France as far south as the Pyrenees. English kings looked for vessels that could be arrested for warlike purposes not only among the ports of England and Ireland but also in those of their French lands, particularly Bordeaux and Bayonne.[31] Equally the French king needed to take a similar wider view of possibly vulnerable coasts. The tactical possibilities of a naval battle had arguably changed radically by the beginning of the thirteenth century. By the 1250s the possible area of conflict had also widened. It was much more likely that the strategic possibilities of some naval involvement would be exploited as an element in any new military campaign in northern as in southern waters.

Notes

1 *Icelandic Sagas*, Vol. III, *The Orkneyingers' Saga*, quoted in A.F. Scott, *The Saxon Age*, London, Croom Helm, 1979, p. 167.

2 G.N. Garmonsway (trans.), *The Anglo-Saxon Chronicle*, London, Dent, 1972, p. 108.

3 Snorre Sturlason, *Heimskringla or the Lives of the Norse Kings* (ed. E. Monsen) Cambridge Saga IX, Cambridge, W. Heffer and Sons, 1932, pp. 496–7.

4 *Heimskringla*. Saga X, pp. 541–6.

5 N.A.M. Rodger, *The Safeguard of the Sea*, pp. 2–4.

6 N. Hooper, 'Some observations on the navy in late Anglo-Saxon England', in *Studies in Medieval History presented to R. Allen Brown*, (ed. C. Harper-Bill, C.J. Holdsworth and J.L. Nelson), Woodbridge, Boydell, 1989, pp. 203–13, discusses the methods of raising fleets at this period.

7 S. Duffy, *Ireland in the Middle Ages*, Basingstoke, Macmillan, 1997, p. 10 and p. 30.

8 Discussion of the naval aspects of the events of 1066 will be found in: C.M. Gillmor, 'Naval logistics of the cross-Channel operation, 1066', in R.A. Brown (ed.) *Anglo-Norman Studies VII*, Woodbridge, The Boydell Press, 1984 pp. 105–31: C. and G. Grainge, 'The Pevensey expedition: brilliantly executed plan or near disaster?', *The Mariner's Mirror*, 79, 1993, pp. 261–73: C.D. Lee, 'England's naval trauma: 1066', *The Mariner's Mirror*, 80, 1994, pp. 208–9: N.A.M. Rodger, 'The Norman Invasion of 1066', *The Mariner's Mirror*, 80, 1994, pp. 459–63.

9 *The Anglo-Saxon Chronicle*, (from version C), in R.A. Brown, *The Norman Conquest*, London, Edward Arnold, 1984, pp. 69–70.

10 C. Morton and H. Muntz (eds), *The Carmen de Hastingae Proelio of Guy Bishop of Amiens*, Oxford, Clarendon Press, 1972, pp. 4–10.

11 In 717–8 the second siege of Constantinople by the forces of the Caliph was arguably largely determined by the judicious use of ships armed with Greek fire siphons against the attacking fleet which was attempting to cut the city off from its hinterland. W.L. Rodgers, *Naval Warfare under Oars: 4th to 16th Centuries: A Study of Strategy, Tactics and Ship Design*, Annapolis, Naval Institute Press, 1967, pp. 37–9.

12 A.R. Lewis and T.J. Runyan, *European Naval and Maritime History 300–1500*, Bloomington, Indiana University Press, 1985, p. 111.

13 J.H. Pryor, *Geography, Technology and War: Studies in the Maritime History of the Mediterranean, 649–1571*, Cambridge, Cambridge University Press, 1988, Chap. I, 'The sea', pp. 12–24.

14 N.A.M. Rodger, *The Safeguard of the Sea*, pp. 12–3. G. Hutchinson, *Medieval Ships and Shipping*, London, Leicester University Press, 1994, pp. 4–7.

15 R.W. Unger, 'Admiralties and Warships of Europe and the Mediterranean, 1000–1500', in *Ships and Shipping in the North Sea and Atlantic, 1400–1800*, Aldershot, Ashgate-Variorum Press, 1997, pp. 34–42.

16 See Chapter 1, pp. 12–13.

17 F.W. Brooks, *The English Naval Forces, 1199–1272*, London, A. Brown and Sons, 1932, p. 196.

18 Matthew Paris describes how Ferrand, the Count of Flanders had made a secret pact with John. When Philip heard of this he threw Ferrand out of his court and immediately attacked his county. M. Paris, *Historia Anglorum sive ut vulgo dicitur historia minor*, (ed. F. Madden), Rolls Series, London, 1866, vol. II ,1189–1245, pp. 137.

19 This is Matthew Paris's version of events. F.W. Brooks in 'The Battle of Damme 1213', *Mariner's Mirror*, 16, 1930, pp. 264–71, suggests that the beached vessels were burnt by the orders of the French king, since they were trapped in the harbour by the English fleet.

20 F.W. Brooks, 'The Battle of Damme 1213', p. 264.

21 John Gillingham, *The Angevin Empire*, London, Edward Arnold, 1984, pp. 80–1.

22 Matthew Paris, *Chronica Majora* (ed. H. Luard), London, Her Majesty's Stationery Office, 1964, p. 26.

23 H.L. Cannon, 'The Battle of Sandwich and Eustace the Monk', *English Historical Review*, 27, 1912, pp. 649–70, provides an account of the whole career of Eustace.

24 Matthew Paris, *Historia Anglorum*, pp. 217–21. This longer version of events in 1217 includes the details of de Burgh's speeches etc.

25 These words are Matthew Paris's, *Historia Anglorum*, p. 220; a French chronicler, William the Breton, called him 'a much admired warrior at sea as on land'. H.F. Delaborde, *Oeuvres de Rigord et de Guillaume le Breton, Historiens de Philippe Auguste*, Paris, Nogent le Retrou, 1882–5, p. 314.

26 M. Paris, *Historia Anglorum*, p. 217–21.

27 The throwing of quicklime on to an enemy ship is included in Vegetius' list of recommended tactics for use at sea. See Chapter 7, p. 123.

28 M. Paris, *Historia Anglorum*, p. 217.

29 N.A.M. Rodger, *The Safeguard of the Sea*, p. 55.

30 Details of this campaign can be found in M. Weir, 'English naval activities, 1242–1243', *The Mariner's Mirror*, 58, 1972, pp. 85–92.

31 S. Rose, 'Bayonne and the King's ships, 1204–1420', *The Mariner's Mirror*, 86, 2000, pp. 140–7.

CHAPTER THREE

Christians, Muslims and Crusaders: naval warfare in the Mediterranean at the time of the Crusades

The Mediterranean Sea, *Mare Nostrum*,[1] to use the name presumptuously chosen by the Romans, had been no stranger to sea fights both in ancient times and in the period from the foundation of Byzantium to the rise of Islamic powers on its eastern and southern shores. It is generally agreed among naval historians of the period up to 1000[2] that the earlier thalassocracy of the Roman Empire in the east[3] had been severely shaken by the advancing forces of the Caliphs leading to the loss of Crete in 826 and the Arab conquest of Sicily after 875. Ibn Khaldun, a later Arab historian, wrote of this period with perhaps pardonable exaggeration, 'the Christian nations could do nothing against the Muslim fleets anywhere in the Mediterranean. All the time the Muslims rode its waves for conquest'.[4] There is also a widely-held view that in the later tenth and eleventh centuries the Christian nations of the northern shores of the Mediterranean regained the initiative in naval warfare and maintained their supremacy over the navies of the southern states at least until the mid-fifteenth century.

The earlier Muslim conquests had broken the Byzantine Empire's domination of the sailing routes most convenient and practical for any vessel of the day whether a peaceful trader or a warship. John Pryor has forcefully pointed out the powerful influence exerted by the patterns of the prevailing winds and currents in the Mediterranean Sea, over the activities of all maritime nations in this period.[5] The disruption caused by the advance of Islam made this increasingly evident and it is a factor which must not be forgotten when examining naval warfare throughout our period. The seasonal pattern of winds, especially the summer *melteme* or North West wind of the eastern Mediterranean, and the currents, generally flowing in a counter-clockwise direction round the shores of the inland sea, served to enhance the importance of certain ports, islands and other coastal features. The possession or control of these could be crucial to the success of a would-be dominant power. Sicily was strategically placed on routes both to the east, to Constantinople and the

Black Sea, and to the west, to the Balearics and to Spain. Crete provided an equally important link between Egypt and the south, the shores of Syria and Palestine and the islands to the north, leading again to Constantinople the centre of both commercial and political power in the early medieval period. It can be argued that, from the time of the explosive eruption of the forces of Islam from the Arabian peninsula, leading to their domination of the southern shores of the Mediterranean, religious and cultural differences lie behind much of the conflict in this area, whether on sea or by land.[6] This, however, to some extent oversimplifies a situation where motives were often confused and complex with economic and political advantage being at least as important as religious and cultural hegemony.

The Eastern Mediterranean

Events in the Eastern Mediterranean in the eleventh century illustrate this point very clearly. On the one hand it can be argued that conflict between Christians and Muslims is the dominant factor. We can point to the continuing wars between Byzantium and the advancing forces of Islam and the intensification of this kind of warfare which was brought about by the First and subsequent Crusades. However we need to remember that the Guiscards, the most prominent of the Norman conquerors of Sicily also turned their attention to the eastern shores of the Adriatic invading Albania in 1085 and were seen as hostile and dangerous by the Greeks even if fellow Christians. Similarly this period sees the relatively rapid rise of Venice, Genoa, and Pisa as sea powers in the Mediterranean, but they were as suspicious of each other and as wary of each other's ships as they were of those from ports in Egypt or the Maghreb. Each city state wished to secure privileges for its traders in the lucrative trade with the East and in the safest ports and anchorages in the Eastern Mediterranean and the Black Sea. Clashes at sea between the vessels of these states were often as violent as those which were part of some wider and grander strategic scheme.[7]

The First Crusade in fact, if one thinks only of the campaign which culminated in the fall of Jerusalem, saw little involvement of naval forces. Their intervention was only crucial as providers of desperately needed supplies. During the siege of Antioch in November 1098 a Genoese fleet managed to get into the harbour of Saint Symeon with reinforcements and building materials for the crusaders which enabled them to extend their siege works around the city.[8] Similarly, when the siege of Jerusalem itself was in danger of ending in failure with a crusader assault on the walls being beaten off by the Muslim defenders, the arrival by chance of Christian ships at Jaffa saved the situation. They had brought with them the materials needed for siege engines and scaling ladders.[9]

Soon after the founding of the Kingdom of Jerusalem most new recruits to the crusading forces, and the increasing numbers of pilgrims reached the

Holy Land by sea. The long march across central Europe was even less attractive than a long sea voyage. It was also clear that the sea-route was the only really practicable one by which to supply the forces in the east. The coastal waters of Syria and Palestine became a centre of naval activity, both commercial and warlike in nature. The Crusaders' hold on the coast was at first tenuous with only Jaffa in their hands until 1101. In that year Baldwin I captured the towns of Arsuf and Caeserea. In 1104 he also gained possession of Acre which had perhaps the best natural harbour on the Palestinian or Syrian coast. For this he needed the help of a Genoese fleet, a fleet which, with ships from Provence, was also crucial in ensuring the success of the siege of Tripoli by both Baldwin and the followers of the house of Toulouse.[10] Askelon remained in the hands of the Fatimid rulers of Egypt, and although not a secure anchorage, this could have been used as a base for attacks on the shipping of the Franks and their supporters from Italian maritime cities making for Jaffa or Acre.

It could, in fact, be seen as surprising that the Fatimid navy was not more effective in opposing the Franks in Outremer. At the end of the eleventh century their fleet consisted in theory of some 70 ships, with its headquarters at Alexandria but also bases at Damietta, Tinnis and Askelon.[11] It was in its home waters in the Eastern Mediterranean at a time when the Italian fleets, which were the main source of naval power for the Crusaders, were only transients returning to their home cities at the end of the sailing season.[12] Yet while these ships did assist Muslim forces in some small operations against the Franks, their presence was not exploited and seemed of no real strategic significance. Hillenbrand, in her discussion of the conduct of Muslim military activities against the Crusaders, lays some emphasis on the idea that there was some inherent aversion to the sea and seafaring in Islam. Proverbs like the Arab, 'it is preferable to hear the flatulences of camels than the prayers of fishes,' can certainly be interpreted like this.[13] Even Ibn Shaddad, Saladin's biographer was so frightened by a winter voyage along the coast to Acre that he remarked that, 'anyone earning his living from the sea must be mad'.[14]

In 1123, however, the Muslim fleet at Askelon was completely defeated by a Venetian squadron in an action off the port. The doge Domenico Michiel who, according to the chronicler, marshalled his ships into two groups with the heaviest vessels in the van, commanded this squadron. The largest vessels included four large merchant ships and galleys called 'cats' because they carried adaptations of the mangonels or *ballistae* used in siege warfare on land, probably on their bows. These would have been used to launch projectiles, stones or pots of flaming liquid, at the enemy. The account of the battle given by William of Tyre is dramatic.[15]

> The Fatimid fleet, at anchor in the roadstead of Askelon, at first saw only the heavy ships and mistaking them for a harmless group of trading vessels made sail in haste, perhaps in the anticipation of

plunder. As the dawn mist cleared they saw the Venetian war galleys, about forty in all, coming up behind. They were now outnumbered and Michiel's galley rammed and sank the ship of the Egyptian admiral.

The chronicler continues gleefully that the sea turned red with blood for two miles around the embattled fleets with the Venetians gaining a decisive victory. The Venetians themselves now cruised on south along the coast and captured Muslim merchant ships laden with the treasures of the East, gold, silver, pepper, cinnamon and other spices. This moment would also have seemed to be propitious for an assault on the town of Askelon thus denying its anchorage to the Egyptians, but the leaders of the Franks wished instead to lay siege to Tyre and bought Venetian assistance at a high price. Their merchants would pay no customs or taxes and could trade freely. They would have their own courts, a subsidy of 300 besants a year and control of one third of the city itself. In July 1124 the city fell to the Christians and the terms of the treaty came into effect. To F. C. Lane their privileges were well deserved since they had, 'won for the crusaders undisputed control of the sea for a generation'.[16]

The concept of control of the sea is perhaps not wholly appropriate to medieval fleets which could neither sustain anything approaching a blockade nor even undertake regular patrols except in exceptional circumstances. These events, however, serve to illustrate well the nature of naval warfare at this period especially in these waters. As we have said the apparent simplicity of a conflict between two religious and cultural entities, Christians and Muslims, existed but was overlaid by a much more complex web of conflicting interests. Byzantium was suspicious of the whole crusading movement which seemed to threaten both her religious hegemony in the East and her territorial control of lands formerly part of the Empire. Venice, as the ally of Byzantium, had no wish for support for the Frankish kingdom to undermine her privileged position in the markets of Constantinople but at the same time did not wish to leave what could prove a source of profitable trade to her rivals in Italy, the Genoese and the Pisans. None of the Italian merchant states desired their support for the crusaders to make it difficult for them to continue trading with the Fatimid rulers of Egypt. There were equally strains between the rulers of the Muslim states with little common purpose between them. If we consider the engagements in which ships were involved, we can perhaps make some generalisations about the value of maritime power to the Franks. Above all ships were needed to maintain the vital supply routes which led back to their European homeland. Only in this way could goods of all kinds but especially military supplies, reinforcements and pilgrims make the journey to the East in relative security. The dangers of the journey were not only those inherent in all sea travel but also those of being attacked by pirates of one kind or another. They were, however, less than those of the overland route. Ships also could give vital help in the siege of a port town and they might, but much more rarely, confront the enemy in battle almost always in coastal waters. Since a large proportion of the fleets of both the crusaders and their allies and the Fatimids were galleys, some kind of base on the coast of Palestine, or within easy reach of it was essential. A galley crew, particularly one operating in the high summer temperatures of this area, needed to slake its thirst at regular intervals: not much water could be stored on a galley.[17] Once the Franks had control of all the ports north of Askelon their opponents were faced with difficulties. Fulcher of Chartres describes an Egyptian fleet in 1126 attempting to harrass Frankish shipping along the coast of Palestine, getting as far north as Beirut but:

> suffering greatly from lack of fresh water ... obliged to make a landing in order to fill their buckets from the streams and springs. ... Our knights with their lances and our bowmen with their arrows drove them into the sea and in this way unexpectedly routed them.[18]

It has also been suggested, as we have seen, that by the twelfth century most Muslims were frightened of the sea and very reluctant to get involved in any naval operations. Even though almost all Crusader reinforcements came by sea, no Muslim leaders in the period 1100–1160 made any concerted attempt to attack the cities of the coast as they fell one by one into Crusader hands.[19]

The loss of Askelon itself to the forces of Baldwin III in 1153 served only to increase the operational problems of any Fatimid commander. His nearest watering point not in enemy territory was now Tinnis in the Nile delta and no large fleet could sail beyond Beirut if it was to have sufficient water for the journey home.[20] Conversely it can be argued that the possession of secure coastal bases, now largely free from the fear of Fatimid raids, as well as the corruption and disunity prevailing in the government of Egypt allowed Amalric I to pursue an active policy against that nation despite the threat posed by the successes of Nur ed-din in the north. In the campaigns of 1167, although the main body of crusaders invaded Egypt by the land route, Frankish ships supported the army at the siege of Alexandria. In 1169 an amphibious operation was mounted with Amalric leading the land forces by way of the isthmus while the grand duke Andronicus Contostephanus in command of a large Byzantine fleet shadowed their progress along the coast. The fleet could not, however, sail up the Nile at Damietta as intended since its way was blocked by a great chain stretched across the river by the defenders.[21]

The flexibility given to an army which could operate like this (even if this particular expedition was disastrous for the Christians), had not escaped the attention of Shirkuh who had seized control of government in Cairo in 1168, or his young nephew, Salah ed-Din Yusuf or Saladin. Saladin had succeeded his uncle in March 1169 and had waited all through the summer for the invasion of the Franks and their Byzantine allies. Their arrival outside the walls of Damietta, only possible because of the presence of the Greek fleet, took him by surprise and although he soon profited by the endemic quarrelling in the Christian camp to ensure the raising of the siege, he learnt the lesson of the advantages which could come of a well disposed fleet.

His own preparations had to start virtually from scratch because the few remnants of the Fatimid fleet and its dockyard at Fustat had been accidentally set on fire during the Frankish siege of Alexandria in 1167.[22] As a first indication of his approach he managed to send a small squadron up the Gulf of Aqaba which captured the small Frankish outpost of Aila. As an exploit this was daring, but it did little to diminish the perceived superiority of the Franks at sea. For this he needed to have a fleet. From 1172 he followed a policy aimed at achieving this. He signed trade treaties with both Venice and Pisa for the supply of naval stores, including iron, timber, and wax. He had better access to suitable timber within his own domains as his rule extended west along the North African coast with access to the forests of the Atlas Mountains. The actual construction of the new fleet began in 1177. By 1179 he had 60 galleys and 20 transports; of these 50 were said to be for defence and 30 for offensive purposes against the Franks.[23]

The immediate use made of this fleet followed the pattern seen before. Raids were mounted on Frankish shipping off Crete and Cyprus and along the Syrian coast. In June more than 1000 prisoners were taken back to Alexandria in triumph and in October Saladin's ships raided the harbour at Acre. The chronicler commented with satisfaction, 'our fleet once destroyed became in turn the destroyer of the enemy'.[24] As well as the Mediterranean fleet Saladin had also deployed vessels in the Gulf of Suez and the Red Sea and had restored and refortified Damietta and Suez. Whether this expenditure and the confident assessment of the chronicler were immediately justified was perhaps not entirely clear. Thirty galleys intended to provide seaward support for Saladin's siege of Beirut in 1182 fled from a crusader squadron with some suggestion that the crews of the Egyptian ships had no stomach for a fight. On the other hand Reginald of Chatillon's adventure into the Red Sea, in 1182, ended in the destruction of all the crusader ships by the Saracens. Reginald had conceived a bold plan; using galleys brought overland almost in 'kit form', he had taken Aila and then raided all down the African coasts of the Red Sea sacking the small towns and pillaging merchant ships. On crossing to the Arabian coast his vessels sank a pilgrim ship on its way to Jedda, the port for Mecca. In Muslim eyes this was not only aggression but sacrilege. Saladin's brother sent a fleet in hot pursuit of the corsairs which caught them off al-Hawra. All the ships were taken; some of the prisoners were executed at Mina at the time of the next pilgrimage. The rest were beheaded in Cairo.[25] By 1187 Saladin's military superiority on land to the rulers of Outremer, seemed undoubted. His overwhelming victory at the battle of the Horns of Hattin left the Kingdom of Jerusalem defenceless. His fleet at first seemed to perform well, protecting his seaward flank and assisting in the taking of Acre where 10 galleys were soon stationed. At the siege of Tyre, however, the last crusader stronghold, its deficiencies became cruelly evident. Saladin intended his galleys to perform the vital function of preventing the defenders of Tyre being supplied by sea. His squadron from Acre was surprised by Christian raiding parties; five ships were taken and the rest fled back towards Beirut pursued by the Frankish galleys. Rather than fight, the Egyptian crews abandoned ship with many drowned or slain in the water.[26]

From the point of view of Saladin, this defeat, perhaps, was of only minor importance. His control of the interior of Palestine and Syria was absolute and Tyre, many miles north of Jerusalem, the focus of Christian dreams of recovering the Holy Land, was not well placed as a base for any future expedition from Europe. Imad ad-Din's comment on this disaster is also revealing in its attitudes to naval matters.

> This incident showed that the naval administration of Egypt did not suffer from a superfluity of recruits and that it could not muster suitable manpower. Instead it tried to reassemble ignorant men, without skill or experience or any fighting tradition so that whenever they were terrified and whenever it was imperative to obey, they disobeyed.[27]

He does not mention any technical or supply problems that bedevilled Egyptian fighting ships; nothing about a shortage of timber or ironwork[28] or inferior ship designs.[29] The problem is the lack of experienced battle hardened crews. We can speculate that the Egyptians probably were forced to rely on crewmen from subject peoples either with little or no tradition of manning war galleys or with no great enthusiasm for the task in hand. We can also point out that given the nature of an encounter between oared fighting ships at this time it is no wonder that an inexperienced crew was terrified and took refuge in precipitate flight. The rowers had little or no protection from the showers of missiles that launched a galley attack. Whether these were quarrels from crossbows, stones from some kind of shipboard mangonel or inflammable material probably made little difference. Among the crowded rowing benches casualties could soon become very high. If the opposing galley managed to get a boarding party in position, the situation would rapidly worsen. If it is the case that Egyptian galleys were little different from those of the Italian cities, it is suggested that these inexperienced crews, if taken by surprise, may well have had all or most of their weapons (which they probably had to supply personally) stored centrally on the ship and not to hand. The crossbow (seen by the Venetians, Genoese and Aragonese as the crucial weapon in galley warfare) is not usually associated with Saladin's armies.

The light bows of Saracen mounted archers, not suited to this style of fighting, may have been all that was available. In the right circumstances, principally when no large scale encounter between warships was likely, Egyptian galleys could perform at least adequately. In 1189, at the beginning of the siege of Acre during the Third Crusade, the Christian forces may have had as many as 552 ships engaged, yet on Christmas day, 50 Egyptian galleys got through the enemy fleet and into the harbour at Acre to bring supplies to the defending forces. Richard I's defeat of a large Saracen supply ship somewhere off Beirut 'excited the hyperbole of the English chroniclers',[30] but had ultimately little real strategic significance. The same incident is also mentioned by Ibn Shaddad, Saladin's biographer. He recounts how the shipmaster, 'an excellent man ... made an opening in the ship and all those in it were drowned, together with all the war machines, provisions and other items and the enemy did not obtain any of it at all'.[31] This puts a different slant on the episode making it seem more advantageous to the besieged than their attackers. Throughout 1190–1 small vessels regularly slipped through with supplies from Haifa, a few miles up the coast, even though Saladin's appeals for more fighting ships from the Al-Muwahidi North African rulers were unanswered. Those ships, however, which were in the harbour of Acre, proved very reluctant to fight their way out against the crusaders' vessels even in the winter when their opponents' vigilance was much reduced.[32] This again could hint at the problem identified by Imad al-Din; there was little enthusiasm for action among their crews of conscripts.[33]

After the partial success of the Third Crusade, there is little sign of either Saladin or his successors reversing this situation. Saladin was content to accept that Askelon should be destroyed and left uninhabited, its anchorage unavailable to either side. Success on land was what was of importance and it is no wonder that the reputation of naval forces was so low among the Mamluks that, as Al Maqrisi commented, it was an insult to address an Egyptian as 'a sailor'. Other recorded comments also concentrated on the failings of crews; Baybars I called the crews of an Egyptian squadron defeated off Cyprus in 1270, 'peasants and rabble' and later claimed that, 'anyone given an oar can row well but not everyone can strike well if given a sword'.[34] He laid his finger on the difference between the attitudes of the Mamluk rulers and those of the maritime states of Europe to naval warfare when he stated somewhat enigmatically, 'for you your horses are your ships whereas for us our ships are our horses'. Occasionally the building of a fleet might seem propitious to a Mamluk ruler; this did happen in 1365 following a Frankish attack on Alexandria but the ships, under construction at Beirut in a new yard, were abandoned half-finished and soon looted of any useful fittings.[35] In general, however, from the thirteenth to the fifteenth centuries, the rulers of Egypt saw little purpose or profit in building and equipping warships. We should not, however fall into the trap of seeing in this some characteristic of Muslim nations as a whole or some manifestation of

European naval supremacy. It was a reasonable response to the particular geographic and strategic situation of the Mamluk state at this period.

Of the strategic islands and narrows in the Mediterranean identified by Pryor none of those in the eastern part of the Sea was in Muslim hands in this period with the exception of the isthmus of Suez. Crusader attacks in the Nile delta, however, for example those of Louis IX, were defeated by land forces. In the Red Sea there was no challenge to the domination of Arab traders until late in the fifteenth century. The wind and current patterns also described by Pryor did place the states of the southern coast of the Mediterranean at a disadvantage but the crucial point is perhaps that the real threat to Mamluk rule came eventually not from overseas opponents but from the forces of the Ottomans advancing overland. European merchants, especially of course those from Venice and Genoa, could not afford to neglect the trading opportunities to be found in Alexandria and certainly had an ambivalent attitude to any warlike threats which may have disrupted this. By the end of the thirteenth century to some extent neither the Christian nor the Muslim powers wished to disturb the *status quo* which existed in the naval sphere.

The Western Mediterranean

In the Western Mediterranean, the religious divide between the dominant powers can be presented as the determining factor. The process of the *Reconquista*, the recovery of formerly Christian lands from the Muslim rulers of Southern Spain and the *Maghreb* by the rulers of Aragon and Castile undoubtedly is one important strand running through the history of this period in this area. However, if our main concern is naval warfare the conflicts between Christian states and Christian rulers are of at least equal consequence. Possession or control of the Balearic Islands or the Straits of Gibraltar was of great strategic importance while the islands of Corsica, Sardinia and Sicily also loomed large in the calculations of local rulers. In a maritime context, the most important of these local rulers was probably he who controlled Barcelona. By the end of the twelfth century this was the ruler of the combined realm of Aragon and Catalonia, Alfonso II of Aragon and I of Catalonia.[36] Castile, the other major Christian ruler in the Iberian peninsula had, at this date no access to the Mediterranean. The coastline of the Castilian kingdom lay in the north along the Bay of Biscay and the Atlantic in the territory of Galicia and Asturias. Also on the Atlantic was the small kingdom of Portugal, while in the south were Muslim emirates in close connection with the rulers of the *Maghreb*; from the mid-twelfth century these were members of the Almohad dynasty whose empire at its greatest extent included Morocco, Algeria, Tunisia and Al-Andalus (southern Spain). Further east beyond the somewhat fluid frontiers of Catalonia lay the county of Provence and the territories of Italian city states, most importantly Genoa and Pisa.

At the level of individual seafarers and merchants, a rough, often lawless and violent, maritime community seems to have existed along the shores of the western Mediterranean.[37] The control which rulers had over this community often seemed minimal although it did perhaps increase over the period. Historians of piracy or privateering or the *guerre de course* have pointed out how difficult it is to distinguish unadorned theft and murder at sea from the same acts dignified by some sort of commission that made them part of a low level but officially sanctioned warfare. In all periods up to the end of the fifteenth century and beyond, any vessel at sea was liable to be attacked, boarded and plundered. Christians attacked Christian ships and Muslims their co-religionists. While at the same time attacks on the ships of members of another religious community, indistinguishable in their practical effects, could be officially seen as justified by the crusading ideal, and as part of the holy war of Christianity against Islam. Hélène Ahrweiler described the whole Mediterranean as, 'un vaste théâtre des luttes entre les puissances maritimes de l'Occident' and went on to characterise piracy as warfare which was not only between states but between two groups within a pan-Mediterranean society, Merchants on the one hand and anti-merchant pirates on the other hand, both obsessed with the need to increase their wealth.[38]

The rulers of states in the western Mediterranean did not begin to take real advantage of the opportunity to use ships to good effect in warfare until the thirteenth century. Before this period, naval interventions that bore real fruit seem almost accidental. In June 1147, a group of English, Flemish and Frisian ships, carrying crusaders who had been inspired by the preaching of St Bernard of Clairvaux to join the Second Crusade put into the mouth of the Douro in Portugal to shelter from a storm. Their arrival was greeted with enthusiasm by Alfonso-Henry, count of Portugal who enlisted their aid in the siege of Lisbon, then a Moorish stronghold. The city fell to the Portuguese and their crusader allies in October.[39] Few of the ships then continued to the East but the episode was a demonstration of the key role which could be played by ships in the siege of a city on a waterway. Only with their aid could the investment be complete; only by using ships could supplies be prevented from reaching such a city by water and on the other hand their presence made much easier the reinforcement of the besiegers. In rather similar circumstances, a fleet of northern crusaders also including Germans, and Danes helped in the taking of Sives and Alvor again by the Portuguese in 1189 and of Alcacer do Sal in 1217.[40]

The first steps, however, in the process of the Christian rulers of Iberia becoming naval powers in their own right were taken by the king of Aragon, Jaime or James I known as the Conqueror. When he succeeeded his father, Peter II in 1213 he also inherited his plans to conquer the kingdom of Majorca. The Balearic Islands, in Muslim hands, had long been the base of raiders who could prey very effectively on trading vessels from the North Italian cities, Provence and Catalonia. There had been earlier attempts to wrest control of them from the Muslims by the rulers of Catalonia acting with the Pisans and Genoese.[41] James, however felt confident that the vessels and expertise now available to him among the seamen of Catalonia enabled him to mount an invasion of the islands without the aid of Italian allies. In his own account of his deeds, the *Libre dels Feits*, James describes the fleet put together for the invasion as comprising 25 *naus complides* (translated 'large ships' by Foerster Laures), 18 *tarides* (horse transports) and 12 *aleras*. He also describes how the galleys towed 12 *tarides* into the chosen disembarkation beach where 150 horses and 700 men were landed.[42] There is no difficulty in accepting that horses were routinely transported by sea for war-like purposes. If cavalry was the most effective arm of a medieval army with the mounted knight the most valuable component, clearly an amphibious assault, whether part of an invasion or part of the siege of a town, would hardly be likely to succeed if the attackers were deprived of this weapon. There are many references to the transport of horses in this way and the existence of specialist ships (usually known as *tarides*, *huissiers* or *uixers)* is also well attested. There does, however remain a lingering doubt as to whether the process was quite as trouble free and routine as is sometimes suggested. The landing of horsemen on an open shore cannot have been easy; first of all the vessels, by all accounts large and unwieldy, would have had to have been manoeuvred so as to be stern first to the beach. Laures suggests that in early *uixers*, 'their number of oars was reduced only to position the ship for the landing of the horses', implying that normally the vessels used sail power.[43] This, however, does not greatly diminish the amount of skill and effort needed to get these ships into position. Then, if the horsemen rode away up the shore as if disembarking from an early version of a 'roll-on roll-off' ferry, as some chronicle illustrations undoubtedly suggest, the vessels must have been beached in sufficiently shallow water to allow this to happen in reasonable safety. While all this was happening the ships and their crews would have been very vulnerable to attack from the defenders of the shore in a contested landing. If several vessels were involved the potential for chaos and mishaps of one kind or another must have been very high. Have the chronicles misled us and were in fact horses normally disembarked at a quayside using some form of gangway? A trained warhorse was a very valuable possession; the dangers of a beach landing may only have been contemplated in unusual and extreme circumstances.

The importance of a war fleet became even more obvious to king Peter III of Aragon during the War of the Sicilian Vespers which broke out in 1282 after the Sicilians had rebelled against Charles of Anjou, the papally-backed contender for the throne of the island. Peter's interest in the struggle was ostensibly in right of his wife, Constance, daughter of Manfred, the last Hohenstaufen ruler of Sicily, although it is probably correct to see it also as an aspect of the struggle between Angevin and Aragonese interests for the domination of the western Mediterranean and its trade routes. The most important commander of the Catalan-Aragonese fleet during this conflict was Roger of Lauria, an admiral for whose talents the most extravagant claims have been made. He has been described as, 'a war leader deserving to be ranked with Richard Coeur de Lion, the Black Prince and Nelson',[44]and as having no rival in medieval history, not even among the Genoese and Venetians, as a naval commander.[45] It is certainly the case that, unusually for the commander of a galley fleet at this period, he was involved in at least six major engagements in the period 1283–1300. These are not the sum total of his seafaring exploits over a long and notably successful career as a war leader but they do allow an assessment to be made of his approach to the management and deployment of galleys in battle.[46] It is also possible from a consideration of his career to try and reach some general conclusions about the nature of galley warfare in the Mediterranean in the late thirteenth century.

One problem that has to be faced in any attempt to do this is the nature of the evidence on which to base these conclusions. Lauria was a major figure in the Mediterranean world. The War of the Sicilian Vespers involved participants from and the interests of several European states: in Italy, Genoa, the Regno (the kingdom of Naples and Sicily), and the papacy; in Spain, the joint realm of Aragon and Catalonia and also the kingdom of Majorca; in France not only the king himself but also the lands and interests of Charles of Anjou, especially Provence; and finally the Empire in the east, Romania as contemporaries called it, and both its Greek and its Latin (Frankish) rulers. There is no shortage of chronicles from all these varied realms which include accounts of Lauria's battles but few if any of the writers had any experience of naval warfare or even in some cases the sea itself and we may suspect that the details given of a battle are either merely conventional or based on no more than current rumours. The most reliable of all the chronicles may well be that of Ramon Muntaner.[47] He was present at some of the fights described including the battle of Malta and was a loyal servant of the Aragonese crown. However he wrote between 1325–8, when he was over 60, recalling the events of his adventurous youth, and begins his chronicle in 1208 with the birth of James I some 50 years before his own. His account therefore is not always that of an eyewitness. There are some official letters and other documents in the archives of Aragon relating to Lauria and his exploits. Among the papers of the house of Anjou, which are dispersed in various archives, there is also relevant material including shipbuilding accounts of vessels built for the Angevin fleets. To some extent, however, conclusions must have an unavoidable speculative element based not only on this material but also on a general appreciation of the seaworthiness and manoeuvrability of medieval galleys and the geography of the battle sites and likely sea conditions.

The first naval battle in which Lauria was involved as commander or admiral (Muntaner always refers to Lauria by this title) took place in the Grand Harbour of Malta on 8 July 1283. The Angevins occupied the Castel

St Angelo and were under attack from the landward side by Aragonese forces led by Manfred Lancia; a relieving force of approximately 20 galleys from Provence, commanded by Bartholomew Bonvin and William Cornut, was beached beneath the castle walls.[48] Although the various chronicle accounts are not in complete agreement, it seems that Lauria's first action on reaching Malta was to reconnoitre the situation, slipping a barge with muffled oars between the two Provencal guard ships at the harbour mouth under cover of darkness.[49] When the news came back that the Angevin galleys were beached with their oars unshipped, Lauria ordered his forces to action stations and went into the attack at dawn. At this point Muntaner cannot restrain his amazement at Lauria's next orders. Instead of surprising the Frenchmen he ordered all the trumpets to be sounded thus rousing the enemy; something 'which should be counted to him more for madness than for sense'.[50] Muntaner then explains the action as a reflection of Lauria's wish, 'to show his boldness and the prowess of the worthy people with him'. He also suggests that it very effectively terrified the Provencal commander who is described as exclaiming, 'Ah, God, what is this? What people are these? These are not men, rather are they devils whose only wish is a battle'.[51] Pryor more prosaically points out that Lauria could have had less chivalric motives. In his view in the kind of amphibious action, which was characteristic of galley engagements at this period, beached vessels had an advantage. They were more or less invariably beached stern first so that their high prows with their beaks faced the enemy. This made them 'virtually unassailable' in the kind of hand-to-hand fighting which was usual in the closing stages of a naval battle; it was much easier for men to rush from one danger point to another or for reinforcements to come aboard from the land and the whole group could much more easily be commanded as a unit. He, therefore suggests that Lauria intended to lure the enemy to abandon the safety of the shore and to face the dangers if not in this case of the open sea then at least of the waters of Grand Harbour.[52]

Pryor also takes up three other features of the battle as described by Muntaner which have considerable significance for Lauria's other seafights and also for naval warfare in general. First of all Muntaner tells how Lauria entered the harbour, 'formed in line and all galleys lashed together'.[53] Pryor relates this to the tactic of forming galleys into a 'bridled line'. In this galleys were linked together bow to bow and stern to stern by lines and also by passing the handles of the oars over to the adjacent galley and lashing them in place.[54] The effect would be to create a kind of platform and it is easy to see how this could effectively block a harbour mouth or, in very sheltered waters, provide a good base for the hurling of missiles at an enemy. It is not so easy to understand how this would be a good tactic in any situation where mobility was required or where a fleet was exposed to the effects of wind and wave. Muntaner goes on to describe Lauria closing with the enemy under sail (something not possible if the vessels were lashed together), and how 'they came to the attack so vigorously that the prow of every galley was shattered'.[55] This seems to imply some kind of head-to-head collision of the fleets which might have been a way of leading up to a boarding action with the opposing forces pouring over the prow and beak into the enemy ship. Muntaner, like other chroniclers writing of seafights, mentions the 'bridling' or lashing together of galleys in other places; for example in an encounter between four galleys commanded by Conrad Lancia and 10 Moroccan galleys the Aragonese commander encourages his crew and urges them on, 'roped together as we are, we attack resolutely ... and assuredly we shall defeat them'. However when battle was joined Conrad's forces 'advanced towards the Saracens', 'with great strokes of the rowers'.[56] Similarly, in an encounter with the forces of Charles of Anjou off Nicotera, not long before the battle of Malta, he describes the Aragonese preparations for battle in much the same way:

> And the twenty-two galleys were within a cross-bow shot and they also unshipped their masts and cleared the decks for action and hoisted the standard in the admiral's galley, and all armed themselves and lashed every galley to the next, so that all the twenty-two galleys, thus lashed together and hauling the wind, began to row towards the fleet of king Charles ready for battle.[57]

From these examples it is hard to be sure what is meant by the 'lashing together' of galleys but it cannot have been any process which made it impossible to use the oars. If the oars could be used, any 'bridle' would have had to be of a considerable length and it is hard to see how the tactic can have been of any real benefit. Moreover the danger of loose ropes trailing in the water and snagging on other equipment would also have existed.

Much better attested is the second factor specifically mentioned by Pryor, the value of crossbowmen in sea battles. There is copious evidence that naval encounters usually began with showers of missiles launched by the combatants at each other. These could be stones flung by some form of 'engine', darts, arrows, lances, fire-raising devices, and most effectively the quarrels fired by crossbows. Muntaner claims that the Catalan crossbowmen were, 'so dexterous that they did not discharge a shot without killing or disabling the man they attacked'.[58] The third factor is the presence of *almugavars* as the marines on the Catalan galleys were called. These were lightly armed soldiers from non-noble backgrounds who had gained a fearsome reputation in land battles against the Moors. They were protected only by leather jackets and were armed with javelins, a lance and a dagger. Pryor suggests that they were much more nimble in close combat on a ship's deck than knights in armour[59] and contributed a great deal to the slaughter wrought on the Provencals who, according to Muntaner included 'a hundred men of rank' from the Castel St

Angelo.[60] Certainly on this occasion as on others the victory lay with the Catalans who apparently suffered far fewer casualties than their enemy.

Do Lauria's remaining battles show similar skill in the tactical disposition and in the control of a galley fleet? All were fought against the enemies of the house of Barcelona in the context of the War of the Sicilian Vespers. They include the battle in the Bay of Naples in June 1284, that off the Catalan coast probably near the islands of Las Hormigas in September 1285, the so-called battle of the Counts in June 1287 and a battle off Cape Orlando in July 1299 and off Ponzo in June 1300. All were fought off shore in relatively sheltered waters; this is a common characteristic of virtually all naval warfare at this period. We can compare the fighting at sea in the eastern Mediterranean where the most common use of ships was in support of the siege of a coastal town. To Pryor a common feature of the battles is also the clear tactical thinking of Lauria as demonstrated in the actions of the Aragonese fleet and the close control that he seemed to have over his fellow galley commanders. The problem with this interpretation is that it does depend on placing trust in the accuracy of the account of a battle derived from chronicle evidence, and, as Pryor freely admits, the chronicles seldom agree. The number of vessels whether Angevin or Aragonese involved in an action can be either a matter of some uncertainty or wildly exaggerated.[61] Lauria, for example, is credited at the battle of Naples with luring the fleet of Charles of Salerno out from the relative safety of his anchorage at Naples, apparently against the express orders of his father, Charles of Anjou, largely by the tactic of a feigned flight towards Castellamare.[62] A tactic like this could have been decided on in advance at a council of commanders but once battle was joined communication between the admiral and his subordinate commanders would have been extremely difficult. The use of signals at sea was hardly developed and there is no evidence of any training of galleys in complex concerted manoeuvres. It is, perhaps, more to the point that Lauria was a battle hardened commander with a squadron of similarly experienced galleys and crews, while the opposing commander was young, inexperienced, anxious to impress both his father and the people of the Regno who had not shown any great enthu-siasm for the Angevin cause. Once battle was joined the chroniclers on this occasion state that the Angevin fleet was suddenly surrounded by Lauria's forces. Those who could, fled back to safety in Naples and the remainder was taken. Pryor sums this action up as, 'another triumph for Lauria's tactics and handling of his fleet as a controlled unit, for the discipline of the fleet and for the fighting qualities of his crossbowmen and *almugavars*'.[63]

Lauria certainly deserves the credit for the victory even if in strategic terms it made little difference to the course of the war as a whole but the evidence for his tactical skill, as a fleet commander, is suspect. A feigned flight could credibly have been decided on in advance, as has been said, but to imagine that a medieval galley fleet could then have turned as a unit to form a battle line in a crescent moon formation to face a pursuing enemy seems doubtful.

The battle more probably became a series of individual fights, galley versus galley, where skilled experienced crews would have had an advantage. The very fact that the crescent shaped line abreast is the tactic recommended by Vegetius, arouses suspicion.[64] Chroniclers, well read in the classics and the works of their predecessors, knew how a sea battle should be fought and therefore may have provided a conventional description, especially if they had little or no contact with anyone present at a particular encounter.

The battle of Las Hormigas occurred when king Philip III of France had led a force over the Pyrenees to support his uncle, Charles of Anjou against Peter III of Aragon. Philip had a supply base at Rosas well protected by a large galley force since he was aware how vulnerable were his lines of communication. Lauria had returned from Apulia at the urgent entreaty of Peter III when the French invaded his territory. Pryor points out that there is no consensus at all among the various chronicles concerning the details of this battle.[65] Muntaner states that Lauria's forces were beached for the night but came out when the mast top lanterns of the French were seen out at sea at day break. Desclot has a story of the French pursuing a smaller Catalan galley force which was then joined by Lauria's forces. Neocastro recounts how the French were beached and then lured to sea by Lauria. The only recurring fact seems to be that the battle took place before or about daybreak. Pryor sees this, which was certainly unusual at this period, as another demonstration of Lauria's astuteness as a naval commander; he could and did take advantage of darkness or poor light to confuse or surprise his enemy. He links this with the ability of the *almugavars* to fight at night but at sea this skill would not have been a deciding factor.[66] Much more to the point would have been the ability of Lauria's ship masters to navigate along a rocky coast in the dark or half-light so that the galleys were not in greater danger from running aground or striking rocks than from the enemy. If Lauria's fleet could engage the enemy in these conditions, it is a great tribute to the skills of Catalan seamen.

The battle of the Counts in June 1287 (so-called because the Angevin forces were commanded by Count Robert of Artois assisted by the counts of Avella, Brienne, Montpelier and Aquila) took place in the Bay of Naples probably in much the same area as that of 1284. This has led to the suspicion that in some chronicles the accounts of the two engagements are conflated. There seems to be general agreement that Lauria's forces were outnumbered and that the battle was lengthy and hard fought, but it is, as usual, difficult to get a clear and reliable picture of the tactics employed. The crucial factor in Lauria's eventual victory may well lie in Villani's comment that the French, although valiant, were much less experienced in fighting at sea than Lauria's men.[67] In a confused melee with groups of galleys engaged in boarding actions, the fighting spirit and expertise of both the galley crew and the specialised fighting men on each could well have determined the outcome. What is notable about this battle is that it did have strategic importance; the

Angevin attempt to invade Sicily was abandoned, leaving James II, second son of Peter III, as ruler of the island.

The two final encounters of Lauria's career took place in rather different political circumstances from those already discussed. The policy of the Sicilian and Spanish branches of the Aragonese royal house had diverged to the extent that James II, now ruler of Aragon had allied with the Angevins headed by Charles II against his younger brother Frederick III, king of Sicily from 1295. Lauria was loyal to Aragon so that these battles were fought between an Aragonese-Angevin fleet commanded by Lauria and a Sicilian one commanded by the Genoese Conrad Doria. The first took place off the Sicilian coast when Lauria's fleet was supporting an invasion of the island by James' forces, the second in the familiar waters of the Bay of Naples. Both were victories for the Aragonese but, although the second seems to have led to the destruction of the Sicilian fleet, neither had long term strategic importance. Despite these defeats at sea Frederick consolidated his hold on Sicily and was recognised as king by the Treaty of Caltabellotta in 1302. From the tactical point of view the battle of Cape Orlando is of greater interest not least because as well as the chronicle accounts there also exists a report of events written by James and a letter concerning his defeat written by Frederick, both being present at the battle with their forces.[68] From these it appears that Lauria's galleys were beached in the bay of San Marco di Val Demone, a secure position but, in this case probably complicated by the fact that a strong on-shore wind made leaving shelter difficult. Niccolo Speciale speaks of Lauria's galley being in fact moored securely to the shore. The Sicilian fleet spent the night off-shore in stormy conditions but was able to enter the bay to engage Lauria on the morning of 4 July. Both fleets engaged, drawn up in the crescent moon formation with the galleys 'bridled'. This again raises problems; why should a fleet entering a bay with the wind in all probability behind it adopt a tactic which gravely reduced its mobility? If we also consider that the Sicilians could not have bridled their galleys until they were within the bay and may well have been under attack by missiles thrown from Lauria's forces while attempting this complex manoeuvre, it seems even more unlikely that this was done. On the other hand given the tactical advantages that accrued to galleys with easy access to the shore, why should Lauria have ventured out even into shallow water at this stage of the battle? Better to wait until the opening exchanges of missiles had done their work and then allow galley commanders to board enemy vessels as opportunity served. It is notable that Frederick's own report of the encounter accounts for his defeat by saying that his galleys could not attack the enemy because they were, '*sic intra seipsas remis involutae*'. This would seem to describe not 'bridling' but a situation where his galleys under oars had failed to keep sufficiently far from each other and had ended up tangled one with another; not a situation that reflects well on individual galley masters but one which could easily arise in the confusion of battle with the crew exposed to showers of crossbow bolts and flaming arrows.[69]

Even if one does not accord Lauria quite such extravagant praise for his skills as a fleet commander as Pryor, it is nevertheless clear that this series of battles reveals the use which could be made of sea power at this time.[70] In suitable circumstances the possession of a fleet could be of considerable strategic importance especially where the lines of communication between a land army and its base were vulnerable to attack from the sea. The difference between defeat and victory did not depend so much on the sheer number of vessels available to the combatants as on the determination and steady nerves of all those on board whether the crossbowmen, the rowers or the commanders. The issue of the importance of conflict between religious blocs does not arise at all in the connection with this series of battles. This does arise, however, if the interest of Castile in naval matters during the same period is discussed.

The Kingdom of Castile had had control of the north coast along the shores of the Bay of Biscay from the time of its union with Galicia in 1230. Despite the fact that this was an area with an active seafaring tradition and some excellent harbours, the origins of the royal Castillian navy are traced to the campaign to recapture Seville from the Moors led by Ferdinand III in 1247–8. The *Primera Cronica General* includes an account of how *Remon Bonifaz, un omne de Burgos,* came to the king and suggested that ships must be used in any attempt to capture Seville which had a chance of being successful. This suggestion appears to have been acted upon and Bonifaz is recorded as being present with vessels which may have been hired in the northern ports. These helped in the investment of the city and two eventually managed to break through the bridge of boats which had linked the Moors in Seville with those on the other side of the Guadalquiver in Triana, an action which was crucial in ensuring Ferdinand's success. Remon was no seaman, despite the fact that he is often described as the first Admiral of Castile, and came in fact from Montpellier rather than Burgos but the fame of his exploits helped encourage the use of ships by the Castillians.[71] The whole lower course of the Guadalquiver was soon in Castillian hands including Cadiz and Sanlucar. This provided more ports and access to the Straits of Gibraltar, opening up a whole new maritime world to the Castillians.

Considerable effort was devoted by Alfonso X, who succeeded to the throne in 1252, to the establishment of naval facilities in Seville and to the creation of an Admiralty administration. The first Castilian to hold this title was Don Ruy Lopez de Mendoza from December 1254.[72] The aim of this new fleet, one which had already been under active discussion in the last months of Ferdinand III with the encouragement of the Pope, was to cross the Straits and assist the invasion of Moorish territory. Nothing was done for some time but at last in 1260 an expedition set out for Sale, on the Atlantic coast of Morocco, a notorious base for pirates. The Castillian fleet held the town for nearly three weeks but retreated laden with booty and prisoners when the forces of the Marinid emir approached. Castillian fortunes in the south of Spain however suffered a reverse from the success of a rebellion in 1264 of the Moors in conquered lands supported by the Marinid leader Ya'qub and the king of Granada. Alfonso used his own naval forces to help recover lost territories and also turned for help to the Genoese who were well established as merchants in Seville. Of the details of the action undertaken by the Genoese galleys in the service of Alfonso nothing is known.[73]

By 1278, Castillian rule in the south still faced the challenge of incursions by the Moors from across the Straits. Any attempt to use their naval forces, which Alfonso had never ceased to support, against the Moors came to nothing because of the Moorish possession of Algeciras. This town dominated its bay and was the favoured port of arrival for Marinid incursions. According to the chronicle, Alfonso ordered the preparation of an enormous fleet including 80 galleys, and 24 large sailing vessels (*naves*) without counting all the smaller boats. The naval blockade of the town began on 6 August 1278 and it was completely surrounded by land and sea by February 1279. A relief fleet collected from all the Moroccan ports, eventually numbering about 72 ships, was ready by July. The chronicles then have a story of how a Moorish embassy, sent from their fleet at Tangiers in a single galley, visited the Christians forces off Algeciras to offer peace. While diplomatic niceties were exchanged between the adversaries, other men disguised as ordinary seamen took careful note of the disposition of the Christian galleys. Two days later the Moorish forces attacked and completely defeated Alfonso's galleys. The admiral Pedro Martinez de Fey was made prisoner and most of the galleys taken or sunk except a few which fled to Cartagena. The Castillians had no alternative but to abandon the siege.[74] This fleet had not perhaps distinguished itself but the awareness of the potential benefits of a 'royal navy', which Alfonso undoubtedly possessed, produced a great change in Castillian attitudes. Seville was a city whose prosperity depended on seamen and ships. Castile now had the opportunity and the motivation to become not only a land power but a sea power as well.

In some respects it is possible to see similarities between the aims of rulers engaged in war at sea in both the eastern and western Mediterranean. In both areas the religious conflict associated with crusading was an important factor. In the East, however, although the Christian states could be portrayed as having naval superiority, the situation of both the Empire and the kingdom of Outremer on land deteriorated during the thirteenth century, leading to the elimination of the latter in 1291. The relative weakness of the Mamluks in naval matters may more probably be interpreted as a lack of interest, since victory was theirs without the need to build and maintain a fleet. In the West the same period saw the rise of an aggressive and expanding state, the combined realm of Aragon-Catalonia, whose rulers fully appreciated the value of naval power but who employed it with greatest effect not against

Muslim powers but against the house of Anjou. The largest Iberian state, Castile, also began to exploit the use of ships in war but in her case, against the Moors of the Maghreb, the result was the total destruction of her fleet and the abandonment of the land campaign which it was supporting. The assessment of the tactical details of naval encounters in whatever part of the Mediterranean is hampered by lack of confidence in the available sources but even so we can perhaps discern a growing interest in naval warfare among rulers even if its style and methods showed little change.

Notes

1 Our sea.

2 B. Kreutz, 'Ships, shipping, and the implications of change in the early medieval Mediterranean', *Viator*, 7, 1976, p. 87. Kreutz also draws attention to the extreme fragility of naval power in this period.

3 H. Ahrweiler, *Byzance et la Mer*, Paris, Presses Universitaires de France, 1966, p. 395, speaks of the Byzantine 'armée de mer et la flotte' as being 'au service de la politique d'expansion ... elles sont l'arme du rêve Romain de Byzance'.

4 Ibn Khaldun, *The Muqqadimah: An Introduction to History* (trans. F. Rosenthal), Princeton, Princeton University Press, 1958, vol. II, p. 41; quoted in J.H. Pryor, *Geography, Technology and War: Studies in the Maritime History of the Mediterranean, 649–1571*, Cambridge, Cambridge University Press, 1988, p. 103. Ibn Khaldun (c.1333–1408) wrote a considerable time after the events described, and is generally thought to have been guilty of a degree of exaggeration. Y. Lev, 'The Fatimid navy: Byzantium and the Mediterranean Sea 909–1036 C.E./297–427 A.H.', *Byzantion*, 54, 1984.

5 J.H. Pryor, *Geography, Technology, and War*, Chapter III, pp. 87–101.

6 F. Fernando de Bordeje Morencos, 'La Edad Media: Los años obscuros del poder naval', *Revista de Historia Naval*, Año XI, 1993, Part II, pp. 101–22.

7 The importance for naval warfare of the prolonged conflict between Venice and Genoa will be discussed in a later chapter.

8 H.E. Mayer, *The Crusades*, second edition, Oxford, Oxford University Press, 1988, p. 50.

9 H.E. Mayer, *The Crusades*, p. 55.

10 H.E. Mayer, *The Crusades*, pp. 68–69. In the view of William Hamblin, 'the Franks were able to conquer Fatimid-held maritime cities only when the presence of a large Christian fleet operating in the region ensured Frankish naval superiority and paralysed Fatimid naval capacities'. 'The Fatimid navy during the early Crusades 1099–1124', *American Neptune*, XLVI, 1986, p. 77.

11 Hamblin, *loc. cit.*, feels that this number may have existed on paper only.

12 J.H. Pryor, *Geography, Technology and War*, p. 114.

13 C. Hillenbrand, *The Crusades: Islamic perspectives*, Edinburgh, Edinburgh University Press, 1999, p. 557.

14 C. Hillenbrand, *The Crusades*, p. 559.

15 William of Tyre, *A History of Deeds Done Beyond the Sea* (trans. and ed. E.A. Babcock and A.C. Krey), New York, Columbia University Press, 1943, Vol. I, Book XII, pp. 22–3.

16 F.C. Lane, *Venice: A Maritime Republic*, Baltimore and London, Johns Hopkins University Press, 1973, p. 34.

17 J.H. Pryor, *Geography, Technology and War*, pp. 75–7. Pryor discusses the whole question of the water consumption of medieval oarsmen in a hot climate in some detail and comes to the conclusion that two quarts (c.2 litres) per man per day was required.

18 Fulcher of Chartres, *History of the Expedition to Jerusalem*, quoted in J.H. Pryor, *Geography, Technology and War*, p. 116.

19 C. Hillenbrand, *The Crusades*, p. 562.
20 J.H. Pryor, *Geography, Technology and War*, pp. 116–9. Pryor includes a full discussion of the water supply problems of Fatimid naval commanders and calculates that these, in fact, ensured that it was virtually impossible for any effective action to be taken at sea by Egyptian ships between the coast of Palestine and Cyprus.
21 S. Runciman, *A History of the Crusades, Vol. II, The Kingdom of Jerusalem*, Harmondsworth, Penguin, 1965. For the siege of Alexandria in 1167 see pp. 374–5; for the events of 1169 see pp. 382–8. Runciman goes into full details of the negotiations and conflicts between all the parties involved, Shia Syrians, Sunni Egyptians, the Franks of Outremer and the Byzantine Greeks.
22 A. Ehrenkreutz, 'The place of Saladin in the naval history of the Mediterranean Sea in the Middle Ages', *Journal of the American Oriental Society*, 75, 1955, p. 103
23 A. Ehrenkreutz, *op. cit.*, p. 106
24 A. Ehrenkreutz, *loc. cit.*
25 S. Runciman, *A History of the Crusades, Vol. II, The Kingdom of Jerusalem*, Harmondsworth, Penguin, 1965, pp. 436–7. The incident, which is found only in Arab Chronicles and that of Ernoul is also described in H. Labrousse, 'La Guerre de Course en Mer Rouge Pendant les Croisades: Renaud de Chatillon (1182–3)', in *Course et Piraterie*, Paris, Institut de Recherche et d'Histoire des Textes: Centre Nationale de la Recherche Scientifique, 1975.
26 C. Hillenbrand, *The Crusades*, p. 569.
27 A. Ehrenkreutz, *op. cit.*, p. 111.
28 W. Hamblin, 'The Fatimid navy during the early Crusades', p. 79. M. Lombard in 'Arsenaux et bois de marine dans la Mediterranée musulmane c.viii–c.xi' p. 98 in M. Mollat du Jourdan (ed.) *Le Navire et l'Economie Maritime du Moyen Age au XVIII Siècle, Principalement au Mediterranée*, also claims that in an earlier period (the end of the tenth and beginning of the eleventh centuries) Muslim forces had lost their preponderance in naval matters because of a shortage of suitable timber for shipbuilding in Muslim lands.
29 J.H. Pryor, *Geography, Technology and War*, pp. 62–8. Pryor discusses what is known about Muslim and Arab ship types in some detail and argues that while there is some evidence that later Turkish galleys may have been smaller and slower than their Western equivalents, the information on earlier Fatimid and Mamluk vessels is too scanty to come to any definitive conclusions. What evidence there is suggests that there were no very great differences between them and those of Byzantium or the Italian maritime cities.
30 N.A.M. Rodger, *The Safeguard of the Sea: A Naval History of Great Britain, Vol. I, 660–1649*, London: HarperCollins, 1997, p. 46.
31 C. Hillenbrand, *The Crusades*, pp. 565–6.
32 J.H. Pryor, *Geography, Technology and War*, p. 129, feels that the problem was not a reluctance to fight but the fact that the galley crews were conscripted into the ranks of the defenders as soon as they reached the port of Acre. He goes so far as to claim, 'when Acre capitulated and the entire Egyptian fleet in the harbour was captured, the survival and recovery of the Crusader states was virtually assured', *ibid.* p. 130.
33 J.H. Pryor, *Geography, Technology and War*, p. 76.
34 D. Ayalon, 'The Mamluks and naval power: a phase of the struggle between Islam and Christian Europe', *Proceedings of the Israel Academy of Sciences and Humanities*, I(8), 1965, p. 5.
35 D. Ayalon, *op. cit.*, p. 6.
36 D. Abulafia, *The Western Mediterranean Kingdoms 1200–1500: The Struggle for Dominion*, London and New York, Longman, 1997, p. 34. At this date the union of crowns was personal with each realm possessing different systems of government. Abulafia points out that the 'central puzzle' of the 'rise of Aragon' is how far it was inspired by the interests of merchants and how far it was driven by the desire of the house of Barcelona to expand its influence and territories.

37 C.–E. Dufourq, 'Chrétiens et Musulman durant les derniers siècles du Moyen Age', *Anuario de Estudios Medievales*, 10, 1980, p. 209, describes what he calls 'an innate tendency to maritime piracy' as characteristic of medieval seafarers in the Mediterranean.

38 H. Ahrweiler, 'Course et Piraterie dans la Mediterranée aux IVième–XVième siècles (Empire Byzantin)', in *Course et Piraterie*, Paris, 1975. Robert Burns sees piracy, 'both as privateering and bloody robbery' as 'a constant in Mediterranean history', 'Piracy as an Islamic–Christian interface in the thirteenth century', *Viator*, 11, 1980, p. 165.

39 S. Runciman, *A History of the Crusades, Vol. II, The Kingdom of Jerusalem*, p. 258.

40 J. Riley Smith, *The Crusades: A Short History*, pp. 139 and 141.

41 D. Abulafia, *The Western Mediterranean Kingdoms 1200–1500*, p. 39.

42 F. Foerster Laures, 'La tactica de combate de las flotas Catalano-Aragonesas del siglo XIII segun la describe Ramon Muntaner (1265–1315)', *Revista de Historia Naval*, V(16), 1987, p. 30. Another version of this article, which is not a complete translation, appeared in the *International Journal of Nautical Archaeology*, XVI, 1987, pp. 19–29, under the title, 'The warships of the Kings of Aragon and their fighting tactics during the 13th and 14th centuries AD'.

43 F. Foerster Laures, *op. cit.* (English) p. 25, (Spanish) p. 30.

44 J.H. Pryor, 'The naval battles of Roger of Lauria', *Journal of Medieval History*, 9, 1983, p. 179.

45 J.H. Pryor, 'The naval battles of Roger of Lauria', p. 211.

46 Lauria's family were supporters of the Hohenstaufen emperors with a base in Calabria. The family moved to Aragon when Constanza married the Infante Peter (later Peter III). Lauria was a loyal servant of Peter and a powerful man at the Aragonese court for his whole career. As well as his naval exploits against the Angevins he was involved with raids on Tunis in 1279 and later in 1292 in the Peloponnese. (G. Airaldi, 'Roger of Lauria's expedition to the Peloponnese', *Mediterranean History Review*, 10, 1995, pp. 14–23.) On his death in 1305, he had a string of fiefs and honours including as well as estates in Aragon, Djerba and Kerkema off the Tunisian coast, Malta and Gozo and Castel d'Aci in Sicily. (J.H. Pryor, 'The naval battles of Roger of Lauria', p. 211).

47 Muntaner's Chronicle has been published both in the original Catalan and in English. R. Muntaner, *Cronica catalana*, (ed. A. de Bofarull), Barcelona, 1890; and *The Chronicle of Muntaner*, (ed. Lady Goodenough), London, Hakluyt Society, 2 vols, 1920–1. Further references are to the English translation of this work. Muntaner much admired Lauria describing him in these terms: 'There never was a man who was not a king's son, to whom God showed greater favour, or who accomplished all things entrusted to him with greater honour to his lord'.

48 This action is fully described in J.H. Pryor, 'The naval battles of Roger of Lauria', pp. 179–89.

49 The action is included in, among others, the chronicles of Muntaner, Desclot (*Chronicle of the reign of King Pedro III of Aragon* (ed. F.L. Critchlow), 2 vols, Princeton, 1928–34), Jacopo d'Oria (included in *Annali genovesi de Caffaro e de' suoi continuatori*, (ed. C. Imperiali,) Rome, Fonti per la storia d'Italia, 1929) and Niccolo Speciale (*Niccolai Specialis historia sicula in VIII libris distributa ab anno MCCLXXXII usque ad annum MCCCXXXVII*, Milan, Rerum Italicarum Scriptores, 10, 1727).

50 R. Muntaner, *Chronicle*, p. 191. Vegetius writes of the advantage of surprise in a naval battle which may account for Muntaner's amazement at a commander who voluntarily relinquished it. Flavius Vegetius Renatus, *Eptitoma Rei Militaris*, (ed. L.F. Stelten), New York, Peter Lang, 1990, p. 293.

51 R. Muntaner, *ibid.*

52 J.H. Pryor, 'The naval battles of Roger of Lauria', pp. 185–6.

53 R. Muntaner, *Chronicle*, p. 191.

54 J.H. Pryor, 'The naval battles of Roger of Lauria', pp. 188–9.

55 R. Muntaner, *Chronicle*, p. 192.

56 R. Muntaner, *Chronicle*, p. 51.

57 R. Muntaner, *Chronicle*, p. 90.

58 R. Muntaner, *Chronicle*, p. 192.

59 J.H. Pryor, 'The naval battles of Roger of Lauria', pp. 187–8.

60 R. Muntaner, *Chronicle*, p. 191.
61 J.H. Pryor, 'The naval battles of Roger of Lauria', p. 195.
62 J.H. Pryor, 'The naval battles of Roger of Lauria', p. 192.
63 J.H. Pryor, 'The naval battles of Roger of Lauria', p. 194.
64 Flavius Vegetius Renatus, *Eptitoma Rei Militaris*, p. 293.
65 J.H. Pryor, 'The naval battles of Roger of Lauria', p. 196.
66 J.H. Pryor, 'The naval battles of Roger of Lauria', p. 199–200.
67 G. Villani, quoted in J.H. Pryor, 'The naval battles of Roger of Lauria', p. 203
68 H. Finke, *Acta Aragonesa*. J.C. Lunig, *Codex Italiae Diplomaticus*, Frankfurt, no publ., 1729–1735.
69 Orders to ensure that the galleys kept their distance one from another when going into the attack were given to the Venetian fleet before the battle of Zonchio in 1499, see below, p. 127.
70 J.H. Pryor, 'The naval battles of Roger of Lauria', p. 213
71 F. Perez-Embid, 'La marina real Castellana en el siglo XIII', *Anuario de Estudios Medievales*, 10, 1969, pp. 141–54. The *Primera Chronica General* was edited by M. Pidal in the series Nueva Biblioteca de Autores Espanolas.
72 F. Perez-Embid, 'La marina real', p. 166.
73 F. Perez-Embid, 'La marina real', pp. 166–71 and 175–7.
74 F. Perez-Embid, 'La marina real', pp. 179–83.

CHAPTER FOUR

The Channel powers in the fourteenth century: the use of seapower by England, France and their allies, c.1277–c.1390

The last quarter of the thirteenth century and the opening years of the fourteenth are, perhaps, characterised by the degree of instability which existed in the relations between states. Alliances were made and unmade with rapidity and this undoubtedly had significant effects on the way in which naval warfare developed. Edward I, as king of England and duke of Aquitaine, in turn opposed and was in alliance with Philip IV of France. The Flemings, whose economic interests tended normally to ensure their friendship with England, became allies of the Scots during their bitter wars against England. The Welsh princes, even if not themselves able to use a fleet against the English, were well aware that Edward I needed access to supplies brought by sea to confirm his conquest of their lands. After the accession of Edward III of England and his intervention in the French succession dispute, the strategic situation becomes much clearer. For the remainder of the century, the dominant conflict was that between England and France, the first phase of the Hundred Years War, and other nations were involved as allies or enemies of the two major combatants. In this confusing situation, it seems best to look at the use made of sea power under three headings: the use of ships as auxiliary forces; transporting men, material and victuals, major encounters between the forces of rival powers, and raids on coastal towns and on commerce.

Ships as auxiliary forces

Given that, of the two states most likely to be in conflict in northern waters one was the major part of an offshore island and the other was a continental state, it is of course, obvious that all wars between them would at some point necessitate the transport of men and supplies by sea. It was, however, much rarer that a whole campaign depended on the ability to use sea routes effectively and keep them open against a determined enemy. Edward I's attempts to subdue Wales and Scotland both illustrate the importance of ships in a logistical role in medieval warfare. Rodger has drawn attention to the existence of a semi-independent 'Norse-Celtic world' in the Irish Sea in the 200 years before Edward intervened in order to enforce English rule over the remaining Welsh princes.[1] In the campaigns of 1277 and 1282 the royal armies depended on supply by sea, largely using arrested ships supplied by the Cinque Ports.[2] Since there was no hostile naval force at large in the Irish Sea, this was successful. Edward was able to make progress along the shores of North Wales with no fear of running out of supplies since his fleet tracked his progress on land. Similarly fleets assisted in the taking of Anglesey, invaluable as a base and also as a source of grain. In the Scots campaigns beginning in 1296, which were, of course, on an altogether bigger scale, the logistical support of ships was of even greater importance. Scotland was, at this time, a poor and ill-developed country where transporting large quantities of military stores and supplies for both armed men and their horses overland was extremely difficult. There was also little prospect of feeding even a moderate force off local supplies. If an army was unable to maintain contact with its supply ships it could be forced to withdraw or face virtual starvation. The aim of the Scots, from 1306 led by Robert Bruce, was to cut the English maritime supply routes and thus fatally impede the ability of their army to fight a successful campaign.

There is little here of naval warfare in an active or heroic sense. The claim that 'ships as men-of-war' were unimportant in these campaigns is, perhaps, based on a misunderstanding of the potential of the use of ships in such circumstances.[3] A naval battle in the conventional sense would have been unlikely to have greatly affected the fortunes of the forces on land. The same cannot be said of interruptions to the supply chain. The sheer amount of provisions which had to be transported north by the English is clear from the amount ordered from Ireland by Edward I in 1301; this included large quantities of wheat, oats, malt, beans and peas, and salt fish.[4] Once Scottish castles were in English hands, ships were arrested to run regular supplies northwards up the east coast as far as Aberdeen and on the west coast, using vessels from both Ireland and the West Country to Dumfries and other strongholds. Bruce found support among the powerful local lords in the Western Isles and in the north of Ireland and was able to use their forces to disrupt this supply route, while on the east coast he had help from Flemish allies. Edward II's failure to hold on to his father's conquests in Scotland cannot be put down solely to his lack of success in maintaining his vital maritime supply routes but this was an undeniably important factor. The final humiliation from the English point of view was the capture of Berwick by the Scots in 1318 after they had prevented English reinforcements and supplies getting into the harbour.[5]

Knowledge of these operations comes largely from accounts kept in this instance by the king's Wardrobe. This section of the royal household became in this period an accounting office which was more flexible and more immediately responsive to royal commands than the Exchequer with its somewhat stately procedures.[6] It was, therefore, highly suitable for war finance. A remaining Wardrobe book for 1314–16 allows a closer look at these operations. Some royal ships are involved, an anonymous barge, the *Welfare*, the *Cog Edward*, the *Red Cog*, the *St John* and the *Swallow*. The others are arrested ships coming from Colchester, Hull, Newcastle, King's Lynn, Grimsby, Yarmouth, Orford and other east coast ports. Despite the often vicious weather on the east coast in the winter these ships were at sea in these months, the master of the *Welfare* being paid for the period from November to February and specifically said to be at sea. One unfortunate Newcastle vessel, the *St Mary Boat*, took four weeks to go from Berwick to Newcastle with Christmas fare for the royal household because of the roughness of the sea. More usually the ships were carrying victuals, horses, carpenters needed for the construction of pavisades, and other supplies for the army. By 1317 a squadron of four vessels, described as war ships, (though none were in royal ownership), manned by 42 men-at-arms and 99 archers, was patrolling off the coast for the protection of the supply route from Berwick to Edinburgh. It is clear from the names of these ships (cog, barge, etc.) and the size of their crews that these were sailing ships. The accounts (which do not cover all naval activity during these years) also imply that quite large sums of money were laid out in this way; over £500 for example in 1314–15.[7] The precise way in which vessels not in royal ownership were provided for these expeditions to the north is also revealed in two documents preserved in the archives of the city of Exeter.[8] The first relates to 1303 and a vessel called the *Sauveye*. This ship was said to have been hired from her owners, five Devon men, by the Mayor and community of Exeter, with her equipment but no crew, to go to Scotland for the king's wars. The city committed itself to paying 'reasonable' hire costs and the full cost of any losses due to the war. The second dates from 1310 and sets out how the *St Mary Cog* of Exmouth has been provided at the royal command to convey Simon de Montagu from the Isle of Man to the Scottish wars. The payment due to the owners, 55 marks (£37 6s 8d) for 40 days service came from the city but longer service would be at the cost of the crown.[9]

The logistical support of shipping was also, of course, of great importance in the Anglo-French wars later in the fourteenth century. English armies had to be transported across the Channel and the capture of Calais can be represented as the acquisition of a secure overseas base from which to mount campaigns in northern France. Some forces also had to face the much longer and more difficult voyage through the Bay of Biscay to the coasts of Aquitaine for operations in the south of France or in northern Spain. The crown did have the ability to arrest local shipping, in ports in areas under English rule, for use in wartime and in fact considerable use was made of the maritime resources of Bayonne, but the transport function of English ships was still of great importance. The organisation required to put together the transport for an expedition overseas was very considerable. Ships of sufficient size had to be placed under arrest to serve the crown and then assembled at the relevant port. Some had to be adapted for the transport of large numbers of horses. This involved the supply of wide gangplanks to get the animals on board and then the construction of stalls in the hold made of hurdles and provided with rings and staples for the restraint of the animals. Expeditions almost invariably left long after the date first envisaged for their departure for a variety of reasons including the vagaries of the weather, changes in plans and the need to assemble enormous quantities of provisions. In March–April 1338 the victuals ordered to be collected at Yarmouth or Orwell included 7900 quarters of grain and legumes, 6930 carcasses of fresh and salt meat and 5900 stones of cheese. The following year royal orders were issued requiring 10,000 horseshoes and 60,000 nails to be provided from Nottingham for an overseas expedition.[10]

The most striking example in the French wars of the essential support supplied by ships to a land campaign is, perhaps, provided by the siege of Calais. Both sides desperately needed to keep open supply routes by sea. The French within the town had little hope of getting food through the lines of the investing English army on land; it was much more difficult, however, for the English to prevent French vessels slipping through the blockade into the harbour. If Edward could not keep open his lines of communication with England and, in his turn receive fresh supplies, he ran the risk of being himself besieged by the forces of Philip VI or being forced to retire. The French king had entered into negotiations with Genoa for the supply of 32 galleys and one galiot crewed by some 7000 men in early 1346. These forces under the command of Carlo Grimaldi did not arrive until after the English had crossed the Channel, won a resounding victory at Crécy and marched on Calais. Grimaldi, however, managed to intercept and take 25 English supply ships a fortnight after the siege had begun in early September 1346. He insisted, however, on taking his galleys into winter quarters at the end of October. He had no wish to risk them in winter storms in the Channel. French ship masters from Leure, St Valerie, and Dieppe, however, were prepared to attempt to run provisions into the town. Colin Hardy had some success as did Guillaume Dauvelle but the ships used were very small (Dauvelle's averaged seven crewmen each) and some were driven ashore and wrecked.[11] By January, the English crown had taken steps to arrest over 738 ships to victual the besieging army. Of these 700 were English vessels and 38 came from Bayonne, Spain, Ireland, Flanders and Gelderland; they were crewed by over 9300 mariners. These figures seem extraordinarily high but come not from the fertile imagination of a monastic chronicler writing far from the scene of battle but from a copy of the account roll of the Treasurer for War.[12] In April 1347, Philip made a determined effort to replenish Calais' supplies. A squadron of ships was assembled including at least seven royal ships. These went into Dieppe harbour probably to load more supplies but were delayed when one very heavily laden barge ran aground. It took the concerted efforts of over 300 local women to pull her free. The ships then crept along the coast in stormy weather losing one of their company on the way. At Boulogne further reinforcements joined the squadron and two Calais mariners (or perhaps more properly pirates) agreed to act as pilots for the tricky approach to the town. They found, however 120 ships commanded by Suffolk and Arundel awaiting them and also discovered that the English had managed to fortify the Risban (a sandbank lying across the entrance to Calais harbour) with a new wooden tower. Nevertheless 30 French ships made it through the opposing forces into the safety of the harbour avoiding missiles and sunken blockships alike. This was the last convoy to reach the town though other attempts were made including one from Crotoy,[13] led by Genoese galleys in June which ended with the Genoese fleeing from a superior English force even dumping their weapons overboard in their frenzy to escape.[14] By the end of the month, the English had clear confirmation of the degree of distress in the town. Two vessels attempted to break out through the blockade to take letters to the French king. One, when attacked, managed to retire safely to the town, the crew of the other threw letters overboard before being taken. These were retrieved at low tide and, according to Knighton's Chronicle, included one from the Captain of the town to Philip VI suggesting that cannibalism would soon be the only alternative left to the starving townspeople.[15] By the beginning of August the town had capitulated and Edward III set about converting it into an English colony with vigour. The French inhabitants were expelled and English settlers installed in their place along with a permanent garrison. All this certainly gives the impression that the town was seen as having a military and strategic function but the maintenance of strong maritime links with England would be as important for its future development as they had been for its successful capture.[16]

Major encounters at sea

Major encounters between rival fleets which can be dignified with the name of battles are, of course, much rarer occurrences in this area and at this period than the kind of unglamourous but essential support role which we have already discussed. The possible important strategic implications of a naval battle which had been demonstrated by the battle of Dover in 1217 were to some extent understood. It was also the case, however, that problems in communication and in the acquisition of accurate intelligence severely limited the circumstances in which a sea fight on a grand scale could have such consequences. Rulers were, perhaps, prepared to take a greater interest in their realm's capacity to engage in naval warfare. The most striking demonstration of this was the foundation by Philip IV of France of the *Clos des Galées* at Rouen. Even if the number of vessels built there for the French Crown was small, they were in the main vessels intended primarily for war and thus signified a new acceptance of the importance of sea power. The response of the English king to the threat that this development posed, his order to 26 towns to share in the building of 20 galleys for the Crown, reveals a different solution to the problem of providing for maritime forces but also a similar appreciation of the need for increased provision of warships.[17]

The first major battle to consider in detail occurred in 1304 in the waterway leading to the town of Zierikzee in Zealand. The protagonists were Philip IV of France and Guy de Namur the Count of Flanders. The French had been attempting to extend their control over Flanders at least since 1297; the situation was complicated both by the involvement of the English, the major trading partners of the Flemish towns and the semi-independent status of the major cloth-producing towns of the region. In 1302, a major rebellion against French rule in the region had led to the defeat of the French land forces at the battle of Courtrai. The English had used this moment of weakness on the part of France to conclude a treaty with them. Thus when the French began a new campaign in Flanders in 1304 the English were at least temporarily allies of France while the Flemings had turned to Scotland for support. Guy de Namur had in the meantime attempted to take over the lands of John d'Avesnes, the Count of Holland and Hainault. These included Zealand while John himself was also allied with the French. Guy's forces were laying siege to the town of Zierikzee, part of d'Avesnes' territories, when the French fleet approached.

The events of the battle were recorded in a metrical history written c.1306, by one Guillaume Guiart who seems to have had access to good information.[18] The attacking French fleet consisted of two diverse squadrons. One consisted of what the author calls 'grands nefs', one variation on the round sailing ship type of northern Europe; this was led by Pedrogue from Calais and consisted of eight Spanish ships and French vessels arrested along the Channel coast. The other was made up of 12 galleys hired from Genoa under the command of Renier Grimaldi who also had overall command. Five further ships commanded by Count William, the son of John d'Avesnes joined them at the mouth of the Scheldt. Here the wind and tide turned against them and it took at least eight days to bring all the ships up the waterway to the besieged town. The plan, according to Guiart, was to divide the ships into three groups of about 15 each while the galleys also stayed together. The ships were equipped not only with fore, aft and top castles for the mast but also with springals; a white banner was flown as a recognition signal. The first move was made by Pedrogue who moved forward with his own and three other ships to within crossbow range of the Flemings. The tide, however, was ebbing and all ran aground becoming easy targets both for the Flemings on shore and those on their ships who greatly outnumbered the French. According to Guiart, the response of the remainder of the French fleet to this emergency was to form into one squadron and anchor to avoid being swept on shore by the tide or the wind. He also states that the ships passed cables from one to the other as did the galleys which were behind the *nefs*, tying them into a block. Guy decided to send fireships towards his immobilised enemy but the wind shifted allowing them to drift back towards the town. In the ensuing confusion Guy's shipmasters seem to have realised too late that the tide had turned and Pedrogue's ships were on the move again. The battle now became a confused mêlée with the air thick with missiles of all kinds from the springals, crossbows and archers. Two of the largest Flemish ships were boarded and taken. By this time darkness had fallen but neither side broke off the battle. Grimaldi, whose galleys had taken no part in the fighting as yet, saw that the enemy was in confusion, and now attacked with great success taking at least three more Flemish ships. Guy steered his ship, now under full sail towards Grimaldi's own galley, broke up its oars but failed to grapple it successfully. A second attempt also failed and by this time it was clear that the French had won the day. The account concludes with the lifting of the siege and the return of Pedrogue to Calais.[19]

How much credence can be based on this account and what does it tell us about battle tactics at this date? The account is very nearly contemporary but there is no evidence that the writer had any direct experience of war at sea. An eighteenth century commentator on the poem pointed out that the tactic of 'bridling' warships or tying them together can be found in Livy and thus may be here no more than the conventional following of a classical model.[20] Other aspects of the account are more valuable. Although the battle took place near the shore the action of wind and tide was crucial to the outcome. The ability to handle a vessel under sail in difficult circumstances could decide the issue. Guy's desperate attack on Grimaldi's galley could have turned the fortunes of the battle if it had succeeded. Even if the closing stages were marked by boarding actions the exchange of fire, whether by bowmen or by those operating the big catapaults, was of great importance. The overall consequences of the French victory are less clear-cut. The peace treaty signed in 1305 at Athis-sur-Orge was unfavourable to the Flemings but this in no sense resolved the conflict which continued intermittently until at least 1320.[21]

During the 1330s the tension between England and France came once more to the fore. The underlying cause was, perhaps, the conflict which arose over the position of the English king as Duke of Aquitaine, and thus in relation to some, if not all, the lands of the Angevin inheritance, a vassal of the king of France. The death of Charles IV of France in 1328 had also raised the possibility of a claim to the French throne by Edward III, as heir to his mother Isabella daughter of Philip IV, disregarding the rights of Philip VI of Valois, acknowledged in France as king. War in fact broke out in 1337 precipitated by events in Scotland and on the borders of Gascony.[22] The French quickly took the initiative at sea. In 1338 five of the largest and best armed of the small squadron of English royal ships were surprised and taken in the harbour at Arnemuiden. It is not entirely clear whether this was what later mariners would call a 'cutting-out' expedition or the result of catching the English ships at anchor with most of their crews ashore. Among them was the *Christopher*, the pride of the English fleet. The French also mounted a series of destructive raids on the south coast of England. Although the sheriffs of the maritime counties had set about putting in place the machinery to raise a militia to defend these areas soon after war was known to be imminent, their efforts do not seem to have been very successful. The most serious raid was probably that on Southampton in October 1338. A force which may have included as many as 50 galleys appeared off the town, got the crews ashore and then sacked and burnt the town. Stories of rape and murder circulated fuelling the atmosphere of fear all along the coast. A successful counter-raid on Boulogne in 1339 by ships from the Cinque Ports seemed little compensation for these humiliating events. By the spring of 1340, however, Edward III was in a somewhat better position. He had concluded a treaty with the Flemish wool-manufacturing towns led by Jacob van Artevelde. He had raised a loan to cover naval expenses and orders had gone out for the arrest of shipping, the meeting point being the estuary of the Orwell.

By the middle of June the king was at Ipswich ready to go on board the *Cog Thomas*. On 22 June, after the usual delays the fleet of some 160 ships set sail across the North Sea aiming for the Zwyn, the name given to the more southerly of the branches of the estuary of the Scheldt. They found the French already in possession of the anchorage at Sluys. Froissart describes Edward as being amazed by the size of the French fleet. To him, from seaward, 'their masts resembled a forest'.[23] The French certainly outnumbered the English having at least 200 ships, collected from all the ports of northern France. They also had three Genoese galleys and some barges. Among this force were 32 royal ships, including three galleys and seven *nefs*. The chroniclers do not entirely agree about the course of the battle. The most authoritative account and also the baldest is that to be found in the letter, written by Edward himself on board the *Cog Thomas* four days after the battle.[24] He states that the fleet reached the coast near Blankenberghe on the morning of Friday 24 June. They could see the French at anchor in the Zwyn but could not attack immediately as the wind and tide were against them. The next day with a favourable tide they attacked the enemy drawn up in a very strong formation and with God's help won an overwhelming victory. The *Christopher* and the other ships lost at Middelberg (sic) were retaken. Finally Edward reported with some relish that French mariners and men at arms lay 'dead all along the coast of Flanders'.[25]

He makes no mention of features of the battle of Sluys which are somewhat contentious. Some chronicles describe the English as having the sun behind them. This has led Rodger to suggest that the English approached the French from the east not from the North Sea.[26] This could have been achieved if the fleet had taken the channel between Cadzand and Wulpen and then gone about into the channel known as *Zwarte Gap* and approached from the north east. This would, however have been a highly complex manoeuvre for the fleet to perform and one perhaps dependent on a wind shift since a wind favourable for entry to the Scheldt estuary would not have allowed the fleet to come up on the rear of the French. The ability of ships of this period to lie close to the wind was very poor thus increasing the problematic nature of such tactics. Some chroniclers also suggest that the French had adopted the tactic of mooring the ships together into a block already described as being used by the Flemings at Zierikzee. There again seems some reason to doubt this, despite the added circumstantial detail that the Genoese commander refused to do this and thus was able to flee and save himself and all his ships. The Zwyn is a tidal estuary with many sandbanks; high tide on 24 June 1340 was at 11.23 a.m. Edward III in his letter states that the English entered the port with the tide 'well after Nones'. This implies a time between c.12 and 2 p.m. To face an enemy in a confined waterway on a falling tide with the possibility of any manoeuvring so severely limited seems unlikely if the seamen had any control over the deployment of the French forces. Edward's emphasis on the hard fought nature of the battle and its length (it lasted the remainder of the day and into the night) is significant. A factor in the English victory may have been the arrival of reinforcements for them in the form of the northern squadron of English ships commanded by Robert Morley.[27] What is not in doubt is the later fame of the battle at least among the English. Edward issued a great gold noble with the image of himself carrying his sword and shield on board a cog on the obverse. This served to perpetuate the impression of a great victory gained and in fact the great nineteenth-century historian of the navy Sir Nicholas Harris Nicolas declared that, 'the name of Edward III is more identified with the naval glory of England than that of any other of her sovereigns'. [28]

Edward III may in fact better deserve this reputation for his actions in the much less celebrated action at sea known to contemporaries as *les Espagnols sur Mer*[29] than for Sluys. Sluys was a naval encounter in the old style; a battle off shore in an estuary where one participant found the other at anchor. It was, perhaps, unusual in the scale of the casualties suffered on the loser's side but otherwise was decided by an exchange of missiles followed by boarding actions. *Les Espagnols sur Mer*, as its name suggests, took place offshore in the Channel with the sailing ability of the vessels and the seamanship of the shipmasters being of great importance. In the late summer of 1350 a Castilian fleet, allied to the French was known to be preparing to leave Flanders for the return voyage to Spain. Froissart paints a vivid picture of Edward preparing to mount an attack on this fleet in the Channel explaining that he felt 'they have done us many wrongs and far from making amends they go on arming themselves against us. They must be intercepted on their way back'. Froissart seems to have obtained much of the detail of the course of the battle from

Robert of Namur who was present himself. He states that the king, the Prince of Wales, and John of Gaunt (only 10 years old at the time) were all present along with many other nobles and 400 knights. The Spanish came into view sailing freely with a north east wind behind them. Although the Spanish ships were larger and better armed than the English (Froissart mentions particularly the large supplies of missiles ready in their fighting tops) Edward was apparently in tearing spirits as battle was joined at around four in the afternoon. According to the chronicler, the king directed his shipmaster to steer straight for one of the enemy ships and hit it in such a way that one of the Spanish topcastles was sheered from the mast. The force of the collision also sprang the seams in the king's *Cog Thomas* so that she was in danger of foundering. The king and his companions, however, managed to draw off from this ship, and to grapple with another and take her, abandoning their own damaged ship. This makes for dramatic reading, as does the rather similar account of the actions of the Prince of Wales.[30] However, the particulars in the account of William Clewer, the clerk of the king's ships, note when the ships' crews went on 'war' wages for what is called the voyage against the Spaniards. They then record the *Cog Thomas* and also the Prince of Wales' ship the *Bylbawe*, almost immediately after the battle, setting off to London to return to their anchorage at Redcliff. There is no mention of special repairs or indeed of any losses due to the battle. The same applies to the other royal ships said to have taken part in this battle, the *Cog Edward*, the *Plenty*, the *Miguel*, the *Isabel*, the *Gabriel*, the *Barge Welfare*, the *Godsbyte*, and the *Laurence Bichet*.[31] Froissart may well have exaggerated the severity of the encounter but the overall account rings true. To the English it was a further demonstration of the superiority of their ships and seamen; the Spanish has lost vessels and had had to flee from their determined and persistent attackers. The most important aspect from the point of view of developments in naval warfare was a continuation of the tactics first seen at Dover in 1217. Some crews at the very least now had the confidence and ship handling skills to lay one ship alongside another in a seaway and then mount a successful boarding action despite the best efforts of the crossbowmen or the troops in the enemy's fighting tops hurling stones or other missiles.

If we look for the long-term consequences of the victories of either Sluys or *Les Espagnols* for the English and their war with France, later historians have tended to lay emphasis on those of Sluys while almost completely ignoring *Les Espagnols*. Perroy, the distinguished French writer, states that victory at Sluys 'secured to the victor the command of the sea ... but it was a success without decisive effect'.[32] As he goes on to explain Edward still had to conquer France by land and lacked the means to achieve this. Richmond sees it as allowing England to move 'on to the offensive'.[33] Rodger categorically denies that it gave England command of the sea; 'no such command was possible'. In his view the French, even after loosing large numbers of ships had a more intelligent 'appreciation of the uses of naval power' than their adversaries.[34] The lack of attention paid to *Les Espagnols* is almost certainly due to the fact that Philip VI of France died in the same month. This certainly affected the course of the war as a whole far more than the brief, bloody action off Winchelsea between the English and the allies of France rather than the French themselves.

The engagement between an English squadron carrying the newly appointed Lieutenant of Aquitaine, the Earl of Pembroke and 12 Castilian galleys in the vicinity of La Rochelle in 1372 involved the same protagonists but with a different result. The English vessels were all destroyed and Pembroke and the sum of £20,000 in gold which he had with him to pay for an intended campaign in Poitou fell into the hands of the Castilians. The engagement also raises some interesting problems regarding naval warfare at this period. First of all is that of the nature of the evidence for the events of a battle. Here the best accounts are to be found in Froissart and the French *Chronique des Quatre Premiers Valois*.[35] As before neither chronicler had personal experience of naval warfare and must have been supplied with information from unknown participants. Their accounts do not agree; crucially Froissart makes no mention of the grounding of Pembroke's fleet and the use of fire as a weapon by the Spanish, both important features of the other version of events. The two chronicles also differ quite markedly on the number of ships involved. Second, it is plain that the English ships were all round ships, probably small cogs (the order for the requisitioning of ships for Pembroke's voyage mentions vessels of less than 50 tuns burden with only three larger escorts with 'castles'). The Spanish vessels were all galleys with crews of around 180 men which were much more specialised warships than anything available to the English crown. Third, the conditions of the tide and the precise location of the battle were of great importance in the eventual outcome. Sherborne sees the battle beginning very near the harbour mouth and then moving within the haven itself at La Rochelle.[36] This was not navigable by Pembroke's ships at low water, though the galleys with a much shallower draught could still manouevre and were not, of course, dependent on the wind. The initial encounter near the harbour mouth took place on 22 June and seems to have shown no clear advantage to either side. The next morning the Castilians set fire to the English ships and all were burnt out with Pembroke, some other lords and the treasure chests falling into their hands. Although the tide was rising it does seem that the English may have been caught still aground in the harbour and thus were defenceless against an attack in which flaming arrows were fired on to decks previously sprayed with oil. The news of the complete loss of the fleet caused consternation in England and every effort was made to assemble a further expedition which would prevent the town falling into French hands. This never sailed because of contrary winds; by 27 August Edward III was still at Sandwich. On 7 September the town fell to Charles V while on 18 September Edward had got no further than Winchelsea. Sherborne denies that the action was a naval disaster on a grand scale; rather he sees it as stimulating the English to take more seriously the need to provide ships to defend the realm. Russell, looking at the overall effects of the alliance between French and Castilian seapower on the war with England, saw it as 'bringing home to the English people the disadvantages of the war in which they were engaged'.[37] This does indeed seem to be the case if one looks not so much at the results of the relatively rare naval battles but at the effects of coastal raids and attacks on commerce.

Raids on commerce and coastal towns

Rodger, in fact, sees the raiding tactics of the French and their allies as having a great measure of success.[38] Trade was interrupted, merchants lost ships and the stocks in their warehouses and the people of coastal towns were left fearful and resentful of the apparent inability of the Crown to offer adequate protection from these brief but very violent incursions. The normal form of a raid at this date was that a fleet consisting mainly of galleys left a French channel port, and after a swift crossing appeared off a coastal town. Few English ports had walls or other fortifications before the 1360s;[39] the galley crews thus could enter the harbour more or less unopposed and having fired any moored or anchored ships could turn their attention to burning and looting the town. By the time the news of the raid had reached any forces in the neighbourhood and they had made efforts to mount a defence, the galleymen would have often re-embarked with their booty and set sail to find another vulnerable and terrified community.

A survey of raiding activity in the Channel from 1337 to the end of the century makes clear how realistic these fears were. In England the towns of Rye, Winchelsea, Portsmouth, and Plymouth and the Isle of Wight all seem to have been particularly unfortunate being raided more than once. The dangers were not confined to the south coast, however; northern ports were threatened by the Scots and their allies and the enemy could also appear off Orwell and other towns on the east coast and as far west as Bristol. The most devastating attacks on English towns had more than local resonance. In October 1338, as we have already heard, a mixed force of French galleys and their Genoese allies burnt Southampton. This event is described in one of the poems of Laurence Minot in dramatic terms. The French king's plan was to destroy England; thus he sent his galleys forth with orders to:

> Bot brin and sla both man and wife
> And childe, that none suld pas with life.

The galley commanders were apparently delighted with their orders but when they reached Southampton, although they caused great destruction:

> But not so mekill als sum men wend ...

Sum (attackers) were knokked on the hevyd
That the body there bileved:
Sum lay stareand on the sternes
And sum lay knokked out thare hernes ...[40]

They then took to flight in the direction of Flanders and Zealand. Equally shocking to the English was the burning of Winchelsea in 1360. This probably caused particular dismay since it occurred just before the signing of the Treaty of Bretigny after a lull in this kind of activity.

How should this use of coastal raiding as a tactic in naval warfare be regarded? Why does it seem the French used it much more successfully than the English, who, contrary to the more common expectation, had greater success with land-based expeditions? Two explanations have been put forward; the first being that Edward III lacked any understanding of the use of sea power while the French had a much better grasp of the possibilities presented by this kind of activity at this time. The second explanation relies on the differing nature of the forces available to each monarch. Edward, it is suggested, relied largely on arrested merchant ships, the great majority of which were cogships prepared for war by the addition of fighting tops and fore and aft castles. The French king had his own force of galleys from the shipyard of the *Clos des Galées*. He also had the help of galleys from Genoa under the command of members of the Grimaldi and Doria families and the assistance of the expert seamen of the Castilian squadron. Galley squadrons were particularly suitable for coastal attacks; they could get into most harbours whatever the state of the tide; they were not at the mercy of the wind direction and could leave as rapidly as they had appeared if the need arose. It is also suggested that, since the French king had a professional fleet more or less continuously in being, a much more rapid response could be made to favourable intelligence while the English often took weeks if not months to gather a fleet together by which time the opportunity for a successful operation had passed.[41] There may well be some truth in these ideas but they also perhaps paint too black and white a picture of the situation on the naval frontier between England and France.

The French could and did raid English coastal towns extensively as we have heard. This occurred mostly in two periods; between 1338–45 and between 1377–80. In the first period as well as Southampton, Portsmouth (twice), Harwich, Bristol, Hastings, the Isle of Wight, Plymouth (twice) and Teignmouth were all attacked. In the second, beginning in June 1377, a single devastating raid led by Jean de Vienne, with allied ships from Castile and Genoa, swept along the south coast. Folkestone, Rye, Rottingdean (with a push inland to Lewes), Portsmouth, Plymouth, and Dartmouth all suffered damage. On the return voyage in August, Poole and Hastings were also burnt although Southampton, Dover and Winchelsea remained safe behind their walls. During the first period, however, the English also raided French coastal towns, for example Boulogne, Dieppe and Tréport in early 1340, while the second took advantage of the undoubted period of weakness which followed the death of Edward III. The first attack in fact took place three days after his death. It also must be said that while galleys were excellent in some sea conditions, there were also times when their design, originally adapted for conditions in the Mediterranean, was not suitable for more northern waters. In any kind of a sea the vessels were in danger of swamping, while there was little if any shelter for the rowers. The perception that galleys were the best ships for use in war in these northern seas also does not seem to have been shared by contemporaries. Though as we have seen they could be very successful, by the 1370s the vessels known as balingers and barges seem to have been more favoured for coastal defence by the English crown. Edward III ordered 70 barges to be built by coastal towns in 1373 and 32 balingers were similarly ordered and in fact mostly built in 1378. Edward I in 1294–95 had ordered galleys. If the Crown did acquire a galley it was soon left to rot on the mudflats. This was certainly the fate of the *Jesus Maria* in the early years of the fifteenth century.[42] It is also the case that the French king ceased to invest money in his galley yard at Rouen by the end of the century. The accounts for 1382–4 reveal that although the yard did contain various galleys most were unseaworthy and in need of extensive repairs for which the funds were not forthcoming.[43] It can be argued that this was at least partly due to the tailing off of the war effort but it can also be argued that galleys were thought of as essentially a southern design successful in the hands of the Castilians or Genoese but not in those of northerners. After the first decade of the fifteenth century galleys do not figure at all in war at sea in these waters. Cogs or other round ships might not be so well adapted to coastal raiding but they were greatly preferred for transporting men, arms, horses and all the other equipment of an invading force by sea. Jean de Vienne, the French admiral, appointed in 1373, was undoubtedly an energetic and effective leader, but despite the terror caused by raiding, he was not able to get an invasion fleet across the Channel and make a successful landing. His attempt in 1383 collapsed perhaps due to the failings of his Scots allies. In 1386 and 1387, news of the preparations being made in France caused widespread dismay in England but neither fleet in fact sailed. On the other hand English expeditions successfully crossed the Channel or made the longer voyage to Gascony or Spain on many occasions in the fourteenth century, the last being that of the Duke of Lancaster in 1386.

Edward III, in fact, did have until the end of his reign a substantial group of royal ships. Between 1369–75 this amounted to nearly 40 ships; most, however, were cogs or related designs, seven were barges and only one a galley. The vessels the king did own were much used; 27 were at sea in 1369; others were involved in voyages in 1370, 1372, 1373 and 1374 when 13 royal ships formed part of a fleet led by William Nevill and Philip Courtenay.[44] If Edward or his commanders had felt a particular need for galleys, these could have been found at Bayonne without the need to obtain them from southern mercenary captains. This had been done earlier in the century but after c.1350 little or no attempt was made by the English crown to raise a fleet from Gascony.[45] The only foreign ships employed were 10 Portuguese galleys chartered in 1386 for the expedition of Lancaster. If a notional 'balance sheet' were to be drawn up of the respective gains and losses of ships and other goods by each side in this conflict, it might well be quite evenly balanced. How does one balance the loss of five of Edward III's ships, including the *Christopher* and the *Cog Edward*, to a French 'cutting-out' expedition in the harbour at Arnemuiden, in February 1338, against the success of Morley off Sluys in 1339?[46] Similarly in 1375 a Castilian fleet took 37 English ships in the Bay laden with salt.[47] In late 1377, however, after the disastrous raids mentioned above, Sir Thomas Percy took 22 prizes from a Castilian fleet near Sluys, and in the following year a fleet successfully relieved Brest and blockaded the Seine. Ten years later, another English fleet under the earl of Arundel chased a French fleet into the Zwyn and took no fewer than 70 prizes with an enormous cargo of wine.

There is little doubt, however, that, despite Minot's warning in his poem that casualties were not always as high as rumour had it, coastal raids caused uncomfortable losses to those directly involved and a general feeling of insecurity. While it is doubtful that they had much impact on the conflict as a whole in military terms, they conveyed the impression that little could be done to defend coastal districts. The reaction from areas which felt vulnerable is well exemplified by a petition to Parliament from Scarborough in 1383. The 'poor burgesses' of the town plead that the town is 'open to the sea' and 'from one day to the next' is attacked by French, Flemish and Scots raiders. Vessels worth 2000 pounds have been taken and the town will be destroyed if no action is taken. They then plead for the right to press crewmen for a barge and a balinger which some burgesses have themselves provided for the town's defence and the right to raise a levy on fish and other goods in the town to pay for the vessels' upkeep. By this date clearly little could be expected from royal forces and local initiatives attempted to fill the gap.[48]

The prevalence and location of piracy in northern waters was, of course, directly related to the patterns of seaborne trade in the area. Small coasting vessels seem to have been very numerous. A great deal of international traffic was concentrated in the waters between England and Flanders, the principal cargoes being wool and cloth. Longer routes went from northern Europe to the Bay of Biscay for salt, woad and the wines produced near Bordeaux. Spanish merchants from Bilbao traded in iron ore, as well as oil and more exotic produce, as did Portuguese traders. The most imposing merchant ships were probably the carracks of the Genoese and the galleys of the Venetians and Florentines bringing both exotic luxury cargoes and essential raw materials like alum to the ports of Southern England, especially Southampton, and Flanders. The frequent attacks on merchant ships were certainly both unsettling and damaging to the whole commercial community. Some were opportunistic with individual sea captains preying on commerce for their own profit. In many cases, however, there might well be an element of official condonation at the very least. Such attacks were only justifiable in law against the king's enemies but truces were often ignored as were letters of safe conduct. The career of John Crabbe, a Fleming, illustrates well how easily robbery on the high seas shaded into service to the crown. He first appears in the records in 1305 when he took a ship belonging to a Zealand merchant of La Rochelle. Five years later he took a cargo worth the enormous sum of £2000 from an English ship in the Straits of Dover, the property of Alice the Countess Marshall. He put himself beyond the reach of any English court in Aberdeen and can be traced for the next 15 years or so either in Scotland or in Flanders usually connected with some violence at sea. By 1332 he was serving the Scots as leader of a squadron intended to attack the supply lines of English forces then besieging Perth. At the end of the year he was captured by the English and the parliament then sitting in York vociferously demanded restitution for all the losses he had caused English merchants and ship-owners. This was not the end of the story, however, for he managed to assist the king at the siege of Berwick in some way and was fully pardoned for all his many felonies. For the remainder of his life (he lived in fact until 1352) he seem to have served Edward III even being credited in some chronicles with the pursuit of French ships fleeing from the battle of Sluys.[49]

Piracy was also seemingly endemic in the Baltic with trading vessels being at risk from attacks either by lawless individuals or by those with some commercial or political axe to grind. The very earliest German traders in the first years of the thirteenth century making their way up the Neva towards Novgorod faced problems from Swedish and Karelian pirates.[50] The first treaties between the Wendish towns, Lubeck, Rostock and Wismar, in 1259 and 1264, had as one of their major purposes common action against sea raiders.[51] A more obvious political element, using commerce raiding as a means of attack, is evident in the activities of the *Vitalienbrüder*. The origins of the problem lay in the conflict between the Hanse and Denmark which had culminated in the peace of Stralsund in 1370. Valdemar IV of Denmark's seizure of Visby seemed to threaten the power of the Hanse in the Baltic. The towns of the league with allies including Albert of Mecklenburg managed to mount a successful campaign against Denmark using both land and sea forces. After Valdemar's death, however, the Hanse supported his daughter Margaret as Regent, much to the fury of the Mecklenburgers, who now began a sustained series of attacks on Hanseatic shipping. By 1389 Margaret was ruler of Denmark, Norway and Sweden with only Stockholm still supporting the Mecklenburgers. Their reaction was to issue a general appeal to all sea raiders to attack Denmark and her allies and their shipping so that legitimate trade in the Baltic all but ceased. Rostok and Wismar, even though notionally members of the league, became the main bases of the pirates. The commercial effects of this action were considerable and it was not until the end of the century that the situation improved. The exploits of the *Vitalien-brüder* became legendary, as had those of Eustace the Monk in an earlier period, but details of their tactics or even of their methods of handling their ships are hard to come by.[52]

The merchants of the Hanse also had strained relations with both England and the Netherlands with frequent mutual accusations of piracy or the unwarranted arrest of shipping. Lloyd has pointed out that though the diet of the Hanse presented Richard II with a list of no fewer than 22 piratical incidents for which compensation was demanded in 1386, many were concerned more with commercial negligence or even embezzlement than with violence at sea. The theft of a Prussian cargo wrecked off Romney in 1381 by the local villagers was illegal perhaps but not piracy.[53] More clearly a matter of condoned violence against a rival power might be the events off Brittany in 1378 when men from 'English warships' boarded a ship from Danzig, killed the captain and threw his body in the sea but not before they had cut off his fingers to steal his rings.[54] The English for their part complained equally vigorously about the *Vitalinebrüder*, in 1395, when they had transferred some of their activities to Frisia.

The fourteenth century, therefore, displays all the characteristics of naval warfare in northern waters with which we have become familiar from earlier times. Piracy may affect any trade or any area sometimes with serious effects. Ships are most widely used and most useful to warring rulers in their role as transports. Supplies for armies of all kinds could often be most easily moved by water. The successful siege of a city or castle accessible by water often depended on the ability to make good use of this means of approach and to deny it to the enemy. Raiding and piracy would seem to have made both life on the coast and trading by sea insecure and stressful. Fleet actions, to use the language of a later era were relatively rare and their outcomes hard to predict. The tactics used show little development from the showers of missiles followed by boarding used since the days of the Vikings. Yet this picture, perhaps, overstates the conservatism of seafarers. Between 1405 and 1457 there were no raids on the English coasts: and in fact after the French raid on Sandwich of that year no further raids for the remainder of the century. The fourteenth century for all intents and purposes sees the end of a tactic which had been a mainstay of campaigns of the French against the English. Similarly, though trading galleys from Florence and Venice visit English ports, principally Southampton, in the fifteenth century, war galleys virtually disappear from the waters between France and England by the 1420s. New ship types with new fighting methods begin to dominate the Channel and the North Atlantic. As Charles VI of France became increasingly unable to deal with the burdens of royal rule and Henry IV attempted to establish himself securely on the throne naval concerns seemed to have faded into the background of public life. It can be argued, however, that this pause heralded a period of rapid and exciting developments in naval warfare in these waters.

Notes

1 N.A.M. Rodger, *The Safeguard of the Sea*, p. 73.
2 Although the Cinque Ports, like all other English ports supplied ships for this kind of operation Nicholas Rodger has convincingly demonstrated in 'The naval service of the Cinque Ports', *English Historical Review*, CXI, 1996, pp. 636–51, that they cannot be regarded as an essential part of the naval strength of England. They had in fact a geographic, diplomatic and political value which led to them being more 'dangerous troublemakers' than 'providers of valuable naval services'.
3 W. Stanford Reid, 'Sea power in the Anglo-Scottish War, 1296–1328', *The Mariner's Mirror*, 46, 1960, pp. 7–23, fully discusses the strategy and tactics of both Edward I and Edward II in these campaigns.
4 Reid, *op. cit.*, p. 9.
5 N.A.M. Rodger, *The Safeguard of the Sea*, p. 87.
6 J.F. Willard and W.A. Morris (eds), *The English Government at Work, 1327–1386*, vol. I, p. 226, Cambridge, MA, Medieval Academy of America, 1940.
7 Wardrobe Book for 8 and 9 Edward II: British Library, Cotton Collection, Nero C, VIII, ff.264r–266d.
8 M. Jones, 'Two Exeter ship agreements of 1303 and 1310', *The Mariner's Mirror*, 53, 1967, pp. 315–19.
9 M. Jones, *loc. cit.*
10 H.J. Hewitt, *The Organisation of War under Edward III 1338–62*, Manchester, Manchester University Press, 1966, pp. 84–5.
11 'La marine au siège de Calais', *Bibliothèque des écoles de Chartes*, 58, 1897.
12 The Hon. G. Wrottesley, *Crécy and Calais from the Original Records in the Public Record Office*, London, William Salt Archaeologoval Society, 1898.
13 C. Bréard, *Le Crotoy et les armements maritimes des XIV et XV siècles*, Amiens, no publ., 1902, pp. 9–10.
14 'La marine au siège de Calais'.
15 J.R. Lumby (ed.), *The Chronicle of Henry Knighton*, Rolls Series, London, 1889, p. 48.
16 S.J. Burley, 'The victualling of Calais, 1347–65', *Bulletin of the Institute of Historical Research*, 31, 1958, pp. 49–57, explains the effect the need to supply the Calais garrison had on the food market in England but does not discuss the continuing need for shipping to transport the goods to the town.
17 G. Hutchinson, *Medieval Ships and Shipping*, London, Leicester University Press, 1994, pp. 23–4. C. Allmand also discusses the naval objectives of both England and France during the fourteenth and fifteenth centuries in *The Hundred Years War: England and France at War c.1300–c.1450*, Cambridge, Cambridge University Press, 1989, pp. 82–7.
18 The poem is entitled *Branche aux royaux lignages*. Its concentration on a naval battle is unusual since as has been pointed out (by J. Sumption, *The Hundred Years War*, vol. I, p. x), chronicles usually include 'next to nothing on naval actions'.
19 Le citoyen Legrand d'Aussy, 'Notice sur l'état de la Marine en France au commencement du quatorzième siècle; et sur la tactique navale usitée alors dans les combats de mer', *Mémoires de l'Institut de France, Classe des Sciences Morales et Politiques*, Vol. II, year VII, pp. 302–75.
20 Legrand d'Aussy, *loc. cit.*, p. 330.
21 D. Nicholas, *Medieval Flanders*, London and New York, Longman, 1992, pp. 195–7.
22 A. Curry, *The Hundred Years War*, Basingstoke, Macmillan, 1993, pp. 42–53.
23 J. Froissart, *Chronicles* (ed. and trans. G. Brereton), Harmondsworth, Penguin, 1968, p. 62.

24 J.B. Hattendorf *et al.*, *British Naval Documents 1204–1960*, London, Scolar Press for the Navy Records Society, 1993, no. 14, p. 22.

25 J.B. Hattendorf *et al.*, *loc. cit.*

26 N.A.M. Rodger, *The Safeguard of the Sea*, pp. 98–9.

27 S. Rose, 'Edward III: Sluys 1340', in E. Grove (ed.), *Great Battles of the Royal Navy as Commemorated in the Gunroom at Britannia Royal Naval College Dartmouth*, London, Arms and Armour Press, 1994, pp. 24–30.

28 A very full discussion of both contemporary and later perceptions of the battle including views on what caused the defeat of the French and the victory of the English can be found in K. DeVries, 'God, leadership, Flemings and archery: contemporary perceptions of victory and defeat at the battle of Sluys, 1340', *American Neptune*, 55, 1995, pp. 223–42.

29 It is sometimes also called the battle of Winchelsea.

30 J. Froissart, *Chronicles* (ed. and trans.G. Brereton), Harmondsworth, Penguin, 1968, pp. 113–19.

31 P.R.O. E 101/24/14. Roll 3. Expenses of William Clewere 18–32 Edward III.

32 E. Perroy, *The Hundred Years War*, London, Eyre and Spottiswoode, 1962, p106.

33 C. Richmond, 'The war at sea', in K. Fowler (ed.), *The Hundred Years War*, London, Macmillan, 1971, p. 99.

34 N.A.M. Rodger, *The Safeguard of the Sea*, p. 99.

35 J. Froissart, *Chroniques* (ed. S. Luce), Paris, Société de l'Histoire de France, 1888, vol. VIII, pp. 36–44 and 293–300. *Chronique des Quatre Premiers Valois*, (ed. S. Luce), Paris, Société de l'Histoire de France, pp. 232–4.

36 J.W. Sherborne, 'The battle of La Rochelle and the war at sea', *Bulletin of the Institute of Historical Research*, 42, 1969, pp. 17–29.

37 P.E. Russell, *The English Intervention in Spain and Portugal in the Time of Edward III and Richard II*, Oxford, Clarendon Press, 1955, p. 227.

38 N.A.M. Rodger, *The Safeguard of the Sea*, p. 91.

39 The need for a continuous circuit of walls was investigated at Southampton from 1360 but the wall were not in fact finished until 1385 when Jean de Vienne's feared invasion was causing much concern. L.A. Burgess (ed.) *The Southampton Terrier of 1454*, London, Her Majesty's Stationery Office, 1976, p. 21.

40 T.B. James and J. Simons, *The Poems of Laurence Minot*, Exeter, University of Exeter, 1989, p. 32.

41 N.A.M. Rodger, *The Safeguard of the Sea*, p. 105.

42 P.R.O. E101/44/17. Particulars of account of John Starlyng.

43 Charles Bréard, 'Le compte du clos des galées de Rouen au xiv siècle, 1382–84', in Blanquart, Bouquet, Bréard, De Circourt, Regnier, Sauvage, *Documents: Deuxième Serie*, Rouen, Société de la Histoire de Normandie, 1893, pp. 93 *et seq.*

44 J. Sherborne, 'The Hundred Years War: the English navy, shipping and manpower 1369–89', *Past and Present*, 37, 1967.

45 S. Rose, 'Bayonne and the King's ships, 1204–1420', *The Mariner's Mirror*, 86, 2000, p. 144.

46 It is of course also the case that these English ships were recovered after Sluys.

47 This occurred despite the truce in existence between England and the 'bastarde d'espaigne' (Henry of Trastamara) at the time according to a document printed by N.H. Nicolas in his *History of the Royal Navy*. This also lists 21 ships from the West Country and 16 from the East Coast ports as taken by the Spanish.

48 *Rotuli Parliamentorum*, VII Richard II, p. 162.

49 H.S. Lucas, 'John Crabbe: Flemish pirate, merchant and adventurer', *Speculum*, 20, 1945, pp. 334–50.

50 P. Dollinger, *The German Hanse* (trans. D.S. Ault and S.H. Steinberg), Basingstoke, Macmillan, 1964, p. 27.

51 Dollinger, *op. cit.*, p. 46.

52 Dollinger, *op. cit.*, pp. 78–82.

53 T.H. Lloyd, *England and the German Hanse 1157–1611: A study of Their Trade and Commercial Diplomacy*, Cambridge, Cambridge University Press, 1991, pp. 62–3.
54 Dollinger, *op. cit.*, pp. 289–90. Extract from *Hanserezesse*.

Plate 1 Shipbuilding in a northern post from a fifteenth century manuscript.
© *The Bodleian Library, University of Oxford, MS. Douce 353 fol. 31 recto.*

Plate 2 An early fifteenth-century carving of a two masted vessel orginally from a
church icon King's Lynn.
© *V&A Picture Library.*

Plate 3   A battle at sea from the Warwick pageant, produced at the end of the fifteenth century. Cannon as well as bowmen can be seen on the ship on the left.
© *The British Library, Julius E IV art 6 f 18v.*

Plate 4 These galley sheds in the Darsena Vecchia, the oldest part of the Arsenale of Venice, date from 1560–2. Their earlier counterparts would not have been greatly different and the scale of shipbuilding operations in Venice is clear.
© *S.P. Rose.*

Plate 5 The Battle of Zonchio, anon., woodcut (1499)
© *The British Museum.*

CHAPTER FIVE

The fifteenth century in northern waters: conflict and commerce raiding on a wider scale

At the outset of the fifteenth century, the rulers of the states bordering on the Channel and the North Sea, principally England, France and the duchies and counties which made up the Netherlands, can easily be represented as largely indifferent to the imperatives of successful naval warfare. This did not mean that the waters which divided them were peaceful and undisturbed, the preserve only of merchant ships and fishermen. On the contrary, it has been argued with justification that the early years of the fifteenth century saw a notable increase in lawlessness and piracy. Royal and other governments spent very little on the building or maintenance of ships, and seemed to have little understanding of the possible strategic value of sea power. If we turn, however, to the final years of the century in many ways the situation seems to have been transformed. Particularly in England the intervening years had demonstrated to at least some of those in power, the value of ships and the ability to use them with drive and imagination. Ships themselves, and the techniques of navigation and ship handling, had developed very considerably. The armaments of vessels also, and consequently the tactics of sea battles, had changed decisively in a way which heralded a new era in naval warfare.

The first decade

Despite the upheavals in England, which had led to the deposition of Richard II and the usurpation of Henry IV in 1399, little at first seemed to be new in the naval sphere. The truce between England and France remained at least notionally in being. France itself, ruled by a king plagued with periods of insanity, was preoccupied, as had been the case for some time, with the growing tensions between various parties at court rather than with the demands of naval defence. The *Clos des galées*, under its last four masters, Guillaume de la Hogue, Jean de Lesmes, Guillaume Blancbaston, and Robert d'Oissel saw little activity. De la Hogue briefly presided over period of bustle and excitement in the winter of 1405–6 when the vessels of Pero Niño, the Castilian corsair took shelter in the galley sheds of the *Clos* but on his departure the more normal torpor returned. From 1409–11 the post of *maitre* of the *Clos* was vacant but once appointed neither de Lesmes (1411–12) or Blancbaston (1412–14) was active. When the English took the galley yard and burnt it to the ground in 1418, it was more or less empty of both vessels and arms.[1] D'Oisell, the last *maitre*, had enjoyed a comfortable sinecure which brought with it the occupation of a splendid *ostel*, the embellishment of which, especially the windows of the hall and chapel, was more important than repairing ships.[2] In the sheds themselves, there was little except mouldering cordage and hulls beyond repair.

In England, the condition of the few remaining royal ships was hardly better. Richard II had owned in the final year of his reign four ships, the *Trinity of the Tower*, the *Gracedieu*, the *Nicholas*, and the *George*. His clerk of the king's ships, John Chamberleyn, rode out the disturbances of 1399 and remained in office until 1406. His responsibilities under Henry IV were more concerned with the elaborate decoration of the tiny squadron of royal ships than with their preparation as ships of war. The *Nicholas*, for example was painted black with white ostrich feathers picked out in gold leaf; there was also a large royal coat of arms and another of St George and finally a gilded figure of St Christopher.[3] All this creates the impression that these ships were regarded more as a means of display, of increasing royal prestige or of 'conspicuous consumption' than as an element in the defence of the realm. By 1409, in fact only the *Trinity* and a ceremonial river barge gorgeously decked out in scarlet and gold, remained in the ownership of the Crown.[4]

Naval activity in these years seems to have become confined to a form of semi-official piracy. There was, of course, nothing new about the robbing of cargoes at sea with a greater or lesser degree of violence. Any merchant knew the risks very well and stories like those associated with Eustace the Monk make clear how piracy and seaborne trade had long gone together in the public mind. The open sea was not, however, completely outside the operation of the law. Our knowledge of the losses suffered by merchants comes largely from the lawsuits which were brought in an attempt to recover either the goods themselves or proper compensation from the perpetrators.[5] The key factor in these cases would often be the unspoken one of the degree of hostility which existed between the states to which those concerned owed allegiance. Was a truce in operation? Did one party or the other desire revenge for some earlier attack? Did the owner of the goods or the ship qualify as 'an enemy'? The answers to these questions were not always easy when goods, for example, of a French merchant were taken out of a Flemish ship and brought into Fowey and there sold to an Englishman[6] or a so-called pirate was acting with royal encouragement.

The ease with which an individual could move from being a law breaker to being in the royal service is made clear in the first decade of the fifteenth century by the careers of Harry Pay of Poole and John Hawley the elder and the younger of Dartmouth.[7] Pay seems to have almost specialised in preying on the Bilboa trade in iron but was also commissioned in 1404 by the king to go to sea to 'provide for the destruction of the king's enemies'. In the following year he was at sea with Lord Berkeley off Milford Haven to prevent help coming by sea from France for Owen Glendower's rebellion. These official commissions did not alter the Spanish view of him. When the raiding squadron of Castilian galleys led by Pero Niño attacked Poole the same winter they were seeking revenge on 'Arripay' the pirate who had robbed Spanish merchants, sacked the town of Gijon and carried off a crucifix from St Mary of Finisterre. The careers of John Hawley, senior and his son John Hawley junior of Dartmouth show many similarities with that of Pay. The elder John was mayor of Dartmouth many times and an MP but he was also in trouble over goods seized at sea from foreign merchants in the reign of Richard II and in that of Henry IV when compensation was demanded in the courts for cargoes of olive oil and wine valued at £398 and £210. The younger John was also an MP and a Justice of the Peace from 1422–31 and took part in royal expeditions to keep the seas in 1419 and 1420. All this did not prevent him being involved in incidents like the seizure of a Breton ship in 1414 and a similar case involving a Scottish vessel in 1427. William Soper himself, who later in his career became Clerk of the king's ships, was accused with others of piracy against a Spanish ship in 1413–14. Her owners claimed to be sailing under a safe-conduct but, although Soper did return some items to the merchants and ship-owner concerned including the ship's dog, the vessel herself seems to have been treated as a prize lawfully taken. It was, in fact, handed over to the Crown and rebuilt as one of Henry V's prized great ships the *Holyghost de la Tour*.[8]

A close analysis of the recorded incidents of so-called piracy in the opening years of the fifteenth century has led to the suggestion that rather than being just the result of the activities of some notable freebooting individuals the losses recorded by both English, Flemish and French merchants should be seen as part of low level naval warfare. Ford has claimed that far from being any form of piracy or private enterprise, the situation in the Channel was the result 'of the conscious policies adopted by both the English and French governments in their pursuit of wider political objectives'.[9] If this is the case, the pursuit of this policy marks a distinctive shift in the strategic use of naval warfare. Previously states had gathered fleets from both their own resources and those of the wider ship-owning community and, as we have seen, used them for both logistical and more strictly warlike purposes. They had not, however, used commerce raiding as an officially inspired and directed tactic. Ford's evidence is in many ways persuasive, particularly the wording of a draft agreement between the English government and the deputies of the Four Members of Flanders. This, with its emphasis on the need for clear identification of Flemish vessels in the waters of the Channel, implies that something like a state of war existed between the English and the French.[10] He also makes clear the degree of official involvement in French attacks on English shipping in 1400 and 1401 when Henry IV was still regarded as an usurper by France. There is still room for doubt as to the degree with which any royal control could be maintained over individuals like Pay, Hawley and the other West Country seamen living far from the centre of power and with a respected position in their local communities. It is plausible, however, that the results of law suits against these individuals could reflect royal desires even if not formal royal policy. The aid given by the French to the earl of Crawford in 1402, providing him with vessels for his return to Scotland, was more clearly treated as a matter of policy. This fleet was intended as much for action against England as it was for the support of Scotland; it took many English merchant ships in the Channel. On this occasion the commission to Hawley and Thomas Rempston to set out on a retaliatory sea-keeping expedition was quite explicit; there was no question of this being a 'piratical' expedition. Raids on Plymouth and the Isle of Wight by the French in the following summer made even clearer that the so-called Hundred Years War was once more entering an active phase at sea if not on land.[11]

In this context it is worth taking a closer look at the activities of Don Pero Niño. Although it is probably the case that his cruise in the Channel in the summer of 1406 has little strategic importance, however much trouble it caused locally, the account of it written by Niño's standard bearer contains important operational details. His account of a raid on a Cornish village makes clear how much success depended on surprise. *Chita* (unidentified, but the approach described is not unlike the Helford river) was in fact occupied for three hours.[12] Its outskirts were defended by the galleymen hidden behind a protective palisade while other crewmembers plundered the town. They finally left having set fire to the houses taking two ships with them which were in the harbour. On their way back to sea, at the mouth of the estuary, the Spanish galleys faced tough opposition from the local population who had, by this time, collected their forces together. Spanish consternation at the strength of the tides, particularly the tidal race at the entrance to *Chita* also hints at the difficulties of operating galleys in northern waters.[13] The account of an action in the Channel later the same summer is even richer in details of the way galleys and other ships were handled in battle. Niño's squadron was at sea not far from Calais when they caught sight of an English fleet 'drawn up in a circle because it was calm'. The decision was taken to attack even though the commanders knew that their galleys would be at a disadvantage in the open sea if the wind got up. The English fleet which included both great ships and balingers, was then deployed in a line with the great ships on the wings and the balingers in the centre.[14] The initial Spanish attack was an attempt at boarding reinforced by the use of flaming arrows and a fire ship; at this juncture, however, the wind got up and the galleys became increasingly vulnerable to attacks by the great ships. Most of them turned to flee but the galley of Niño himself was trapped between two English balingers and was in great danger of being boarded and taken herself. A French balinger, sailing with the Castilians, realised the gravity of the situation. Although the description of the manoeuvre then undertaken is not entirely clear, it seems that this vessel went about, sailed between the galley and her attackers and then rammed one with such force that the bowsprit was sheared off and the forestay severed thus causing the collapse of the mast. The ensuing confusion allowed the galley to escape, sailing for the coast of France where the English could not pursue them as the wind was dropping and also blowing onshore. As before this account makes clear the problems galleys faced from the strong winds in the Channel. It also emphasises the importance of skilled and determined seamanship. The weapons used, however, are still those familiar to earlier centuries. The same account describes how Niño could not enter Calais harbour because of the effectiveness of the bombards on the fortifications; no guns were used at sea, it seems on this occasion, where the preferred missiles were 'bolts, arrows and darts'[15]

Henry V and the war at sea

The first few months of Henry V's reign gave little indication that any radical change in the appreciation of naval power was in the offing. The clerk of the king's ships for the period March to June 1413, one William Loveney, stated in his accounts that he had neither received nor spent any money. The eight ships for which he was notionally responsible were not very impressive; three were very small balingers of between 24 and 30 tuns capacity and the remaining five, single masted cogships of between 220 (the *Cog John*) and 80 tuns. These might have played a useful role as transports but would have done little to stiffen a fighting squadron. From the date of Catton's appointment, however, the number of ships in royal ownership began to rise; the first of Henry V's great ships, the *Trinity Royal*, a vessel of 540 tuns, was built at Greenwich and others were acquired by purchase or as prizes. Seven royal ships were among the enormous fleet, said to be over 1500 strong, which carried the English forces to France in the summer of 1415.[16] After the great success of the Agincourt campaign, the tempo increased even more with large sums being spent on the royal ships both in repairs and in building new ships. Between 1416–19, 36 ships of various kinds were in the possession of the Crown, some for relatively short periods, and over £12,000[17] were received both from the Exchequer and from other sources for their maintenance. The building programme undertaken by both Catton (at Winchelsea and Small Hythe) and Soper and his associates (at Southampton) was notable not only for its extensive nature and cost but because at least some of the vessels concerned were more truly warships than any others built previously for the Crown in England. This applies most forcefully to the 'king's Great Ships', the *Trinity Royal*, the *Holighost de la Tour*, the *Jesus* and the *Gracedieu*. These were not only considerably larger than all other ships in royal possession with the exception of carracks taken in action from the Genoese but had also more advanced rigging and more fearsome armament. The *Gracedieu* was three-masted and at 1400 tuns by far the largest vessel afloat in northern waters.[18] She carried cannon and iron darts for hurling from her topcastles as did her sister ships which were two masted. There was a clear strategic purpose in the building and arming of these ships.[19] They were intended to counter the might of the Genoese carracks hired by the French to pursue the war at sea and make plain the extent to which northern rulers had turned away from employing galleys for warlike purposes. To some extent English victories in the Channel from 1416–19 might seem to demonstrate the success of this policy although, as we shall see, smaller English royal ships also played their part. It is also notable that accounts of these sea fights are found not only in English chronicles as might be expected but, often in greater detail, in Venetian and Genoese ones as well.[20] Events in the Channel were now of interest much further afield.

The first encounter occurred off Harfleur on 15 August 1416. This port of entry had been taken by Henry V the previous year but was now under siege with the garrison suffering badly from lack of supplies and much reduced by disease. The Duke of Bedford was put in command of a relieving fleet of some 300 vessels which included the *Holyghost de la Tour* and four other royal ships. This fleet faced considerable initial difficulties in assembling all its forces. The writer of the *Gesta Henrici Quinti* describes how one squadron, assembled off the Camber, was faced with contrary winds, in the end relying on a favourable tide to round Beachy Head and join the squadron from Southampton.[21] No fewer than eight Genoese carracks in the pay of the French were assisting in the investment of the town. A force of 12 galleys, commanded by Gioanni de' Grimaldi had also been hired by the French but had withdrawn after the death of Grimaldi in an attack on an English convoy of wine ships sailing for Bordeaux.[22] It is not clear what other vessels were involved on the French side. It seems that a Spanish squadron fled when it saw the size of the English fleet while French vessels seem to have remained in harbour at Honfleur, taking no part in the action. This went on during daylight hours and ended with three carracks taken by the English, one driven aground and wrecked and the remainder put to flight. A German hulk was also sunk. Antonio Morosini, a Venetian chronicler, whose account is the most informative, gives no further details apart from the fact that the battle was very cruel with high casualties on both sides. The site of the battle, not far off shore in the sheltered mouth of the Seine, is typical, as we have seen, of this kind of encounter. It was not so usual for a force largely composed of smaller vessels to be so successful against carracks which, with their great size, large crews and high-sided hulls, could dominate a boarding action. Perhaps on this occasion good boat handling skills (enabling the English to lay their vessels alongside the enemy) and determination carried the day. It may also be the case that the smaller English craft drawing less water were able to trap the carracks against the coast on a falling tide. This is hinted at in Morosini's account of the wreck of Zoane Spinola's ship which 'was wrecked because she took refuge in a place where she ran aground at low tide'.[23]

Further understanding of the realities of naval operations in the Channel can be deduced from the story of an action which took place about six weeks after the successful relief of Harfleur. A large Genoese carrack was sighted in mid Channel probably making for Sluys. A force of six English balingers set off in pursuit under the command of the Richard Beauchamp, Earl of Warwick, the Captain of Calais. Nothing was known of the outcome of the affair until one balinger came into Calais reporting that she had lost the rest of the squadron in the night. The next day a further balinger limped into port with the full story. The remaining five ships had caught up with the carrack at dawn on Friday 27 September; the decks of the carrack loomed above the balingers exposing them to a hail of missiles from her defenders. They had, however grappled with her again and again until forced to break off the engagement from lack of missiles and boarding ladders. In the end the carrack 'made off at speed on a straight course towards Sluys'.[24] An easterly gale had then got up further separating the English ships but by 30 September all managed to return to Calais. In the open sea the sailing ability of a balinger matched that of a carrack; indeed the smaller ships may well have had the edge for speed but a carrack had to be very greatly outnumbered and her crew almost completely disabled for her to fall victim to a boarding action on the high seas.

In the next four summers, 1417–20, English naval activity in the Channel was well organised, purposeful and clearly directed at supporting the king's campaigns on land. The French relied more or less exclusively on forces provided by Genoa and Castile. The English tactic was to send out patrolling squadrons composed of a core of royal ships and also arrested shipping. The commanders were operating under a system of indentures very similar to that used for the retinues of captains in land operations. In many ways this system was extremely successful. An impressive list of vessels was captured. The Earl of Huntingdon in 1417 took four more Genoese carracks in one three-hour engagement. His squadron included two of Henry's 'great ships' the *Trinity Royal* and the *Holyghost* but otherwise was mainly the useful balingers.[25] Other commanders in the same summer took a further five ships, at least three being Castilian and one another carrack.[26] These vessels were then added to the royal fleet increasing its strength considerably. Later years saw less action as by 1418 most of the Channel coast was in English hands. Clearly, however, the possibility of a Castilian fleet allied to France reaching the Channel still worried English commanders. By 1420, the largest and newest of all Henry's ships, the *Gracedieu*, was ready to put to sea under the overall command of the earl of Devon. This patrol had little strategic significance; Henry had completed the conquest of Normandy while a political change in Castile had put an end to their alliance with the French.[27] Events when the expedition was on the point of putting to sea cast some light on the way in which these expeditions were put together, expanding on the rather terse information available in formal royal writs and commissions. A report to the Council of May 1420 explains what had happened when an attempt was made to take the muster of the crews and men-at arms and archers enrolled for the cruise. The Earl of Devon flatly refused to muster his men at all. The commissioners then went on board the *Gracedieu*; they were not greeted with enthusiasm. The quartermaster seized the muster roll from the ship's clerk and threatened to throw it into the sea. The ship was now in the Solent but before it could clear the Isle of Wight, some members of the crew from Devon mutinied and insisted on being put ashore at St Helen's on the island. The commissioners tried to intervene and for their pains were assaulted and sworn at. What was at the root of these disturbances? Were the Devon men serving reluctantly with no wish to spend most of the summer patrolling the Channel? We know the weather was bad, since the commissioners could not even get on board another ship because of the state of the sea. Did the Devon men fear that the *Gracedieu* was not seaworthy?[28] A muster roll was the basis on which the members of an indentured retinue were paid; had the numbers been inflated fraudulently to increase the sums available? We cannot answer these questions but the existence of the report does make plainer the rough, often violent world of early fifteenth-century mariners.[29]

The death of Henry V and the completion of the conquest of Normandy brought to an end this period of rapid expansion in the use of royal ships by the English. As well as actions between opposing squadrons at least on occasion in the open sea this had included the support of land forces at the siege of coastal or riparian towns and the usual transport and messenger duties. The entire Channel coast was now in the hands either of the English crown or its allies, Burgundy and Brittany. Henry V's will had treated the royal ships as his personal possessions and directed that they should be sold to pay his debts. His executors complied leaving only the four 'great ships' laid up, at first at anchor in the Hamble river and finally beached on the 'woses' and a single balinger the *Petit Jesus* based at Southampton. The French crown had had little or no interest in the direct ownership of ships after the destruction of the *Clos des galées*; by 1436 the same could be said of the English.

Naval warfare by contract

This state of affairs did not mean that naval operations became rare in northern waters. It did mean that they changed in nature and in scale. The conflict between England and France widened with other states and rulers being drawn into a more complex web of alliances and enmities. Burgundy, which from 1384 had included Flanders and from 1428 Hainault, Holland, Zeeland and Frisia, pursued an independent foreign policy. The conflicting demands of economic links with England, of great importance to the Flemish towns, and relations between the Dukes of Burgundy and the kings of France ensured that neither of the two main powers in the Channel could count on their friendship. Equally uncertain were the relations between the towns of the Hanseatic League and the rulers and merchants of England and Burgundy, especially the Four Members of Flanders and Holland and Zeeland. From the 1450s onwards a further element in the tangled network of links between rulers was the internal instability in England which found expression in the Wars of the Roses. Aid to one or other claimants to the throne, in exile on the continent, often took the form of help in the provision of ships for the all-important Channel crossing.

To the ordinary seafarer, ship-owner or trader, the period from the summer of 1435, when the Burgundians abandoned their alliance with England, followed shortly by the recapture of Dieppe by the French, must have been characterised by an increase in the dangers apparently inherent in seaborne trade. The chances of ships being attacked whether or not they travelled in convoy, whether or not they were ostensibly covered by safe-conducts from a neighbouring ruler certainly increased. Similarly the vessels of any merchant might at times be liable to arrest for naval purposes. English shipping was arrested usually for the transport of reinforcements to France in five out of the seven years 1435–42. The Duke of Burgundy, Philip le Bon, assembled a fleet in 1436 for the purposes of completing the investment of Calais from the sea. This included not only eight ducal ships, of which one was probably a prize taken from the English and another was originally Portuguese, but also two arrested Italian carracks, one from Venice and the other from Genoa, and 38 other vessels from Flanders, Germany, Spain, Brittany, and Portugal. It can have been no comfort to the owners involved that the expedition was a failure largely because of the bad storms in the Channel in July 1436. The way in which an independent trader and ship-owner could almost become a servant of the Crown is also illustrated by the career of Thomas Gille of Dartmouth. In the 1430s ships he owned were engaged on trading voyages, licensed as privateers and requisitioned on at least four occasions for royal purposes. In 1440, while attempting to put a fleet together for another royal expedition he was also asked to provide transport for a royal envoy to Gascony, Edward Hull. The ship used for this voyage, the *Christopher*, was a large and well-found ship of 400 tuns eminently suitable for such a journey.[30]

The apparent exasperation of English merchants at the effect of the lack of security at sea on lawful trade found expression in the petition presented by the Commons in the Parliament of 1442. This sets out an elaborate plan, 'to have upon the see continuelly for the sesons of the yere fro Candilmas to Martymesse, viii ships with forstages; ye whiche shippes, as it is thought, most have on with other, eche of hem cl men'. The plan also includes provision for each of the large ships to be attended by a barge and a balinger with four pinnaces probably to ensure communication with the shore. Not only are the wage scales of the shipmasters and men set out but also a detailed list identifying by name the vessels to be supplied by English ports from Bristol to Newcastle.[31] The petition also significantly includes provisions aimed at dealing with the problems caused by the disposal of ships and goods whether of friends or enemies taken at sea. It piously hopes that 'harme ne hurt' will not be done to friendly shipping but also includes a clause aimed at protecting ship-owners against claims in the courts relating to goods taken at sea. They would only be liable if actually at sea personally or found to have some interest in the goods and even then could be acquitted by their own oath supported by that of two or three of their 'credible neyghbours'. The ambivalence of merchants and the seafaring community in general to the issue of piracy seems evident here. This is also demonstrated by the activities of Gille's *Christopher* just before she sailed with the king's envoy to Gascony. In January 1440, she had rammed and sunk another vessel off Dartmouth and had only attempted to pick up survivors when their cries that they were English were heard by the crew.[32]

The possibility of a more formal kind of naval defence seemed beyond the power of any ruler in this region at this period. Richmond points out that to meet the threat of the Burgundian attack on Calais in 1436 the English crown issued sea-keeping or privateering licenses principally to London ship-owners. In 1440 when the English were intent on retaking Harfleur from the French, prodded into action by Sir John Fastolf, Sir John Speke of Haywood in Devon was bound by indenture to keep the sea. It is not entirely clear whether his force was of material use in the recapture of the town but it is clear that this expedition was the only real attempt to organise an 'official' naval force for many years. 'Constructive naval defence' was 'beyond the power of a government which lacked a royal navy'. Henry VI was not the monarch to undertake the work needed to bring such a navy into being.[33]

Naval forces as a political weapon

In the absence of royal initiative in England, however, there were others who were willing and able to wield the strength derived from a force of ships to intervene in the increasingly complex struggles between competing factions and claimants to the throne. This is most clearly seen in the case of the Earl of Warwick, but the Duke of Burgundy and the king of France were also prepared to provide naval forces to support their favoured candidate for the English throne. Richard Neville, Earl of Warwick had been captain of Calais since 1456 and had taken the opportunity afforded by a relatively secure base to build up a squadron of ships. These were used in the manner most likely to advance the fortunes of the Earl himself and the Yorkist cause, which, at that time, he supported. To many English men his naval exploits in the Channel were a welcome sign of 'enterprise upon the see'.[34] Jack Cade's proclamation in 1450 at the outset of the Kentish rebellion had bewailed the facts that, 'the sea is lost, France is lost'.[35] The French raid on Sandwich in August 1457 had been a humiliating reminder of the impotence of English defence.[36] Now John Bale, himself a merchant and a ship-owner, could laud Warwick in his chronicle, praising his 'greet pollecy and dedes doyng of worship in fortefieng of Cales and other feates of armes'.[37] To modern writers Warwick's deeds seem at least semi-piratical but to his contemporaries his attack on a Spanish squadron of 28 sail off Calais in early June 1458 and his taking of around 17 prizes out of the Hanse fleet returning with Bay salt later the same summer were victories to savour. It even seems not to have affected his reputation that the first engagement was not entirely successful. John Jernyngham's letter to Margaret Paston which gives details of the encounter, recounts how he and his crew boarded a large Spanish ship but were unable to hold her. He concludes, 'and for sooth we were well and truly beat'.[38] The point to contemporaries was that Warwick, who was in fact bound by an indenture of November 1457 to keep the seas, seemed to be acting energetically and speedily even if not all his opponents were clearly 'the londes adversaries'.[39]

His activities in 1459 and 1460 demonstrate with greater force the way in which the possession of a squadron of ships with experienced crews was greatly to the political advantage of both Warwick personally and the Yorkist cause. After plundering Spanish and Genoese shipping in the Straits in the summer of 1459, Warwick, who had joined the Yorkists in England, seemed to have miscalculated when he was forced to flee from the battle of Ludford Bridge. He reached his base in Calais safely, however, and from that point acted with great skill. Lord Rivers and Sir Gervase Clifton for the king had by December managed to impound Warwick's ships in Sandwich harbour. The Crown also mustered a small force under William Scott to patrol off Winchelsea to repel any attack by Warwick. Warwick had many friends in the Southern counties, perhaps beneficiaries of his earlier actions in the Channel. Through them he was well aware of the Crown's plans. In January a force from Calais commanded by John Dinham, slipped into Sandwich early in the morning, while Rivers was still abed, and persuaded Warwick's erstwhile shipmasters and crews to return with them to Calais.[40] The royal government attempted to counter this loss by commissioning further forces to serve at sea against Warwick. The Duke of Exeter in May 1460 in fact encountered Warwick's fleet at some point to the east of Dartmouth and arguably had the opportunity at least to damage very severely the Yorkist cause if not put paid to it entirely. Yet as the Great Chronicle of London put it 'they fowght not'.[41] Richmond sees this as 'one of those critical moments when action was essential but was not forthcoming'.[42] In his view Warwick had what the Crown did not, a fleet and a fleet which was used to keep the sea. The use of that fleet was an important factor in the course taken by the domestic politics of England and to Richmond sealed the fate of the Lancastrians.

In 1470, Warwick was personally in a much weaker position. He may still have had some vessels of his own; on his flight from England, after the failure of his intrigues on behalf of the Duke of Clarence, pursued by Lord Howard, he had taken prizes from the Burgundians.[43] He could not, however from his own resources hope to mount an invasion of England to restore his new master Henry VI. He and Queen Margaret were dependent on the aid of Louis XI of France to provide such a fleet. This aid was forthcoming because of the seeming advantage to France in the restoration of the Lancastrians and their adherence to an alliance against Burgundy. Both English and Burgundian naval forces, however, were at sea all summer in an endeavour to keep Warwick's French fleet in port. Their efforts seemed successful; by August Warwick's men were demanding their pay and the people of Barfleur and Valognes had had enough of their presence. A summer gale then dispersed the Yorkist ships at sea and Warwick sailed across unopposed landing on 9 September near Exeter.[44] By the end of the month Edward IV was himself a fugitive restlessly watching the North Sea from his refuge at Bruges with Louis de Gruthuyse, the Burgundian governor of Holland.[45] If he in his turn was to regain his throne his need also was for ships. The Duke of Burgundy was perhaps more discreet in his support for his brother-in-law than Louis XI had been for his cousin, Margaret of Anjou. In March 1471, however, Edward left Flushing with 36 ships and about 2000 men and once ashore at Ravenspur by guile and good luck recovered his Crown.[46]

In the 20 or so years from 1455, therefore, it can be argued that the possession of the potential for naval warfare could be of great advantage to those who wished to be major players in both internal and external politics. No very great or glorious encounters between the vessels of rival powers took place in the Channel or the North Sea. The typical action was that of the commerce raider; a brief violent boarding action ending probably in the surrender of the weaker crew in an attempt to save their skins. Kings and other rulers possessed very few or no ships of their own and were reliant on the general resources of the maritime community. Yet, despite this, the perception of the pressure, which could be exerted by a fleet in being, was more widely appreciated. Warwick has been held up as the individual whose actions demonstrate this most clearly and it is hard to argue against this opinion. He, perhaps, until the fatal moment on the field at the battle of Barnet, also had luck. Would he have fared well if Exeter had attacked off Dartmouth in 1460? The reasons for Exeter's loss of nerve are not really clear. Exeter had many warships including the *Grace Dieu*, built by John Tavener of Hull and formerly Warwick's own flagship. The *Great Chronicle of London* speaks vaguely of Exeter's crews being unwilling to oppose Warwick while the *English Chronicle* states baldly that Exeter was afraid to fight. Waurin, a Burgundian chronicler, has a circumstantial account of Warwick approaching the coming conflict with great circumspection, sending out fast small vessels ahead of the main fleet to gather intelligence and then calling a council of war of all his ship masters.[47] The decision was taken to attack with vigour and maybe the sight of Warwick's ships coming on at speed with the advantage of the wind terrified Exeter. His lack of courage was certainly a disastrous blow for his party.

On a wider canvas, the situation in these waters as far as the relations between rulers goes has become much more open. In the first third of the century the conflict between England and France was the dominant factor with other states being drawn in as allies of one or the other combatant. After the middle of the century states pursued their own commercial and political interests in a more fluid situation. Naval power was diffuse, not necessarily concentrated in government hands, and the advantage might swing quickly from one state or group of traders to another.

The Hanse and its opponents

Conflict at sea undertaken for purely commercial reasons undoubtedly became more common and in many ways more disruptive of trading links. As we have seen at the end of the fourteenth and early fifteenth centuries the seizing of the trading vessels and cargoes of those designated 'enemies' was almost routinely a feature of wider conflicts with political roots. In the fifteenth century low level maritime war was also waged at various times between the towns of the Hanseatic League, and the county of Holland, and the League and England. This 'warfare' arose over questions of access to markets and reciprocity in the payment of customs dues and other privileges for merchants. It was divorced from considerations of territorial aggrandisement or rivalry between monarchs. The state of war between Holland and the Wendish section of the League caused political difficulties for the Duke of Burgundy in 1438–41 but little naval action beyond the mutual seizure of ships and cargoes. The conflict with England, as well as involving political considerations in the reign of Edward IV raises some problems concerned with the nature of naval war.

The privileged position of merchants from the Hanse towns had long caused a degree of resentment in England especially in London where their base in the Steelyard was a constant and visible reminder of their power. The rate of duty which they paid on the export of woollen cloth was lower even than that paid by denizen merchants. They also gained exemption in 1437 from the poundage applied to all other goods both alien and denizen. To the fury of English merchants they received no reciprocal benefits of any kind in Hanse towns, rather they faced petty harassment especially in Lubeck, Rostock and the other Wendish ports. The importance of commercial traffic between the Baltic and England ensured that the authorities of the League and English rulers made attempts to resolve these difficulties both by negotiations and trade boycotts and other sanctions. Piratical attacks on shipping from Hanseatic towns or on the goods of Hanse merchants carried in the vessels of another state greatly increased in frequency as the situation in the Channel became more and more anarchic. The English Crown's lack of its own shipping and the practice of sea-keeping by licence contributed to what the Hanse saw as intolerable attacks on their lawful trade and English seafarers saw as justifiable retribution.[48] In 1447-9 matters seemed to be reaching a possible resolution with English envoys pressing the League and the Grand Master of the Teutonic knights hard for reciprocal rights. The English position was weakened by the re-opening of the war with France which increased the need to maintain a healthy trade with the Baltic. At this point with new talks pending in Deventer, and Parliament exerting pressure on the king to annul Hanseatic exemptions from poundage, Robert Wenyngton, a respectable man of substance in Dartmouth and a former mayor of the town led a squadron which captured the whole fleet coming from Biscay laden with Bay salt bound for the Baltic ports. Not surprisingly, this had a disastrous effect on relations between the League and England but Wenyngton's own account of the affair also raises some interesting points on how such a capture was achieved.[49]

He had put to sea, in the early summer of 1449, for the kind of sea-keeping patrol much desired by all English seafarers and had had a degree of success taking two ships from Brest on a return voyage from Flanders. This had stirred up the maritime community and the authorities in Brittany to put together a force to oppose him. He mentions in a letter that this was made up of 'the great ship of Brest, the great ship of Morlaix, the great ship of Vannes with another eight ships, barges and balingers, to the number of 3000 men'. Wenyngton was cruising off the coast preparing to meet this force when instead he came up with, 'a fleet of a hundred great ships of Prussia, Lübeck, Campe, Rostock, Holland, Zeeland and Flanders between Guernsey and Portland'. His letter is not entirely clear but the sequence of events can be reconstructed. Wenyngton's squadron was clearly prepared for battle but was small in number with no 'great ships'. With the opposing fleets already at close quarters (Wenyngton went on board the 'admiral', the enemy commander's ship, to state his terms before battle commenced), the English demanded that the opposing force should 'strike' (lower their colours) to acknowledge English claims to sovereignty of the seas in the Channel. When the enemy contemptuously rejected this claim, hostilities commenced with the use of both guns and crossbows by the enemy and heavy casualties on the English side. Wenyngton, however, then had a good wind and with over 2000 men in his fellowship made ready, 'to over sail them'. This had the immediate effect of causing the commander of the Bay fleet to launch a boat and begin negotiations for a truce. With no further blows struck the whole Bay fleet surrendered to Wenyngton and was escorted to the waters off the Isle of Wight.[50] What, therefore caused a larger fleet, well armed and with its ships still seaworthy to give up the fight so completely and so abruptly? Wenyngton seems to have been threatening to board or perhaps to ram and sink his opponents but he could not have dealt with all the enemy ships at once. Why, as far as we know, did none try to escape? We can only speculate about precise answers to this problem but one thing is clear; the initiative lay with the fleet with the weather gauge, especially if this fleet was made up of well-handled vessels with determined and aggressive commanders. The suggestion that the attack was other than entirely fortuitous has been rejected but it is also the case that contemporaries strongly suspected that most of the proceeds of this attack found their way into the pockets of some royal councillors.[51] We have fewer details of Warwick's rather similar taking of 18 ships from Lübeck from the same salt convoy in 1458[52] but the same excuse was put forward by Warwick for his actions.[53] We may also speculate that Baltic merchants preferred to surrender and take the chance of recovering their goods by an action in the English Admiralty court rather than face the horrors of a boarding action.

The running sore of the Hanse privileges in England was not soothed by these relatively spectacular actions. Retaliation and retribution ensured that trade between England and the Baltic was likely to be interrupted whether by official embargoes or semi-official piracy. In 1468 relations between the two trading partners reached a crisis. A group of English ships laden with wool were surrounded by hostile ships and forced to surrender in the Sound. The Danish king accepted responsibility for the incident but furious English East Coast merchants blamed their old opponents the Danzigers. In an atmosphere of high emotion, the leaders of the Steelyard were summoned to Westminster to the king's Council and informed that they would have to pay a large fine or face imprisonment. Despite nearly a year of attempts to settle things amicably, by the end of the following summer the Hanseatic merchants in Bruges had set about fitting out privateers to attack English trade. This so-called English-Hanseatic war (which also drew in both the Burgundians and the French)[54] was indeed fought entirely at sea but was in reality no more than a series of raids on individual ships and traders, a *kaperkrieg* to use the German term.[55] It occurred at a time of great instability in English internal politics with alliances shifting to such an extent that Edward IV was chased by Hanseatic ships as he fled into exile from Warwick in 1470 and then assisted by vessels from the same ports on his return in 1471. By 1473 both sides were looking for peace despite the continuance of attacks including the episode when the Hanseatic freebooter Beneke chased two Burgundian galleys, hired by the Medici bank, en route from Zeeland to Florence. Beneke caught up with them off Southampton. One got safely into port, the other was taken with its rich cargo, much the property of English merchants. Also on board was the Memling altarpiece, *The Last Judgement*, commissioned for a Florentine church. This was soon hanging in the church of St Mary in Danzig but despite protests from all sides little action was taken against Beneke and his men.[56] When a treaty, the Treaty of Utrecht, was concluded between Edward IV and the League in 1474, it did little more than confirm the ancient privileges of the Hanse in England with some vague hints at reciprocity for the English.[57] In Lloyd's view, the attitude of Denmark, 'the master of the Sound' was of far greater importance to England and other maritime states than the friendship or enmity of Prussia.[58]

It is possible, however, to be too disparaging of what seems like a futile and expensive conflict. After the treaty was signed Anglo-Baltic trade recovered its prosperity. Although he had only a small group of ships of his own Edward IV did have some success in suppressing the worst excesses of pirates especially those operating out of west-country ports. Neighbouring states followed similar policies and by the end of the century northern waters were safer for traders and mariners in general. State-owned ships, however, remained a relative rarity with decisive maritime intervention into politics largely confined to the provision of transports for invading forces, as in the case of the future Henry VII in 1483. There was, perhaps little of the interest in warships and their use which can be found at the time of Henry V or even earlier when Philip IV set up the *Clos des galées*. Naval tactics, compared with the use made of fleets in the Mediterranean, seemed to have developed little since the days of the 'great ships' in the early years of the century. Although cannon were undoubtedly carried on ships it is hard to find any action where their presence made a definite contribution to the outcome. The only mention of the use of guns at sea in an English source is in Wenyngton's letter about the capture of the Bay fleet.[59] Pero Niño's squadron was, much earlier, driven off from Calais by artillery but here shore-based bombards are involved not guns on ships.[60] In the kind of close contact action, which seems to have been usual in the final stages of sea battles in northern waters, two tactics seem to have been used; one the boarding action which involved laying a vessel alongside its opponent and grappling with her, while the attackers poured over the side and the other 'sailing over' an opponent, the risky and dangerous manoeuvre of ramming combined with attempts to bring down masts and rigging. Both required high standards of ship handling among the crew and well-found ships that could withstand the impact of a collision. These qualities were evidently as likely to be found among the mariners and vessels of traders as among royal ships and shipmen.

The future, however, clearly lay with the development of the use of artillery at sea and of ships designed with this in mind. Only cannon had the power to deliver a 'ship killing' blow at a distance, something beyond the capacity of crossbows or even mangonels. Henry VII's *Regent* and *Sovereign* come into this category, the first carrying 151 iron serpentines and 29 in brass[61] and the second having 'serpentynes of yron', 'serpentynes of brasse' and 'stone gunnes' in the forecastle, the waist, the summer castle, the deck over the summer castle, the stern and the poop.[62] The *Sovereign* also carried moulds for making lead pellets on board. In the same way, although little is known about the details of the campaign, many of the ships involved against Scotland in 1497 were provided with cannon and shot. The *Anthony of London* carried a *curtowe*, a heavy gun, and 150 iron shot and 50 stone shot for the same. In all 57 guns, not including 180 'hakbusses' were provided by the royal ordnance; some were clearly intended for use on shore (mention is made of 'horsharness' for them and some are described as being 'expent' in the taking of the 'Tour of Aiton') but this is not the case for all the guns mentioned.[63] Equally all the king's ships listed in the accounts for 1485–8 are armed with guns of varying types. What was, perhaps, lacking was understanding of the best way to deploy these new weapons at sea, a skill which could increasingly be found in the Mediterranean.

This period, therefore, in northern waters, while it does perhaps demonstrate a retreat from participation in war at sea by rulers with their own ships, does show an increasing understanding of the strategic use of ships. Whether in the kind of struggle for commercial domination undertaken by the Hanse or in the use of ships to apply political pressure undertaken by the Earl of Warwick, things have developed considerably from the almost random raids and piracies of earlier periods. An important factor in this may well be the increased sophistication in the design of both ships and the weapons they carried. It is also clear that the skills of seamen not only in general navigation but also in the specialist handling of ships in action had increased. All this perhaps pointed to the development in the sixteenth century of navies designed for war at sea employing the deadly weapon of the broadside.

Notes

1 A. Merlin-Chazelas, *Documents Rélatifs au Clos des Galées de Rouen*, 2 vols, Paris, Bibliothèque Nationale, 1977–8, Vol. I, pp. 68–73.

2 A. Merlin-Chazelas, *op. cit.*, Vol. II, texte XCI, p. 205 and see Chapter 1, p. 14.

3 John Chamberleyn's enrolled accounts can be found P.R.O. Exchequer L.T.R. E364/39 and E364/43. The particulars of account are at Exchequer Accounts Various, E101/42/39, E101/43/2 and E101/43/6.

4 John Elmeton's Accounts; P.R.O. Exchequer L.T.R. E364/46; documents subsidiary to the accounts are at E101/44/12.

5 Statutes to compensate those who suffered from robbery at sea were passed in 1353, and 1414, which, in fact, laid down that the breakers of truces would be guilty of treason.

6 C.L. Kingsford, 'West Country piracy: the school of English seamen', in *Prejudice and Promise in XVth-century England*, Oxford, Clarendon Press, 1925, p. 80. This was the situation in the case of Symon Rydoul of Amiens in c.1426.

7 The careers of Pay and John Hawley senior and junior are detailed in articles by Susan Rose in the *New Dictionary of National Biography* (forthcoming). They can also be found in C.L. Kingsford, *op. cit.*, pp. 83–7.

8 S. Rose, *The Navy of the Lancastrian Kings, Accounts and Inventories of William Soper, Keeper of the King's Ships, 1422–1427*, London, George Allen and Unwin for the Navy Records Society, 1982, p. 20.

9 C.J. Ford, 'Piracy or policy: the crisis in the Channel, 1400–1403', *Transactions of the Royal Historical Society*, 5th series, vol. xxix, 1979, p. 64.

10 C.J. Ford, *op. cit.*, p. 65.

11 C.J. Ford, *op. cit.*, p. 77.

12 *Chita* has been identified as St Ives by Joan Edwards whose *Unconquered Knight*, London, George Routledge, 1928, is a translation of extracts from *El Victorial*. This identification is followed by the editor of the Spanish edition, but it seems unlikely on geographical and topographical grounds. The Helford river suits the description in the Chronicle much better.

13 The biography of Don Pero Niño by his standard bearer Gutierre Diez de Gamez, *El Victorial*, has been published in its entirety in Spanish by Juan de Mata Carriaga (ed.), Espasa-Calpe, Madrid,1940. The incident at *Chita* has been translated in J.B. Hattendorf *et al.*, *British Naval Documents 1204–1960*, London, Scolar Press for the Navy Records Society, 1993, no. 16, pp. 25–6. Joan Evans' translation is not always accurate on maritime technicalities.

14 This fleet must have been composed largely of ships owned by merchants; Henry IV did not own more than five or six ships at this date and there is no trace of payments in the clerk of the king's ships' accounts for any repairs following an action in 1406. The accounts in question are P.R.O. Exchequer L.T.R. E364/43.

15 This action in the Channel is no 17, pp. 26–9, J.B. Hattendorf *et al.*, *op. cit.*

16 S. Rose, *The Navy of the Lancastrian Kings: Accounts and Inventories of William Soper, Keeper of the King's Ships, 1422–1427*, London, Allen and Unwin for the Navy Records Society, 1982, p. 34.

17 S. Rose, *op. cit.*, p. 36.

18 I. Friel, 'Henry V's *Gracedieu* and the wreck in the R. Hamble near Bursledon, Hampshire', *The International Journal of Nautical Archaeology*, 22, 1993, pp. 3–19, discusses the building of the *Gracedieu* and her later history in detail.

19 S. Rose, *op. cit.*, p. 247 and G. Hutchinson, *Medieval Ships and Shipping*, London, Leicester University Press, 1994, pp. 156–9.

20 Mention of the battle can be found in J. Stella, *Annales Genuenses*, in L.A. Muratori (ed.), Rerum Italicarum Scriptorum, 27 vols, Milan, 1723, 17, p. 1268; A. Morosini, *Chronique, Extraits rélatifs a l'histoire de France* (ed. G. Lefevre-Pontalis), Société de l'Histoire de France, 4 vols, Paris 1898–1902, I, p. 107 and A. Guistiniani, *Annali della Repubblica di Genova* (ed. G. Spotorno), 2 vols, Genoa, 1854, p. 277.

21 F. Taylor and J.S. Roskell (eds), *Gesta Henrici Quinti*, Oxford, Clarendon Press, 1975, p. 145.

22 S. Rose, *op. cit.*, p. 49.

23 Morosini's account of this battle is no.18, pp. 29–30, J.B. Hattendorf *et al.*, *op. cit.* The *Gesta* adds the comment that the English ships did not pursue the enemy into Honfleur because 'of the untried channels, unknown sandbanks and peculiarities of an unfamiliar river', *Gesta Henrici Quinti*, p. 149.

24 *Gesta Henrici Quinti*, pp. 161–7.

25 An account of this engagement from Morosini's Chronicle is no 19, p. 30 in J.B. Hattendorf *et al.*, *op. cit.*

26 S. Rose, *op. cit.*, pp. 49–50.

27 N.A.M. Rodger, *The Safeguard of the Sea*, p. 144.

28 This was certainly the opinion of later historians who maintained that the enormous clinker-built *Gracedieu* never put to sea at all and was a technological disaster.

29 The report is P.R.O. Exchequer Accounts various E101/49/33. A full translation has been published in S. Rose, 'Henry V's *Gracedieu* and mutiny at sea: some new evidence', *The Mariner's Mirror*, 63, 1977, pp. 3–6.

30 H. Kleineke, 'English shipping to Guyenne in the mid-fifteenth century: Edward Hull's Gascony voyage of 1441', *The Mariner's Mirror*, 85, 1999, pp. 472–6.

31 Rotuli Parliamentorum, vol. V, XX Hen VI, pp. 59–61. The text of the petition is also printed in *The Mariner's Mirror*, 9, 1923, pp. 376–9.

32 H. Kleineke, *op. cit.*, pp. 472–3.

33 C.F. Richmond, 'The keeping of the seas during the Hundred Years War: 1422–1440', *History*, xlix, 1964, pp. 283–98.

34 C.F. Richmond, 'The Earl of Warwick's domination of the Channel and the naval dimension to the Wars of the Roses, 1456–1460', *Southern History*, 20/21, 1998–9, p. 2.

35 Proclamation of Jack Cade, June 1450. *English Historical Documents*, IV, pp. 266–7.

36 R.A. Griffiths, *The Reign of Henry VI*, Stroud, Sutton, 1998, p. 815.

37 C.F. Richmond, 'The Earl of Warwick's domination', p. 2.

38 Hattendorf *et al.*, *British Naval Documents 1204–1960*, 21, pp. 31–2.

39 C.F. Richmond, 'The Earl of Warwick's domination'

40 C.F. Richmond, 'The Earl of Warwick's domination', pp. 3–9, gives a full account of the activities of the Earl of Warwick and his squadron of ships based at Calais.

41 C.F. Richmond, 'The Earl of Warwick's domination', p. 12.

42 C.F. Richmond, 'The Earl of Warwick's domination'

43 J. Gillingham, *The Wars of the Roses: Peace and Conflict in Fifteenth-century England*, London, Weidenfeld and Nicolson, 1981, p. 177.

44 J. Gillingham, *op. cit.*, pp. 180–3.

45 C. Ross, *Edward IV*, London, Eyre Methuen, 1974, p. 153.

46 C. Ross *op. cit.*, pp. 160–2.

47 J. Gillingham, *op. cit.*, p. 109.

48 J.D. Fudge, *Cargoes, Embargoes and Emissaries: The Commercial and Political Interaction of England and the German Hanse*, Toronto and London, University of Toronto Press, 1995, pp. 7–15.

49 His account is found in a letter of 25 May 1449 from himself to Thomas Daniel in the Paston Collection. It is printed in Hattendorf *et al.*, *British Naval Documents 1204–1960*, 20, pp. 30–1.

50 All details come from the above letter.

51 T.H. Lloyd, *England and the German Hanse 1157–1611: A Study of their Trade and Commercial Diplomacy*, Cambridge, Cambridge University Press, 1991, p. 181.

52 C.F. Richmond, 'The Earl of Warwick's domination', p. 7. T.H. Lloyd, *op. cit.*, p. 195.

53 J. Gardiner (ed.) 'A short English chronicle', *Three Fifteenth Century Chronicles*, p. 71.

54 P. Dollinger, *La Hanse, XII–XVII siècles*, Paris, Aubier,1964, pp. 378–9.

55 War of pirates. The term is used by S. Jenks in *England, die Hanse und Preussen: Handel und Diplomatie 1377–1471*, Cologne and Vienna, Bohlau Verlag, 1992.

56 J.D. Fudge, *op. cit.*, p. 73.

57 J.D. Fudge, *op. cit.*, pp. 51–81.

58 T.H. Lloyd, 'A reconsideration of two Anglo-Hanseatic treaties of the fifteenth century', *English Historical Review*, 102, 1987.

59 Hattendorf *et al.*, *British Naval Documents 1204–1960*, 20, pp. 30–1.

60 Hattendorf *et al.*, *British Naval Documents 1204–1960*, 17, p. 26.

61 M. Oppenheim, *A History of the Administration of the Royal Navy and of Merchant Shipping in relation to the Navy from MDIX to MDCLX with an Introduction Treating of the Preceding Period*, reprinted by The Shoe String Press Inc., 1961, p. 41.

62 M. Oppenheim (ed.), *Naval Accounts and Inventories of the Reign of Henry VII*, London, Navy Records Society, 1896, pp. 194–5.

63 M. Oppenheim (ed.), *Naval Accounts and Inventories*, p. 84, p. 129.

CHAPTER SIX

Venetians, Genoese and Turks: the Mediterranean 1300–1500

In the fourteenth and fifteenth centuries the sources of evidence for naval warfare in the Mediterranean are both more copious and more reliable than those for the earlier period. Not only are there chronicle sources but also two of the major players in the field of war at sea at this time, the city states of Genoa and Venice, had well organised and sophisticated bureaucracies whose records have survived in quite large quantities. There are gaps caused by unpredictable events like the fires in the sixteenth century in the Doge's Palace in Venice, where the archives were stored, but much remains. There are also more personal papers, memoirs and reports which allow a clearer view of the intentions or orders of commanders even if the fog of war still hangs thickly over the events of many battles.

Considering the extent of war at sea at the beginning of this period in the Mediterranean, we can perhaps distinguish two theatres of operations, the eastern and the western. The former was dominated by the deadly rivalry for control of the enormously lucrative trade to the East between Venice and Genoa. The latter saw not only the hardly less bitter rivalry between Genoa, Pisa and Aragon for control of trade routes and also the islands in the western Mediterranean, but also the conflicts, sometimes pursued in open warfare and sometimes in ill-defined piratical exploits, involving the Moors of Granada and the Maghreb and the Christian rulers of Iberia. These were never, of course, entirely separate but such a division makes it easier to discuss the unstable and shifting political background to encounters at sea. Later, in the fifteenth century, the growing menace to Christian states of the new naval power of the Ottoman Empire overshadows all other conflicts. This can be presented as a collision between two religions but it was also a conflict between an expanding political entity and others whose powers were declining, and a conflict with an important economic element.

Venice and Genoa

The two states which are our particular concern at this period, Venice and Genoa, were alike in that both lived by trade and both had a republican form of government but were unlike in many other ways. In each state there was a general awareness of how closely the fortunes of the city and its inhabitants were bound up with the sea. In the normal course of events, sea-borne trade was the root of this perception and the origin of each city's wealth but, in an era when the division between commercial and naval shipping was not clearly drawn, war at sea also figured largely in the concerns of the citizens. In the detail of the organisation of trade, shipping and war at sea, however, the differences between the two are marked. In Venice it is noticeable that, by the middle of the thirteenth century the organisation of a fleet whether for commercial or warlike purposes, was a public matter;[1] the protection and promotion of Venetian interests, which were widely construed to include the economic interests of the city state, was accepted as the responsibility of the *Signoria*. It is also noticeable that once a fleet had been organised and dispatched to trade or to deal with the enemy that the authorities in Venice did their utmost to keep themselves informed of what was going on and even attempted to control events, despite the distances sometimes involved and the difficulties of communication with vessels at sea.[2] In Genoa, it seems that individual ship-owners and commanders had a much freer hand especially in the conduct of trading voyages. There was no system like that of the Venetian *muda* or galleys running on predetermined routes to a time-table or the Venetian war galley patrols and escorts to trading ships.[3]

In some ways it might seem surprising that Venice and Genoa became such bitter rivals that the tension between them which had built up since the First Crusade erupted into open war on four occasions between 1253–1381. Each had arguably a 'sphere of influence' in home waters, the Adriatic for Venice and the Tyrrhenian Sea for the Genoese. War with Aragon in the case of Genoa or with the power that controlled the Dalmatian coast in the case of Venice might seem a more natural consequence of the confined geographical position and the restless energy of each state. Each was involved in war with its near neighbours but no conflicts were as hard fought as those involving each other. The origins of the rivalry lay in trade; the trade with the Levant, Romania and the Black Sea which by the thirteenth century was extremely lucrative. The Venetians had first acquired extensive privileges in Constantinople by making a crucial bargain with the Byzantine Emperor in 1082. In return for aid to the Greeks against the incursions into the mainland of the Empire of Robert Guiscard from Sicily, their position as merchants in Constantinople was assured. The Genoese, on their part, had used the opportunity of the First Crusade to establish themselves on the route to the Holy Land and within its ports. Their fleet had given valuable assistance during the taking of Antioch and in 1104 a treaty between the Genoese and Baldwin I king of Jerusalem allowed them tax exemptions and property rights in the port towns of Jaffa, Arsuf, Caeserea and Acre. As the merchants from each city strove to increase their influence with their trading partners and extend their trading networks they had no wish to give way to their rivals but rather wished to oust them from the area. Thus the rivalry spread from the ports of Outremer to Constantinople, and to the islands and ports in the Aegean, the Black Sea and elsewhere where these merchants wished to establish trading bases or negotiate for exclusive privileges with the local rulers.[4]

The success of the fleet commanded by Domenico Michiel off Askelon in 1123[5] from this point of view could be interpreted as an attempt to undermine the dominant position of the Genoese in Outremer. Similarly at the end of the twelfth century the good relations between the Byzantine Empire and Venice deteriorated as the Venetian fleet sacked Greek islands in the Aegean and the Emperor retaliated by arresting Venetians in Constantinople and seizing their property. In the Fourth Crusade the Venetians stand accused of using the Crusaders' need for ships provided by them, to ensure the diversion of the Crusade to Constantinople, the sack of the city and the eventual establishment of the Latin Empire in the east. After the fall of Constantinople to the Crusaders the Venetians acquired not only booty, including the bronze horses which have for so long adorned the façade of San Marco, but the right to three eighths of the city. Their colony there, soon numbered in thousands, was clustered round the port area. Elsewhere in Romania (as the Empire was always called) the Venetians concentrated on consolidating their hold on Crete and establishing bases on the island of Negroponte and the towns of Modon and Coron in the Morea soon known as the 'two eyes of the Republic'. These territorial acquisitions made sense as commercial and naval bases by which trade routes could be controlled and the operations of patrolling galleys supported. It is not surprising to find the Genoese, after these events, emerging as allies of the dispossessed Greek imperial family. They were eventually bound by treaty in 1260 to support Michael Paleologus in his ultimately successful bid for the throne with a force of 50 galleys, and founded their own colony at Pera just out side the walls of Constantinople.

The tension between the rival merchant republics first flared into open warfare in 1257. The murder of a Genoese by a Venetian in Acre, the main port and trading centre of Outremer, led to rioting in the town between the two groups. When the Venetian *muda* arrived it included war galleys as well as trading ships and forced its way into the harbour apparently breaking the chain across the entrance. A large Genoese fleet, including as many as 50 galleys, arrived off the town in the next sailing season and the Venetians commanded by Lorenzo Tiepolo came out to give battle. The action which ensued was the first in a series of encounters between the ships of the two city states which was to last for over 100 years.[6]

Are there any common features to these encounters which can contribute to our understanding of naval warfare? As far as the first Genoese-Venetian war goes John Dotson is of the opinion that it reveals a good grasp of the possibilities of attaining something akin to Mahan's concept of control of the sea among the naval commanders of both states. He does not deny that control of the sea in the conventional sense associated for example, with the

British navy in the nineteenth century, was impossible for fleets largely composed of galleys, which cannot stay long at sea without putting into port for supplies of food and water for the crew. He does point out, however, that the patterns of prevailing winds and currents in the Mediterranean, combined with the fact that sailing was virtually confined to the summer months between April and October, meant that ships on trading voyages could be reliably found at certain 'pinch points' on their routes at well known times.[7] The effect of this was that an opposing fleet need only be 'on station' for a short time to have a good chance of taking a high proportion of the enemy's trading vessels. Since trade was, as has been said, of vital importance to both states, a successful action like this was not just commerce raiding but a severe blow to the losing state's security. Interpreted like this the fact that the admirals of the Genoese fleet showed 'either a fatal timidity or an utter clumsiness'[8] in their handling of their forces in large-scale galley actions loses importance. The Venetians defeated a larger force of Genoese galleys off Acre in 1258, near Settepozzi (Spetsai) in 1263 and Trapani in 1266. The Genoese, however, managed to take a large *nef* and three galleys of the Venetians off Abydos, laden with the proceeds of a year's trade with the Black Sea ports in 1262. In 1263 some of the Genoese survivors of the battle of Settepozzo redeemed their honour by capturing four Venetian traders off Malvasia. In the following year, the Genoese admiral Simone Grillo, by setting up an elaborate ruse which tricked the Venetians into thinking his fleet had gone east when in fact it was cruising off Durazzo in the southern Adriatic, captured all the galleys in the Venetian fleet returning from Constantinople. Only the *Roccafortis*, a large sailing round ship, escaped. In 1266 Obertino Doria hoped to capture the entire Venetian *muda* from Romania off Modon but was driven away by the very heavy escort of armed galleys with the traders. With their war galleys tied down by escort duties to their own convoys, the Venetians, in their turn could pose little threat to Genoese traders.[9]

Details of the formal galley actions rely on chronicle accounts whose accuracy may be doubtful but which do cast doubt on the leadership of the Genoese fleet. At Settepozzi only a portion of the Genoese fleet engaged the enemy; Lane ascribes this to the fact that the admirals were wary of endangering the investment of the contractors responsible for fitting out the galleys. At Trapani the Venetians apparently caused such panic in the Genoese galleys that many of the crews leapt overboard and tried desperately to save themselves by swimming for the shore. There may be much truth in the wry comments of Iacopo da Varagine, archbishop of Genoa from 1292, who described the crews as not Genoese but Lombards, unskilled in seafaring, inexperienced in sea battles, in fact useless at fighting and completely ignorant of ship handling.[10]

The two succeeding episodes in this long running conflict, that from 1294–9 and that from 1350–5, usually known as the Second and Third Venetian-

Genoese Wars have very similar strategic and tactical profiles. By 1294 the Genoese had established themselves with admirable drive and energy as the dominant force as western traders in Romania. The fall of Acre to the Mamluks, extinguishing the last remnants of the Crusader kingdom on the mainland of the Levant, had made it even more essential for merchant powers to maintain good relations with Byzantium and other rulers in the trading zone which now extended right into the Black Sea and the Sea of Azov. As well as their secure base at Pera adjacent to Constantinople the Genoese also had colonies at Caffa in the Crimea and Tana on the Sea of Azov. In the Aegean Chios was in their control. The Venetians had re-established themselves in Constantinople and had the valuable bases in the Aegean and Peloponnese already mentioned as well as Crete. Other islands in the Aegean were ruled by Venetian noble houses but were not part of the territory of the *Serenissima*. Each state had an undoubted desire to eliminate its rival and secure for itself all the rewards of the trade in silks, spices, slaves, and other goods on which its prosperity depended. In 1294 the Genoese caught the Venetian *muda* for Armenia off the port of Lajazzo and captured the bulk of the fleet and the goods it carried. Four years later near the island of Curzola just to the north of Ragusa[11] the Genoese commander Lampa Doria had the better of an encounter between c.90 Venetian and c.80 Genoese galleys taking what were said to be thousands of prisoners. During this whole period each side preyed extensively on the other's commercial shipping, actions which might now be called piratical but which at the time were seen as legitimate and expected. By 1299 divisions in the ruling oligarchy in Genoa led them to make a peace treaty, in effect no more than a temporary truce, with Venice. The real issue of rivalry for trade in Romania was left unresolved.

In 1350 the ostensible *casus belli* seems very similar. The intermittent, opportunistic taking of vulnerable vessels and their cargoes by both sides flared into a more serious conflict when a Venetian fleet of armed galleys sent east under the command of Marco Ruzzini to deal with a quarrel over trading rights at Tana caught about 14 Genoese galleys in the harbour of Castro near Negroponte and took ten. The Genoese response was to dispatch in the following year a fleet of some 64 galleys under the command of Paganino Doria to the Aegean. The Venetians meanwhile, who had had difficulty in manning Ruzzini's fleet because of the aftermath of the Black Death had made alliances with Aragon and the Byzantine Emperor John Cantacuzenus thus creating a fleet of potentially more than 60 galleys, (40 of their own, 12 Catalan-Aragonese, eight Greek in Venetian pay, 12 Greek funded by the Emperor). Their commander Niccolo Pisani was initially at a disadvantage because the Genoese found him at sea before he had joined up with his allies. He retired to Negroponte and successfully held off the Genoese until the Catalans arrived. Doria sailed for his base at Pera leaving the allied vessels uncertain as to their next move. With winter now upon them it might have been expected that there would be no attempt at any engagement until the spring brought calmer seas. However, in February 1352 the allied fleet appeared in the Bosphorus intending to join up with the Greeks in the Golden Horn. The Genoese left the shelter of Pera to prevent this and a long hard-fought action resulted leading to the withdrawal of the Venetians and Catalans. Pisani got his revenge the following year when he destroyed a Genoese fleet off Alghero in Sardinia, supporting the Aragonese invasion of the island. Yet still the tit for tat continued; Pisani's victory at Alghero did not prevent Doria taking a new fleet to the Aegean where it did much damage to Venetian shipping. Pisani followed them but eventually received orders from Venice to avoid battle with Doria since he was now outnumbered and a peace treaty was in the offing. Pisani chose Porto Longo, a small anchorage near Modon as his winter base. Doria appeared offshore and not having the same inhibitions against fighting as Pisani challenged him to come out. Pisani refused but after a Genoese galley had evaded the guard ships at the harbour mouth a confused engagement followed in which all the Venetian ships were taken and Pisani and many others made prisoner.

If we take this succession of naval engagements, some common features do emerge. First of all despite the apparently crushing nature of many naval encounters they could have remarkably few lasting effects. The battle of Porto Longo was followed by a peace treaty which merely bound both Genoese and Venetians to cease trading to Tana for three years and exhorted them to cease attacks on each other's shipping. The equally crushing Venetian defeat at Curzola had no long-term benefits for Genoa while the Venetian victory at Alghero was beneficial to Aragon but did little to advance Venetian war aims. Lane in fact concludes that, 'the outcome of Venetian-Genoese rivalry was not to depend on superiority in seamanship or naval operations'. This was almost irrelevant beside what he sees as the deciding factor, 'their relative skill' in 'social organisation'. In his view the Venetian Republic, for all its faults, was a more robust society than Genoa where factional rivalries were often out of control. It is also the case, despite the wider range of sources available, that it is difficult to find reliable accounts of the events of a battle which might allow one to better understand the tactics employed by either side. Chronicles can be very terse; the *Annales Genuenses* merely says of the battle of the Bosphorus, 'in these parts there was a battle two miles off Constantinople and the Genoese were victorious with their galleys'. The description of Porto Longo is equally brief concentrating on the lack of Genoese casualties and the number and rank of the prisoners and giving as much space to the celebration of the victory in Genoa as to the battle itself. Other chroniclers have apparently longer accounts but are in effect 'padding out' the little hard information available. Iacopo de Varagine exults in the Genoese victory at Lajazzo but spends some time comparing it with the victory of Judas Maccabeus over the Assyrians. As any reading of either chronicles or secondary material soon makes clear there is virtually never any agreement about the number of vessels involved between the different sources. There are, however, administrative sources which may not give details of the battles but which do make much clearer the costs involved, the logistical problems and sometimes also the orders given to the commanders. In relation to the battle of the Bosphorus three account books or registers exist in the Genoese State Archives which relate to this engagement; one is the register of the treasurers of Paganino Doria's fleet, Dario Imperiale and Domenico di Villanucio who seem to have made up most of the register while based at Pera. The other two are examples of the individual accounts kept by the scribes or pursers of particular galleys; one dated from 14 June 1351–13 August 1352, comes from Doria's own vessel; the other comes from the galley commanded by Simone Lecavalla.[12] In the Venetian State Archives the decisions and decrees of the Senate, or *Consiglio dei Rogati*, can be found in registers from the beginning of the fourteenth century; these include the directions sent to fleet commanders and instructions relating to the manning and provisioning of the galleys.[13] These sources allow a clearer picture of the difficulties facing galley commanders at this period. Doria by the time he reached Pera after his unsuccessful attempt to lay siege to Negroponte had a pressing need for supplies especially *biscotti* or biscuit, the hard baked, long-lasting carbohydrate staple foodstuff of galleymen. He needed both grain and flour and facilities to bake this product. Grain came in from Caffa and elsewhere; this was ground in mills belonging to the Turkish emir who ruled the south side of the straits. Biscuit was baked in, among other places, Bulgaria. Balard has in fact calculated that 56 per cent of the cost of the whole campaign went on provisions.[14] The accounts also allow some view of the difficulties in manning galleys, while the register from Lecavalla's ship, because it usually records her whereabouts, allows a reasonably accurate picture to be gained of the course she followed. As a scouting galley charged with trying to keep track of the enemy she scoured the seas; thus before the battle itself, in December 1351, this galley sailed more or less continually up and down the Sea of Marmara from Cap Greco south of Gallipoli to Erekli. She came into Pera from 12–14 December and went as far west as Tenedos on 21 December, returning to Pera itself on 28 December. She remained there for most of January and February but after the battle again began her patrolling, eventually finding the enemy galleys at anchor in Trapanon (Tarabaya) on the Bosphorus on 4 March 1352.[15] A further light on the problems of galley fleets is also shed by a report in the Genoese archives relating to the galley of Nicolini Piconi. This left Genoa on 6 November 1351 with the intention of joining Doria's forces but got no further than Calabria where the crew mutinied saying that, 'no way' would they go to Romania or obey the express orders of the Commune. By 8 January 1352 the galley had returned to Genoa where the officers made every effort to exonerate themselves of any guilt for the turn of events.[16]

The Venetian registers give a very clear view of the nervousness in Venice over the situation in Romania before the outbreak of war even if silent on the war itself. As early as April 1349, the Senate required all the captains of Venetian armed galleys in those waters, the Venetian authorities in Constantinople and the consul at Tana to consult together about the damage done to Venetian merchants and their goods by the Genoese.[17] The problem of manning the galleys is made clear not only by the permission given to galley captains to recruit men in Dalmatian ports but also by the issue of a decree to be read out on the Rialto which gave details of the better diet to be offered to galleymen, including four meals a day, good bread, and meat three times a week on Sunday, Tuesday and Thursday.[18] In March 1350 Venetian ships were forbidden to go to Caffa or Pera for fear of Genoese attacks.[19] By June even though ambassadors had been appointed to negotiate with the Genoese for an end to violence in Romania, which the Senate saw as damaging 'to the whole world'[20] as well as to their interests, the Arsenal was also ordered to speed up the preparation of galleys. Far from appearing as aggressive the predominant tone of these registers and the entries for 1351–2 is one of caution. The Senate's main concern was to keep trade flowing as freely as possible provided this could be done without running undue risks. Their watchwords seem to be 'safety' and 'caution' with negotiation always preferred to battle.

When war broke out again between the Venetians and the Genoese in 1378, there seemed at first little reason to suppose that it would differ from the earlier conflicts of which it could be seen as a continuation. The immediate cause of hostilities was a quarrel over the right to control Tenedos, an island in a strategic position at the mouth of the Dardenelles which, as a fortified galley base, could control access to Constantinople and the Black Sea. This seems very comparable to earlier disputes over Tana or even Acre. This time, however, the Genoese made alliances with Hungary, which was in dispute with Venice over the control of the coast of Dalmatia and Padua, a city which had no wish to be absorbed into Venetian territory on the *terra firma*. These states were well placed to surround and blockade Venetian territory even if the city itself still remained impregnable in the lagoon. The Venetians trusted in their sea defences and put their fleet under the command of Vettor Pisani, nephew of Niccolo a well-liked and experienced leader. The initial mistake of the Venetians seems to have been to allow the Genoese fleet to get access to the gulf of Venice, in practice normally barred to all armed vessels save those of the *Serenissima*. Pisani, after a highly successful cruise off Genoa itself, where he took many prisoners, brought his galleys back up the Adriatic with the intention of basing them for the winter at Pola in Istria.[21] This anchorage had been suggested by the Senate as well-placed for the protection of the *mude* on the final stages of their return voyages. In the spring of 1379, when the fleet was in the middle of being re-supplied and with some of the galleys beached for repairs, the Genoese appeared off the harbour mouth offering battle. The Venetians, who had a force of 16 *galie sotil* and five *galie grosse*, though only 16 were ready to put to sea at once, took up the challenge thinking the enemy had only 14 vessels. They were unaware that a further 10 were out of sight behind a headland. Once battle was joined confusion reigned. Pisani grappled and boarded the galley of the Genoese commander who was killed but when the five remaining Venetian galleys put to sea they found themselves facing the 10 hidden Genoese galleys and fled. Pisani judging the situation hopeless joined them leaving 15 Venetian galleys in Genoese hands with all their crews whom Chinazzo describes as 'the flower of the seamen of Venice'. It is reasonable to suppose that the five galleys who fled from the scene were the *galie grosse*, perhaps laden with merchandise and booty. Certainly they are described as those that Pisani had a duty to protect. By any standards this was a disaster for the Venetians; not only had they lost a considerable number of ships and their experienced crews but a victorious enemy fleet was at the head of the gulf within striking distance of the city itself. Pisani got back safely to the city only to be thrown into prison by the exasperated Senate. In the debates among the *Rogati* over his punishment a considerable number felt he deserved the death penalty (technically the punishment for galley commanders who fled during a battle), though he was in fact imprisoned and declared ineligible for any future office.

The extreme danger which faced the *Serenissima* was soon clear. With no galley fleet of any substance to oppose them, (the only other force of Venetian galleys had been sent west to the Tyrennhian Sea under the command of Carlo Zeno) the Genoese were able to blockade Venice with the help of their allies and take Chioggia in August 1379. Chinazzo's chronicle provides ample evidence of the seriousness of the situation for the people of Venice and also of the way the whole community responded to the challenge to its very existence. From the point of view of a naval historian several aspects of this situation from 1379 to its resolution in the defeat of the Genoese in late 1380 need emphasis. Most obviously Venice could only be secure while her ships in effect controlled the waters of the gulf. Important though the more distant bases and trade routes were to her prosperity, the need to keep adequate forces nearer home could not be ignored. Carlo Zeno and his forces returned eventually to Venice in January 1380 after a very successful series of raids on Genoese bases and commerce but their presence in the city was of even greater importance. Equally for Venice successful war at sea had an important element of community support. After the fall of Chioggia when the city seemed to be staring starvation in the face, Pisani was released from prison and restored to the command of a force of six galleys. He was received by ecstatic crowds in the Piazza and was overwhelmed with eager recruits when he sat, as was the custom, in the Piazzetta enrolling his crews. Important as the galley force was, Pisani then devoted most of his attention to isolating the Genoese forces at Chioggia by blocking the major waterways through the lagoon leaving open only the shallow winding routes used by small vessels whose masters had local knowledge. We must not exaggerate, however, the influence that naval forces could have on the final outcome of a conflict.

The Genoese on Chioggia surrendered in June 1380 because they themselves had been besieged and were running out of supplies. For this blockade of an island site in the watery landscape of the lagoon ships, boats, vessels of all kinds were essential but the engagements between the protagonists were in essence infantry encounters with some credit also going to the increased use of artillery. It can be argued, however, that the failure of the fleet to protect Venice allowed the Genoese to seize Chioggia and that more determined and successful use of a galley fleet eventually cleared most of their vessels from the Adriatic after they had left the island itself, thus demonstrating both the advantages of well used naval power and the penalties of failure. The treaty, however, which ended hostilities, was due as much to the use of skilled negotiators by Venice and the internal situation in Genoa as any victory; it was enough for the city to have survived.[22]

The terms of the treaty, although granting important concessions to the king of Hungary in Dalmatia, left the conflict with Genoa over trading bases in Romania as unresolved as ever; Tenedos was not to be fortified and neither Venetians nor Genoese were to trade with Tana for two years. From the long term strategic point of view, minor tinkering like this with the conditions under which each state operated in the area was almost irrelevant. While they had been locked in rivalry, preying on each other's commerce and undermining the financial stability of their own state as much as that of their rival by incurring the enormous expenses of galley warfare, Ottoman power in the region had been steadily increasing. By the end of the fifteenth century, the conflict between Venice and the Ottoman Empire at sea as on land was of profound importance for the future of the eastern Mediterranean.

Venetians and Turks

The seeming inevitability of the advance of Turkish power in the Balkans was made plain to the rulers of Europe by the crushing defeat of a crusading army, mainly made up of French and Hungarian contingents, at Nicopolis in 1396. Most Bulgarian and Serb lands were now ruled by the Ottomans with the Byzantine Empire confined to small areas around their cities of Salonica and Constantinople. At first this confirmation of the establishment of a major new power in the area seemed to have little influence on the rivalries of naval powers. Venice benefited from extending her rule over coastal towns which sought her protection rather than that of the declining Empire. In this way Venice became the ruler of Durazzo and Scutari in Albania, Lepanto, Patras, Argos, Nauplia and even briefly Athens. To many Venetians an important reason for undertaking the task of governing these places was to prevent them falling into the hands of the Genoese, who were still seen as hostile to Venice.

In Lane's view, Venice was able to recover her dominant position in trade in the Levant and enjoy the prosperity this brought, not because of her 'command of the seas' or the superiority of her galley fleet but because the Turkish advance in the West was halted by the need to deal with the forces of Tamerlane in Central Asia.[23] In the first years of the fifteenth century, therefore, naval warfare in the eastern Mediterranean, apart from the continuing problem of widespread, low-level commerce raiding, consisted largely of shows of force by both Venice and Genoa each intending to overawe the other. Documents from the archives of both Genoa and Venice reveal clearly the degree of mutual suspicion which existed.[24] Throughout 1403 the Venetian Senate was authorising its galley captains to keep a close eye on the Genoese fleet which, or so the Senate believed, had sailed from Genoa. Carlo Zeno, who was now captain general of the Gulf, was given special permission to pursue his own course rather than one prescribed by the Senate for this purpose. He was also given permission to take any Genoese property or vessels if they did harm to the property of Venetians to the value of more than 10,000 ducats. This was the sum of the damage already suffered by merchants in Rhodes and Cyprus which was the subject of negotiations.[25] Later in June 1404, the news of a fleet of three cogs and two galleys being prepared in Genoa, led the Senate to forbid the ships of Pietro Contarini and Fantino Pisani from leaving Venice till 8 July when they might expect to have more information and be able to make better arrangements for the vessels' security. A month later in Genoa one Niccolo da Moneglia was given permission by the governor of the city to take reprisals against Venetian ships. The most revealing of this series of documents is the deposition of Costantino Lercari taken in February 1407 when the Genoese authorities were investigating the loss of three of their galleys, part of the expedition of Marshall Boucicaut, off Modon in 1404. Lercari was the *patronus* of the galley on which Boucicaut sailed and therefore was an eyewitness of the events he describes. From his account, on one level relations between the cities were cordial. He describes the Venetian fleet coming out to meet the Genoese with every sign of honour and the two fleets then sailing together into the harbour and anchoring together. He himself was then involved in discussions with Carlo Zeno, the Venetian leader on the possibility of some joint action presumably against the Turks, though the details of this are not made clear. Zeno declined on the grounds that he could not exceed the very tightly drawn terms of his commission from the *Signoria*, making the remark that his 'lordship did not give such long reins to its captains as was the custom of the Genoese'. The Genoese then left Modon but the seeming amity did not last with both sides becoming suspicious of the other; Lercari in fact has a story that the Venetian *bailus* in Nicosia was sending the *Saracenos* (the Turks) news of the Genoese movements. Finally when the Genoese wished to go into Zonchio to take on water, Zeno refused to let them enter the port and appeared with all his galleys ready for battle with lances and crossbows to hand. Boucicault then ordered his men also to arm but not to strike the first blow. When the

Venetians attacked with cannon (*bombardis*) and crossbows battle was joined and in the ensuing melee the Genoese lost three galleys.

The use of cannon in fact is probably the most significant feature of this encounter almost the last in this area between the rival cities. As the century progressed the ability to deploy artillery was increasingly the deciding factor in war at sea. This did not only mean guns mounted onboard ships but shore batteries which could greatly hinder the use of galleys and other vessels to support or bring relief to the besieged in coastal towns. This was made abundantly clear during the siege of Constantinople in 1453. Venetian galleys were unable to contribute effectively to the defence of the city because of the weight of the Turkish onshore guns deployed against them. The fall of the Byzantine Empire stimulated the development of an Ottoman navy. Using the port and dockyard facilities which had long been in existence in or near the city and largely Greek seamen and shipwrights the Ottoman Empire came to dominate the waters of the eastern Mediterranean as it already dominated the land. The Venetians who, with the Knights of St John from Rhodes, the only other naval power of consequence active in these waters, were faced with a new and aggressive opponent; an opponent who, unlike the Genoese, controlled the greater part of the interior of the Balkans. Venetian bases in the area, without which the operation of galleys was more or less impossible, were vulnerable to attacks both from the sea and from the land. The predominantly amphibious character of naval warfare which is clear from the beginning of our period perhaps became even more noticeable in the second half of the fifteenth century, with battles fought in close conjunction with the taking of port towns and their hinterland.

It should not be assumed, however, that the Venetians were particularly eager to fight the Turks or saw themselves primarily as the protectors of western Christendom. On the contrary their aim was to maintain as good relations as possible with the Ottomans consistent with maintaining their position as merchants and control of their bases, particularly Negroponte and those in the Morea.[26] At first also the Turkish fleet seemed to present little danger to the experienced galley captains of Venice. Pietro Loredano succeeded in destroying the bulk of their ships in their base at Gallipoli in 1416 and the Venetian bases in the Morea, Modon and Coron were extensively refortified.[27] The decision of the Sultan Mohammed II to mount an attack on Negroponte in person, however, was a direct assault on Venetian interests and brought forth an energetic response from the *Signoria*. From early February 1470 orders were flying from the Senate to the Arsenal to prepare supplies, particularly of the essential *biscotti* as well as munitions, for the galleys going to the defence of Negroponte. Reinforcements were sought from Corfu in March and other galleys were to cruise off Dalmatia for fear of the extension of the conflict, particularly a possible attack on Durazzo. An order was even given to a galley going east from Pola that it was to make all speed for Negroponte not even putting into port to take on water. By June, when the Turkish fleet was known to have put to sea the Senate issued a general order that all vessels ready to sail, even including the galleys of the *muda* to Flanders, should make for the island. The details of the preliminaries to the engagement itself are recounted in a letter from a Venetian galley *soarcomito* (commander) Geronimo Longo to members of his family.[28] He describes the Turkish fleet as enormous, over 300 ships including 108 galleys, 'the sea looked like a wood'. He also mentions that the Turkish artillery was different from and superior to that of the Venetians and that their vessels were also better under sail than those of Venice, (he speaks of a mizzen sail) and had larger crews. Before the Venetian fleet came to the town of Negroponte, which was under siege by Mohammed II himself, the two fleets manouevred off the islands but no battle ensued, possibly because of unfavourable winds. In Longo's view the Venetians needed to have 100 great galleys, 70 lighter, faster *galie sottil*, and 10 to 15 great ships if they were to have a chance of defeating the Turks in a set piece encounter. The actual events at Negroponte were a disaster for Venice. The fleet at first retreated to Crete where a council was held on what to do (the Venetian fleet, said to include 52 galleys and 18 *nave* was heavily outnumbered if Longo's figures are to be believed). A return to Negroponte was agreed, where they found the Turks had built a boat bridge from the mainland to allow the besiegers easy access to the defences. The fleet sailed up to the bridge but, although the defenders were encouraged by their arrival, the Venetians again drew off for a further conference. This was the crucial moment; should an attempt be made to break through the bridge despite the Turkish guns defending the crossing? At least one galley captain was prepared to try with the wind and current with him, but the wind dropped. This seems to imply that the galleys would not be under oars but sailing so that all the crew could be employed in hurling missiles at the enemy. As night was coming on this would have been a hazardous undertaking. In the morning when the Venetians made another approach to the town they found that it had fallen to the Turks in the night. Da Canal, the Venetian captain-general, made further attempts to find the Turkish fleet among the islands and to engage them; he also tried to retake the lost island but when news of the disaster reached Venice in August he was stripped of his office and ordered to be sent back in disgrace.

The loss of Negroponte was a severe blow to the *Serenissima*. Anonymous poets excoriated da Canal for his failure to relieve Negroponte or pointed out how dangerous the situation was with the Turks, now '*signori del mare*'. The Senate seemed more confused; on the one hand it ordered the new captain general, Piero Mocenigo, in October to save money by decommissioning old galleys and on the other it issued draconian letters threatening very severe punishment to any galley captain who did not obey orders. Our fleet must be returned to its former integrity, they demanded. The old certainties of galley warfare certainly no longer seemed sufficient. Could these vessels in fact any longer serve a useful purpose at a siege if the enemy possessed artillery? Guns were mounted on galleys but it was hard to bring them to bear on a target and galleys themselves could be holed by shore based batteries or set on fire by hot or flammable shot.[29] Pepper argues that ' Venetian reliance on naval defence became increasingly misguided as Ottoman naval and artillery strength improved dramatically',[30] at this period, but it is hard to see what other alternative existed. The fortifications of towns like Modon could be improved but communication with Venice and supplies and reinforcements depended on keeping open the sea routes. At sea a well-led galley fleet was the most effective force available.

All these factors seemed to come together in what has become known as 'the deplorable battle of Zonchio'.[31] Immediately after the fall of Negroponte the Venetians seemed to have shrugged off their loss; the Turkish fleet sailed back in safety to its bases in the Bosphorus but offered no opposition to Venetian ships raiding in the Aegean. The war at sea had become something of a sideshow to both states more concerned with internal politics, events on land and in the case of Venice the state of trade, than the deployment of war fleets. In the spring of 1499, however, the Venetian authorities were greatly alarmed by the news that the Sultan was preparing a large fleet in the arsenals on the Bosphorus. This could only be intended for use either against the Knights of St John on Rhodes or the remaining Venetian possessions in the Morea. The *Signoria* had good intelligence of these worrying developments provided by Andrea Gritti, the *bailo* or head of the Venetian merchant community in Constantinople who sent frequent coded reports back to Venice.[32] By May the Senate was clearly worried about the 'present circumstances'[33] and making strenuous efforts to prepare round ships and supplies especially *biscotti* for the defence of Venetian interests off the Morea and in the Ionian Sea. Antonio Grimani, although reluctant to serve, had already been made captain general of the Sea in April and had left with a force of galleys on the 28 April. The fleet cruised uneasily off Modon and received news that the Turkish armada was at sea in late June. Its most probable destination was Lepanto already besieged by Turkish land forces. The fleets first came in sight of each other a month later between 24 and 28 July. Battle was eventually joined on 12 August off Zonchio (Navarino). The events of the battle are unusually well recorded. Not only is there a full account in Sanuto's diaries[34] but one of the galley captains present at the fight wrote notes of his experience later written up in the sixteenth century as the *Annali Veneti dell' anno 1457 al 1500*. These *Annali* seem to have been rearranged by their first editor but even so have the immediacy that can only come from an eye-witness account. There is also a large and beautiful near contemporary woodcut, made in Venice, which purports to show the most dramatic episode in the battle. From the Turkish point of view, the battle is also described by Haji Kahlifeh, whose account, written a considerable time after the battle, has been published under the title, *The History of the Maritime Wars of the*

Turks. The outline of events is not in dispute. Grimani had set out an order of battle which seems to have depended on the initial attack being carried out by his great sailing ships and the great galleys. Relying on the usual afternoon onshore wind of these waters, these would attack the Turkish fleet, which was hugging the shore, from seaward (this was only prudence on the part of the Turkish commanders since their main purpose was to deliver the necessary artillery train safely to the siege of Lepanto). As the trumpets sounded the advance, a squadron of light galleys joined Grimani's force from Corfu led by Andrea Loredano who had the reputation of being a dashing and popular commander. His arrival was greeted with enthusiastic shouts of his name from the galleymen who seem to have had no very good opinion of Grimani. Loredano went on board the *Pandora* the largest of the Venetian round ships and with another commanded by Albano Armer attacked the largest Turkish ship believed to be commanded by Kemal Ali (or Camali to the Venetians), a notorious corsair long hunted unsuccessfully by the Venetian galley patrols.[35] The three vessels became grappled together. A fire broke out on the Turkish ship which spread to the others and soon all were in flames.[36] There was no general fleet engagement and contact was broken off. The interpretation and explanation of these events has proved to be less easy. Many contemporaries had no doubts on the matter; Grimani was an ineffectual commander, who owed his position more to his political skills and wealth than his experience of leadership. His orders, full of defects according to Malipiero, had been disobeyed by majority of the galley captains. He fully deserved punishment by the *Signoria* for neglect of duty, as did his insubordinate galley commanders. Sanuto described the galley crews shouting, 'hang them, hang them' when they realised that the galleys were not joining the fray. Malipiero called his fellow commanders dogs and said that the crews shouted, 'attack, attack'. Grimani did return to Venice to face imprisonment and exile but perhaps placing all the blame on his shoulders is unfair. In his full analysis of this battle Lane suggests three further causes for the poor showing of Venetian naval forces in this engagement: the difficulty in 'combining for effective battle action round ships great galleys and light galleys': the difficulty in forcing officers who owed their positions to election within the *Signoria* to obey orders: the difficulty in recruiting suitably experienced crewmen in sufficient numbers.[37] Clearly these arguments have much to recommend them. Even in the somewhat confused accounts that we have of the battle it is clear that there was a need for defining more precisely the role of the large sailing vessels and for using more effectively the speed and mobility of the *galie sottil*. The use of both cannon and an early form of musket (*schioppo*), undoubtedly served to increase the noise and terror of the battle while adequate defensive tactics do not seem to have been worked out. Grimani was expected, as were all Venetian commanders, to hold a council with his officers before battle was joined to work out the plan, almost command by committee. This may have tended to lessen his personal authority. Certainly the unexpected and probably unwelcome arrival of Loredano served to undermine what remained. The question of crews was certainly a long term problem. Venice at this date still had crews of free men not convicts chained to their benches. Even allowing for heavy recruitment in Dalmatia, Corfu and Crete, and the inclusion of landsmen from Lombardy, Lane still estimates that Grimani's fleet may have included more than one tenth of the men of military age from the Venetian lagoons. According to our sources, however, there was no lack of an aggressive spirit among the galleymen at the battle itself even if the Lombards were of questionable quality.

It should also not be forgotten that, as emerges clearly from Malipiero's *Annali*, the battle of Zonchio was part of a series of actions not an isolated engagement. The two fleets had been shadowing each other since the beginning of July and were to continue to be in contact after Zonchio itself until the end of August. In a second engagement on 20 August, the Venetians had been joined by French reinforcements and made strenuous attempts to prevent the Turkish fleet sailing north up the coast towards Lepanto. They prepared fire ships which caused no damage to the enemy but which may have served to lure them from the safety of their anchorage the following day. The great galleys then mounted a bombardment of the Turks but after about two hours when ready to press home the attack and board the enemy the Turks disengaged and made for the safety of *Castel Tornese*. On the 22 and 25 August there were further skirmishes off Cape Papas in the last of which the Venetians did manage to take 10 *galie sottil* form the Turkish rear and inflict heavy casualties. These do not seem like the actions of a completely demoralised fleet nor a totally incompetent commander. It seems at least arguable, however, that Grimani's problems may not only have included those discussed by Lane but also the fact that he was facing an enemy which was more concerned to deliver heavy artillery successfully to the Turkish army outside Lepanto than win a fleet action. They therefore refused battle or broke off action whenever possible. From the Turkish point of view this made sense. The Venetians could not successfully defend their coastal bases if their hinterland was in enemy hands. Establishing greater control over the mainland would ensure that enclaves like Modon and Coron would soon be removed from Venetian control and in Turkish hands. In fact by 1502 Venice had lost all its bases in the Morea.

The end of the fifteenth century in the eastern Mediterranean, therefore, is perhaps a crucial moment in the history of naval warfare. On the one hand the strategic situation was in the middle of great change. A new power, the Ottoman Empire, had emerged which had strength in depth on land as well a sea and which could threaten the declining power of Venice whenever it chose.[38] Venice might maintain itself in the Ionian Islands and in Crete and Cyprus for some time but did not have the means to damage seriously the interests of its opponent. Its former rival Genoa now had no further interest as a naval power in the area. The nature of naval warfare was also on the brink of change. The sailing great ship, as opposed to the galley, was demonstrating its usefulness in battle particularly as a platform on which to mount guns. The use of artillery was not yet fully exploited in a naval context but had progressed beyond the point of merely creating uproar and confusion. A 'ship killing' weapon was available even if the boarding action still remained the expected end to a naval engagement.

The western Mediterranean

Did the strategic balance and the mode of naval warfare show similar signs of change in the western Mediterranean? Here as in the earlier period the ships of the rulers of Aragon-Catalonia and of Castile confronted those of the Muslim rulers of the *Maghreb* and of Granada in the waters adjacent to the Straits of Gibraltar. A complicating factor, however, was the rivalry which existed between Genoa and Aragon for control of bases in the western Mediterranean particularly the island of Sardinia while the king of Aragon also wished to reincorporate the kingdom of Majorca into his territories depossessing the cadet branch of his family. The rulers of Aragon, particularly Peter III the Ceremonious, can be seen as understanding the importance of seapower to the successful control of their scattered dominions. Robson has described this as, 'at once the index and the guarantee of national prosperity'.[39] In a letter to his heir John in 1380, Peter himself wrote, 'If we lose Sardinia, you can be sure that Majorca will be lost too'.[40]

The importance of an effective navy to these possessions of the house of Aragon largely lay in keeping open lines of communication and transporting land forces. Genoa and to a lesser extent Pisa, both of which had claims to Sardinia, and which had exerted some control in coastal areas, had access to probably as many ships as Aragon-Catalonia with experienced captains and crews. It was, however much more difficult for them to raise large land forces than Aragon and this was perhaps the factor which led to the Aragonese crown achieving an albeit imperfect control of the turbulent island in 1323–4. In the same way when Peter took Majorca from his cousin James III in 1343 galleys were needed as transports and were not involved in action at sea. The importance of Majorca to Aragon was undoubtedly as a convenient and well-placed port, dominating trade routes to the south. Sardinia had more natural resources as well as a strategic position on routes east but by attempting to take control of the island the Aragonese had greatly provoked their maritime rivals the Genoese. Thus within the Christian community of the western Mediterranean there were tensions and hostilities. As Genoese relations with Aragon deteriorated so their friendship with Castile grew, often supplying, if for a price, both ships and crews to serve the king. These inter-communal rivalries may perhaps explain why piracy and raiding both officially sanctioned and unauthorised seem to have been somewhat more prevalent in these waters than in the Levant. In an extreme situation, however, when the Christian rulers of Iberia faced a real threat from the Moors these quarrelling powers could co-operate.

This is seen most clearly in the period 1337–44 when war broke out between the Moors of Granada and Morocco and the kingdoms of Castile and Aragon-Catalonia. The rapid advance of the *Reconquista* in the thirteenth century had left the Muslims in Iberia confined to Granada but a successful thrust across the Straits of Gibraltar by the Merinid king of Morocco could rapidly reverse this situation as had happened earlier in the days of the Alomhades. The news that such an incursion was being prepared in the *Maghreb* greatly alarmed Alfonso XI of Castile who turned for help to his fellow rulers particularly Peter III whose southernmost possession, Valencia, was as much at risk as the lands of Alfonso. The alliance was concluded with a treaty signed in April 1339. From the naval point of view the most important aspect of the war which followed was the siege of Algeciras by the combined forces of Castile and Aragon. This involved the use of galleys as a blockading force, something which, as has already been pointed out, was a difficult operation for which these vessels were in many ways ill-suited. The need for supplies for the crew, especially water for the oarsmen, was always pressing. By the mid fourteenth century the Aragonese naval ordinances of the Admiral Bernat de Cabrera stipulated that the normal complement of a galley should include 156 oarsmen, 30 crossbowmen, and 30 'others' including the officers, a total of 223 men. There was also a need for a crew to have some respite from time at sea; there was little shelter in a galley for the majority of the crew, making keeping station in poor weather an ordeal. Despite these problems the original treaty of 1339 laid down that the Castilians should provide 20 armed galleys between May and September and eight during the winter. The Aragonese fleet was originally intended to be half this size but Peter III agreed to fit out 15 armed galleys when the Castilians increased their commitment to 30. The immediate result was that 11 vessels from Valencia and Barcelona went south to join the Castilians in the Straits in July 1339. If, allowing for some slippage in the manning scales laid down above, we calculate that each had a crew of some 200 men, around 8000 men had to be provided for.[41] The nearest Castilian base was in the Guadalquivir river while, of course, supplies from Aragon involved a much longer journey. The difficulties are plain and it betokens a high degree of effective organization that the allies managed to keep a galley fleet in the Straits for a prolonged period.[42] Its size varied from time to time and the relative contributions from the allies but the attempted blockade was never completely abandoned. The most dangerous period from the Christian point of view was the summer of 1340 following the Moorish victory over the Castilian galleys in April of that year. Some 35 vessels were sunk by the Moors including 28 galleys. The Aragonese could not send fresh forces until well into the autumn nor could the Genoese from whom Alfonso hired replacements. The victory of the Christian forces on land at Salado in October ensured the failure of the

Moorish incursion into Iberia but the siege of Algeciras continued until March 1344. The sea blockade was essential to this and it can be argued that the whole campaign is a clear demonstration of the advantages of naval forces, well-led and deployed with conviction. Neither Aragon nor Castile had quite as many galleys available to their rulers as has sometimes been claimed. The Castilian forces in the south in particular after 1340 were largely in fact composed of Genoese ships and crews. It is also clear that the naval forces of the Moors of Morocco were considerable and formidable in a battle, but to some extent by 1344 the balance of power had shifted in favour of the Christian powers as far as formal galley actions went. This did not, however imply that the waters of the western Mediterreanean could be described as peaceful or safe for many traders. Piracy or the *guerre de course* continued to be a problem throughout the fifteenth century.

Perhaps because of the availability of judicial, royal and local sources dealing with this matter, there are a number of studies discussing it in some detail. *El Victorial*, the life of Pero Niño, a Castilian noble, the foster brother of king Henry III, written by his standard bearer, which is a classic of early literature in Spanish, also provides much personal detail of the exploits of an individual corsair. From these sources it is clear how widespread and how intractable the problem was. In September 1401 king Martin I of Aragon wrote to the king of Castile praising him for taking action against pirates and corsairs, 'who go by sea robbing and stealing all they can not less from our vassals and friends than from strangers and yours and our enemies'. Within six months he was again writing to the king complaining bitterly that a man previously welcomed at the Catalan court, and in the Castilian royal service had taken at sea and spoiled a galley and two galiots carrying ambassadors as well as the goods of Valencian merchants and demanding compensation and the punishment of the perpetrator. The archives of Valencia, which include both complaints against pirates and licences to corsairs allow some attempt at quantifying the effects of commerce raiding, both official and 'private enterprise' on the relations between states and on trade itself. The *guerre de course* is characterised by one writer as allowing, 'states which did not always have the means, to carry on a maritime war without assuming the costs'.[43] The identity of those who preyed on others at sea was extremely diverse. They could be Moors from North Africa or Granada, Genoese, Portuguese, Castilians, Catalans, Provencals, Basques; in fact from any state, even quite distant ones, which had seafarers among its citizens. Generally speaking in the opinion of Borras, the Muslim raiders at the beginning of the century tended to be in small ill-found boats preying on coastal traders or even fishermen. Those from Genoa were in large vessels lying in wait for wealthy traders with cargoes of expensive goods. Certainly there was a direct linkage to the political situation at any one time. During the internecine war between Barcelona and Valencia in 1467-72 the incidence of attacks by Catalans and their supporters on Valencian traders reached a peak. At the very end of the century corsairs from Valencia preyed on French shipping as part of the reaction to the French invasion of Italy. At any one time a high proportion of cases involved Muslim privateers; as well as the small scale attackers already mentioned, large fleets could be raised in North Africa including the squadron from Tunis which razed Benidorm to the ground in 1447. An individual city could attempt to protect its merchants and their ships by organising convoys, having watch towers on the coast, sending warnings about the presence of raiders to neighbouring towns, or even owning or renting a 'municipal' war galley. These measures could contain the problem but never succeeded in eliminating it.

The career as a Mediterranean privateer of Don Pero Niño perhaps allows us to understand why this was so. He was of impeccable social standing, the close friend of Henry III of Castile, and in many ways a hero of chivalry. He gained his reputation in the Castilian war against Portugal and, with no experience of naval matters at all, was put in command of an expedition, ostensibly against the depredations of corsairs, by the king in 1404. In three voyages he covered the coasts of the western Mediterranean from Seville to Corsica, Sardinia and Tunis. As expeditions to suppress robbery at sea these were futile. By February 1405 the king of Aragon was furiously demanding restitution from Castile for goods seized by Niño the property of merchants from Barcelona and Mallorca. When Niño chased corsair vessels into Marseilles in the summer of 1404 he found they were in the service of Benedict XIII, the anti-pope, who was supported by Castile. Niño was royally entertained by Benedict but quite unable to act against the corsairs who included a Castilian, Juan de Castrillo. An attack on the galleys of the ruler of Tunis, who was rumoured to be preparing a war fleet, had a degree of success but cannot really be considered as an attack on corsairs. In fact on the return voyage to Cartagena the chronicler laments that they could not find any Moorish ships only many from Aragon. The problem was that one ruler's legitimate corsair was another ruler's pirate and that all rulers found the *guerre de course* a relatively cheap and easy way of attacking their enemies. Truces and other alliances tended to be of short duration so that the definition of an 'enemy' changed frequently. A certain level of commerce raiding, though potentially disastrous for an individual, could be accepted between states and was so common that it can almost be called an accepted risk. For the corsair and his crew, of course, the practice could be indeed rewarding. All Niño's men were well pleased, we are told, when the spoils of their voyage were divided.

Naval warfare in the western Mediterranean, therefore, lacks the strategic importance that did attach to some aspects of naval action in the eastern part of the sea. The Reconquista was advanced by warfare on land with the outcome of sea battles not greatly affecting the final victory of Ferdinand and Isabella. The rivalry for trade routes, ports and political power which divided the Christian nations of the area, however, made it almost impossible for them to combine their forces against a common enemy. The blockade of Algeciras is one of the few examples of an alliance even between neighbouring states, resulting in naval action, which was sustained over a relatively long period. Much more typical of the area is the commerce raiding described above. As Borras has said, 'Many ship-owners ... decided to alternate commercial voyages with expeditions as corsairs against enemies of the king, the faith or, what was worse, any ship which was within their reach'. All the states of the region, irrespective of their religious loyalty, preyed at times on the vessels of others for reasons which went from personal greed to political advantage. The typical encounter was not a set piece galley action but a skirmish where the smaller vessel usually had no alternative to surrender but precipitate flight.

Notes

1 The law code of 1255 contains the provision that ships bound for Romania should gather off San Niccolo on the Lido by the 15 August. They would return in the following spring. Such fleets were known as the *muda*.

2 The *Regeste* of the Senate preserved in the Archivio di Stato in Venice contain the commissions of the commanders of galley fleets which often give precise directions concerning ports of call and the need to send and receive letters from the Senate and the policy to be pursued. A typical example is ASV Regeste, Senato Miste, 1377–81 (Copie 36) ff. 65r–66v, 8 September 1377.

3 A. Agosto in his introduction to the catalogue of an exhibition of documents relating to relations between Venice and Genoa at this period makes the point very strongly that in Genoa private interests tended to drive state policy. *Mostra Documentaria Genova e Venezia tra i Secoli XII e XIV*, Archivio di Stato di Genova and Comune di Genova, 1984.

4 F.C. Lane notes that the Venetians fought wars not to gain territory but to 'effect political arrangements which would be disadvantageous to rival sea powers ... and which would gain them trading privileges permitting commercial expansion into new areas'. *Venice: A Maritime Republic*, London and Baltimore, Johns Hopkins University Press, 1973, p. 27.

5 See above, p. 36.

6 The treaty which ended the war of Chioggia was signed in 1381. This did not mark the complete end of all hostilities between the ships of the two states, for example the skirmish off Modon in 1404 between galleys commanded by Carlo Zeno for the Venetians and Marshall Boucicault for the Genoese. F. Surdich, *Genova e Venezia fra tre e quattrocento*, Genova, Fratelli Bozzi, 1970, contains a documentary appendix dealing with this encounter especially pp. 217–23 containing the deposition of Constantino Lercari who was present.

7 J. Dotson, 'Naval Strategy in the First Genoese-Venetian War, 1257–1270', *American Neptune*, 46, 1986, pp. 84–7.

8 J. Dotson, 'Naval Strategy in the First Genoese-Venetian War', p. 88.

9 J. Dotson, *op. cit.*, p. 89.

10 G. Monleone (ed.), *Iacopo Varagine e la sua Chronica di Genova dalle origine al MCCXCVII*, Roma, Tipografia del Senato, 1941, 3 vols, p. 96.

11 Modern Dubrovnik.

12 These documents are fully described in M. Balard, 'A propos de la Bataille du Bosphore: l'expedition génoise de Paganino Doria a Constantinople (1351–1352)', no. II in *La Mer Noire et la Romanie Génoise XIII-XV siècles*, London, Variorum Reprints, 1989.

13 Two volumes of *Le Deliberazioni del Consiglio dei Rogati (Senato) serie 'Mixtorum'*, edited by R. Cessi and P. Sambin have been published by the Deputazione di Storia Patria per la Venezia,

vol. I ,1960, vol. II ,1961. Volume I includes material for 1300–3 and volume II March 1332–February 1335. The registers for the missing years were burnt in the sixteenth century fire. Registers for later years exist in MS in the State Archives; from 1400 the records were divided into two series, ordinary and *Segreti* and from 1440 three, Senato Mar, including all maritime matters, Senato Terra, all matters to do with mainland Venice, the *terra firma*, and Senato Secreta, all matters to do with all internal and external politics.

14 M. Balard, *op. cit.*, pp. 445–6 and 455.

15 M. Balard, *op. cit.*, Document 1, pp. 461–7 prints the log of Lecavalla's galley for this expedition.

16 A.S.G. Antico Comune, registro n. 360.

17 A.S.V. Senato Misto Copie Regestro 1349–1353, Book XXV, 13 April, ff. 22v–23r.

18 A.S.V. *op. cit.*, Book XXV, ff. 56v–57r.

19 A.S.V. *op. cit.*, Book XXVI, f. 17r.

20 A.S.V. *op. cit.*, Book XXVI,. f. 56v.

21 The details of the following account of events in Venice and Chioggia comes from the *Chronica de la Guerra da Veniciani a Zenovesi*, written by Daniele di Chinazzo. Chinazzo was an apothecary and owner of a spice store in Treviso, his home town. He was in Venice for the duration of the war of Chioggia being an eyewitness of the fall of the town to the Genoese. In the opinion of the editor the chronicle is a genuine expression of popular sentiment during the war. Daniele di Chinazzo, *Chronica de la Guerra da Veniciani a Zenovesi*, (ed. V. Lazzarini), Venezia, A spese della deputazione di storia patria per le Venezie, 1958.

22 The Treaty of Turin signed in 1381.

23 F.C. Lane, *Venice: A Maritime Republic*, p. 199.

24 A selection of these documents has been published by F. Surdich as an appendix to *Genova e Venezia fra tre e quattrocento*, Collana Stroica de Fonti e Studi, Genova, Fratelli Bozzi, 1970.

25 F. Surdich, *op. cit.*, p. 172.

26 As Lane (*Venice: A Maritime Republic*) remarks (p. 235), 'Venice counted among her political necessities not only the preservation of her colonies but the continuation of her commerce'.

27 S. Pepper, 'Fortress and fleet: the defence of Venice's mainland Greek colonies in the late fifteenth century', in D.S. Chambers, C.H. Clough and M.E. Mallett (eds), *War, Culture and Society in Renaissance Venice*, London, The Hambledon Press, 1993, pp. 30–8.

28 The letter is included in, *Dannali Veneti dal anno 1457 al 1500 del Senatore Domenico Malipiero*, (ed. F. Longo), Florence, 1843, vol. I, p. 50.

29 The cannon on a galley were mounted on the bow and, in effect, were aimed by steering for the target.

30 S. Pepper, 'Fortress and fleet: the defence of Venice's mainland Greek colonies', p. 40.

31 This is the title of an article published by L. Fincati, 'La deplorabile battaglia del Zonchio, 1499', in *Rivista Marittima* for 1883 and in *Archivio Veneto*, xxv, 1883.

32 J.C. Davis, 'Shipping and spying in the early career of a Venetian doge 1496–1502', *Studi Veneziani*, XVI, 1974, pp. 97–108.

33 'le occurentie di presenti tempi', ASV, Senato Mar, Regeste 14, 1493–99, f. 181v.

34 M. Sanudo, *I diarii di Marino Sanuto*, Bologna, Forni Editori, 1969–70, pp. 1122–6 and 1130–8.

35 The commander of this ship may have been a Turkish *ghazi*, (corsair) in the service of the Sultan called Burak Reis. J.F. Guilmartin, *Gunpowder and Galleys: Changing Technology and Mediterranean Warfare at Sea in the Sixteenth Century*, Cambridge, Cambridge University Press, 1974, p. 86.

36 Khalifeh states that the Turks were using burning pitch to attack the Venetians but were unable to control the weapon.

37 F.C. Lane, 'Naval actions and fleet organisation, 1499–1502' in B.G. Kohl and R.C. Mueller (eds), *Studies in Venetian Social and Economic History*, London, Variorum Reprints, 1987, VIII, p. 162.

38 A.C. Hess states categorically that after Zonchio, 'the Ottomans had achieved naval supremacy in the eastern Mediterranean'. 'The evolution of the Ottoman seaborne empire in the age of the oceanic discoveries, 1453–1525', *American Historical Review*, 74, 1970, p. 1906.

39 J.A. Robson, 'The Catalan fleet and Moorish seapower (1337–1344)', *English Historical Review*, 74, 1959, p. 386.

40 V. Salaverti I Roca, *Cerdena y la expansion mediterranea de la Corona de Aragon 1297–1314*, 2 vols, Madrid, 1956, vol. I, pp. 213–4, n. 37. quoted in D. Albulafia, *The Western Mediterranean Kingdoms 1200–1500*, London, Longman, 1997, p. 172.

41 Galleymen needed a diet with a very high calorific value to function effectively.

42 The Aragonese commander, Pere de Moncada, wrote wearily to Peter III at the end of 1341 when he had been ordered to stay in the Straits with his fleet, 'it seems that those who attended to the letters you have sent neither knew nor were thinking of what it feels like here at sea'. Canellas, 'Aragon y la empresa del estrecho'. doc. 13, pp. 63–4, quoted in J.A. Robson, 'The Catalan fleet and Moorish sea-power', p. 403.

43 J. Guiral-Hadziiossif, *Valence, Port Mediterranéen au XV siècle*, Paris, Publications de la Sorbonne, p. 97.

CHAPTER SEVEN

Theory and practice: writings on naval warfare and the conduct of fleets

Up to this point we have been considering the way in which ships were used in war at sea almost entirely from a pragmatic point of view, looking at accounts of battles and the management of fleets, largely from chronicles and administrative records. This leaves aside the question as to whether there was any body of theoretical writing devoted to the use of ships in war at this period and whether this had any discernible influence on a commander's approach to the conduct of a sea battle.

De la Roncière in his magisterial *Histoire de la Marine Française* includes a passage in which he lists the 10 principles of naval warfare which can be found, (in his view) in Vegetius' *De Re Militari*, book IV. These were widely known to medieval writers; de la Roncière in fact traces them from a crusaders' manual to the works of Egidius Romanus written for Philip the Fair of France, to Christine de Pisan and, in the fifteenth century, Jean Bueil's treatise *Jouvencel*. According to his medieval commentators, Vegetius suggested that burning tow soaked in a flammable substance (pitch, sulphur or oil) should be hurled at the enemy. Lime and dust should be thrown in an attempt to blind an enemy crew who should also be made to slip on decks coated with soft soap, similarly launched onboard in breakable containers. A great beam should be hung from the mast with iron-bound ends so that it could be used like a battering ram. Divers should try to drill holes in the hull of an enemy ship with augers and then stones should be thrown to increase the leaks and speed up its sinking. Rigging should be cut with billhooks and broad arrows fired to make holes in the sails; a weaker ship should be grappled with. Finally every attempt should be made to catch an enemy unprepared and to trap him against the shore while the attacking ship stood out to sea.[1] This summary makes no mention of Vegetius' one suggestion on the deployment of ships in battle; that a fleet should be drawn up in a half moon formation with the strongest vessels on the wings. If an advancing enemy then tries to break the line in the centre, these ships can envelop it.[2]

It is hard to state with any certainty that these ideas had much influence on medieval seamen, whether in France or elsewhere. Fire was, of course, used at sea as one of the most feared of all weapons but the projection of fire-raising missiles was a commonplace of medieval land war and their use probably has little connection with the suggestions of a Roman theorist even if well-known at the time. No mention is made in Vegetius of the two fire-raising methods that were widely used at sea. The first was the use of fire ships, old vessels packed with inflammable material, set alight and then pushed off to drift down with the current or the wind onto enemy ships often close-packed in an anchorage. This could be very effective in the right conditions and was probably the tactic used by the Castilians against the English at La Rochelle in 1372. The second was the notorious Greek fire used since at least the seventh century in the eastern Mediterranean. Its precise composition is still obscure but devices capable of projecting a flame some distance existed and were used at least until the twelfth century. Anna Comnena described the Byzantine ships armed in this way; ' the Greek fire to be hurled at the enemy through tubes was made to issue from the mouths of these figureheads (gilded lions) in such a way that they appeared to be belching out fire'.[3] She then goes on to discuss the action against the Pisans during the First Crusade when these weapons were used. Their main advantage, apart from the terror caused, seems to have been the way in which the spout of fire could be precisely aimed, 'often downwards and sideways, to port or to starboard'.[4] There is, however, no clear evidence that the ships of the two naval powers in the Eastern Mediterranean in the later medieval period, Venice and Genoa were armed in this way. The woodcut of the battle of Zonchio, however, seems to show tubes projecting flaming material on the oared Turkish ships harassing the *Pandora* and the *Nave del Armer*,[5] while Santi-Mazzini identifies a feature in the topcastle of the *nave Turchesca* with a *trombe del fuoco*, a kind of 'special firework' mentioned by seventeenth-century Italian authors.[6]

Soft soap and lime are not often found among the munitions normally carried on warships. The emphasis is on the normal personal weapons, swords and lances, and bows, both longbows with their arrows and crossbows of various types with their quarrels. Darts, called by the English '*gaddes*', and stones were provided for those men positioned in the top castles on the masts.[7] Showers of missiles seem to have marked the opening moments of most sea battles. There are instances in chronicles when mention is made of the cutting of the standing or running rigging of an enemy ship to cause the masts or sails to collapse[8] but they are rare compared to the description of boarding actions which seem to be the expected conclusion of a naval action. Nothing in the least like Vegetius' beam, with both ends ironshod, to be used like a battering ram, can be found among the inventories of any medieval ships that certainly existed. It can be linked, however with the fantastic machines illustrated by Mariano Taccola in his *De machinis bellicis*. This MS, which probably dates from the early fifteenth century, includes a series of drawings of war machines to place on ships including several with beams for sinking an enemy or for flinging pots of flaming sulphur and pitch on to an opposing ship. There is no evidence that any attempt was ever made to construct these devices.[9] By the time Taccola's MS was finished cannon of various calibre could frequently be found on ships, and these weapons would come to dominate the operation of warships and the tactics used in naval warfare.

Even if Vegetius' writing may have had more influence on those who kept chronicles than on those who fought at sea, there is other evidence of a considered approach on the part of rulers and their advisers to the use of warships. In the thirteenth and fourteenth centuries, in the *Libro del feits* of James I and in the *Partidas* of Alfonso III some clear views on naval warfare were put forward. *Partida II* states that war at sea is a desperate thing and much more dangerous than war on land; it should only be undertaken by those who thoroughly understand the sea and the winds and who have sufficient well-supplied forces. They must not delay in preparing an expedition so that they can take advantage of favourable winds and weather. An expedition must also be well disciplined and well commanded. The system of officers of Aragonese galleys was well established and laid down, most clearly in the *Ordinationes sobra la feyt de la mar* of Bernardo de Cabrera in the reign of Peter IV the Ceremonious. These included the provisions that even noble officers must be experienced seamen while the sailing masters of the galleys must have knowledge of winds and ports in order to pilot the ships.[10] In his Chronicle, Ramon Muntaner, writing of the 1280s and 1290s, also puts forward a scheme for royal dockyards for the Crown of Aragon. Four are suggested in Tortosa, Barcelona, Valencia and Cullera. In his view the great advantage of dockyards at Cullera and Tortosa would be that their very existence could be kept secret; in each 25 galleys could be built without an enemy knowing anything 'until they are outside the rivers'.[11] Muntaner is well aware of the need for ships to be readily available, and for them to be in good repair. His ambitious scheme which envisages that a king of Aragon would have 100 galleys at his disposal would be achievable 'through care and good management'.

Unusually among the chroniclers of naval battles, it is clear that Muntaner himself had personal experience of war at sea. He prefaces his remarks on the vital importance of crossbowmen in naval warfare in the thirteenth century with the remark that 'he who tells you this has been in many battles'.[12] In his view crossbowmen could decide the issue of a battle. In fact the skill of Catalans with this weapon was a very important factor in the success of their fleets. There seems little reason to doubt the truth of this observation which is well borne out by, for example, the way he describes how, at the battle of Rosas, the enemy decks were cleared of anyone capable of offering resistance by the withering and accurate fire of crossbowmen. He makes much the same point in the so-called sermon which he addresses to the king setting out a plan for the invasion of Sardinia and Corsica. He stresses the need for crossbowmen in light galleys to scout before the main fleet and for there to be a clear distinction between the fighting men in the galley and those who are oarsmen and steersmen.[13]

More controversial, however, are his frequent descriptions of galleys being 'bridled' or lashed together in some way which has already been discussed in connection with the campaigns of Roger of Lauria.[14] At Rosas Muntaner also states explicitly, 'the galleys were poop by poop and the other ten were astern of them and no-one could enter between on account of the oars which were lashed together'. He is not alone in suggesting that this tactic was used; other mentions can be found in northern waters, for example, in the verse description of the battle of Zierikzee in 1304[15] and some accounts of Sluys in 1348[16]. Legrand d'Aussy who wrote a commentary on French naval tactics at the beginning of the fourteenth century during the Revolutionary period linked the idea of lashing ships together with a description from Livy of Scipio's encounter with Amilcar at Tunis.[17] It would be easier to dismiss it as a conventional cliché of writing on naval battles, based on a classical model, if Muntaner did not claim to have been present at at least some of the actions mentioned. The fact remains, however that especially in northern tidal waters ships deployed in this fashion could very easily find themselves in difficulties, aground or trapped against the shore, and unable to manoeuvre. The fact that the Mediterranean examples refer to galleys compounds the problem. The oars would be unusable or at least very hard to use, while the vessels were lashed together and even in the calmest waters currents might cause the vessels to drift on to rocks or other hazards. If the battle turned against those whose ships were in this position, flight would be more or less impossible. In victory the pursuit of the vanquished might equally be delayed for vital moments while the ships regained their mobility. The only battle orders, as opposed to a chronicle description, relating to galleys, comes from the much later battle of Zonchio in 1499. The order for the deployment of the galleys requires them to maintain station in the squadron, specifically to avoid collisions and the breaking of oars, while at the same time acting together as far as possible.[18]

It is not easy to find discussion of the aims of naval warfare or the preferred strategy to adopt in Venetian, Genoese or other Italian sources. It can be argued that, particularly in Venice, it was so widely accepted that the health, or even the very existence of the state,[19] depended on seaborne trade that the protection of trading vessels and routes was always a major preoccupation of the authorities and was, therefore, not specifically discussed. Particularly when war had broken out, for example at the times of the war of Chioggia with Genoa or in 1470 when the Venetians lost Negroponte to the Turks, the records of discussions in the Council of Rogati and the *Regeste* of the Senato Mar show attempts to control operations almost on a day by day basis, with prudence and caution often being strenuously urged on captains general. An indication of the importance of the conduct of the galleys and their commanders to Venice is also provided by the treatment of some of them in 1379 after Pisani's disastrous encounter with the Genoese off Pola.[20] The Rogati debated various imaginative punishments for those accused of forcing the flight back to Venice leaving 15 vessels to be taken by their enemies; these varied from hanging to the loss of both eyes, the right hand or the right foot and 5–10 years imprisonment.[21] In November 1470, on the other hand, after the loss of Negroponte, the Council made strenuous efforts to get a new fleet together including 20 new *gallie sottil* and 10 great galleys needed for what was seen as '*tanto atroci et periculoso bello*'.[22]

Another clear indication of Venetian attitudes can be found in the orders issued by Andrea Mocenigo, the captain general of the sea, in 1428. After forbidding any form of blasphemy aboard, Mocenigo sets out his expectations for the conduct of galleys in his charge. Whether proceeding under sail or under oars galleys must stay on station and not interfere with other vessels in the convoy. Only those galleys ordered to keep watch may pass in front of the captain's own ship which will always lead the fleet. Mocenigo also includes clear orders about signals, when sailing at night, for calling other commanders to council, for changing course and in other circumstances. Once at sea each galley commander must place two crossbowmen on the poop, two on the prow and two amidships; moreover should they be attacked no-one must leave his post unless expressly ordered to do so. Mocenigo's battle orders re-iterate this point and go on to explain that at the first blast of a trumpet all must arm themselves, at the second, galleys and their crews must take up their battle stations. At the third trumpet call, all, being brave men, must attack[23] the enemy vigorously and none must break off the fight unless expressly ordered to do so by the captain. Breach of this order incurs draconian penalties. In victory, however, Mocenigo wishes all his men to show mercy to their enemies. The whole tone of the document envisages a well-disciplined and ordered force which can act as a unit. It is a pity for us that Mocenigo does not go into more detail on the precise conduct of a sea action, only emphasising the necessity that all should obey the orders of the captain general.[24]

Malipiero's account of the battle of Zonchio in 1499 and the orders issued by Grimani include elements which seem clearly related to those of Mocenigo issued nearly 70 years earlier. Again the order is issued that no vessel or group of vessels can break off the engagement without express permission; moreover attacks on individual enemy ships must follow the plan decided on and not be left, as it were, to private enterprise. Venetians wished and expected a fleet to be a disciplined force where adherence to orders was of greater importance than individual flair or elan in attacking the enemy.

In northern waters, the clearest expression of the possible strategic purposes of naval warfare are found in English texts dating from the third decade of the fifteenth century and later. This may, perhaps, be because at this period England and English ships were clearly vulnerable to attack but the royal government of the day seemed increasingly unable to protect shipping, the Channel coasts or English possessions overseas. *The Libelle of Englyshe Polycye*, which was probably first written c.1436–8 and then revised c.1438–41, was a popular text among the merchants of London.[25] It includes the well-known passages looking back with nostalgic pride to Henry V's 'grete shippes', and attempts to set out the king's purpose in building them. In the view of the author of the *Libelle*, 'it was not ellis but that he caste to be / Lorde rounde aboute environ of the see'. The poem goes on, extolling the sea, 'which of England is the rounde wall, / As though England was lykened to a cite / and the wall environ was the see'.[26] It is clear in the poem as a whole that by this is intended not the sea in general but particularly the Channel and the Straits of Dover; the writer's original aim was to advocate war with Burgundy at that time laying siege to Calais but the sentiments he expressed had wider applications and undoubtedly struck a cord with the maritime community. Firm English control of the Narrow seas would result in peace for all and prosperity. Sir John Fortescue in the 1470s, after a long period when as we have seen there was very little direct royal involvement in naval matters, made a strong plea for a permanent naval force. As he pointed out, it was too late to build a navy when the enemy was at sea. Moreover by the 1470s warships were becoming larger and more specialised and without 'some grete and myghty vessels' it would be hard to attack carracks or 'a myghty ffloute gadered off purpose'.[27] There is little discussion here of the details of a naval engagement but the necessity of well-organised naval forces for an island state is articulated clearly.

Another fifteenth century text, of uncertain date but which Charles, Duke of Orleans may have written[28] in the form of a debate between the heralds of England and France, raises other points. From this debate a clear picture emerges of the contemporary understanding of the purpose of sea power and the preconditions for its exercise. To be king of the sea, a monarch must have 'deep and very strong harbours for the security of his ships' and as well 'an abundance of great and swift ships' and access to the raw materials with which to build them. There is, however, a tacit assumption that these ships are not necessarily in royal ownership but part of the general resources of the state. The aim is to dominate trade (England is accused of 'obstructing the utility of commerce everywhere'), principally trade in the products of the home country.[29] If hostilities do break out, the herald of France sees the crossbow as a much more suitable weapon for use at sea than the longbow and lauds France's allies, Spain and Genoa, but concludes his argument by pointing out that France has no real need to aspire to seapower while for England it is in fact a necessity. Much of this reads like a rationalisation of the position in the Channel between England and France in the second half of the fifteenth century which has been described in Chapter 6 with semi-official piracy taking the place of naval warfare on a grand scale.

Although written just outside our period probably in 1516, Philippe de Cleves' treatise *L'Instruction de toutes manières de guerroyer sur mer* makes clear how much naval warfare has changed by the end of the fifteenth century.[30] He sets out clearly the chain of command and the 'action stations' for the crew of a three-masted warship. (At the date of writing this would have been the most usual ship type in northern waters.) Each ship would have a captain in charge of fighting the ship and a master in charge of sailing her. The soldiers should be kept quite separate from the crew. Each vessel should be divided into four areas, each under the command of an officer with the help of a lieutenant. In addition there would be a fifth officer in charge of the 'fondz de la nef'. He would have with him a few sailors, carpenters, caulkers and other craftsmen. The other four officers would each have one quarter of the available men and would have responsibility for the defence of their area and the deployment of the artillery. As the opposing fleets drew near to each other before battle commenced, all the armed men should be kept under cover; only the sailors needed to sail the ship and the gunners needed to fire the cannon should be on deck. Before boarding the enemy, the four officers must divide their men into two groups; one would stay under cover with the lieutenant and the officer would lead the other in the attack and also in the defence of their part of the ship. In the hold, the fifth officer and his men would attempt to stop leaks caused by the enemy's guns or by the shock of collision. He must also be in charge of the pumps and all the munitions. Cleves makes clear that a sea battle could go on for one or two days and nights and therefore a reserve of fresh men was essential.[31]

Cleves then makes suggestions on how to protect a ship against the effects of cannon fire. He is also anxious to point out that while fire may be a useful weapon, it should be used with great care since, especially if ships are grappled together, it may easily spread to one's own ship. Above all when boarding an enemy every effort should be made to do so 'au dessus du vent' (with the wind); the collision will have greater force and your ship will take the wind from the enemy.[32] In view of the earlier claims of writers that galleys were lashed together in battle it is interesting to note that, like the orders for the battle of Zonchio, Cleves lays great emphasis on the need for ships going into the attack to be massed together but so that they do not touch, and yet keep on station. Only in harbour, particularly if it is really calm, should ships under attack, (which may in fact be grounded) be drawn up so closely together that one can get easily from one to another.[33] Cleves' 'instructions' are clearly based on his own experience as a naval commander both in the Channel and in the Mediterranean. The way in which fire can spread out of control recalls the fate of the *Pandora* at Zonchio. His suggestions for the deployment of the crew seem practical and efficient. The need to be aware of the wind, the weather and the sea state runs all through his treatise: this is not a re-working of Vegetius but a commander's reflections on the lessons learned in the course of actions at sea both with sailing ships and galleys, both in northern waters and in the Mediterranean.

Notes

1 C. Bourel de la Roncière, *Histoire de la Marine Française*, Paris, Librarie Plon, 1899–1900, Vol. I, pp. 255–6.

2 Vegetius *De Re Militari*, Lib.IV XLV, http://www.gmu.edu/departments/fld/CLASSICS/vegetius4.html. This tactic is said by a chronicler to have been used by Roger of Lauria; see above pp. 48–9.

3 *The Alexiad of Anna Comnena* (trans. E.R.A. Sewter), Harmondsworth, Penguin, 1969, p. 360.

4 *The Alexiad of Anna Comnena*, p. 362.

5 See Plate 5, The Battle of Zonchio.

6 G. Santi-Mazzini, 'A sea fight 500 years ago', *The Mariner's Mirror*, 85, 1999, p. 76.

7 The accounts of the Clerks of the King's ships in the P.R.O. contain detailed lists of the munitions provided for English warships.

8 See above p. 4, note 7.

9 Bibliothèque Nationale, Paris, MS Latin, 7239. The devices illustrated on ff. 26v, 59v and 60v seem particularly close to Vegetius' suggestions.

10 J.C. Pery, *El poder naval en los reinos hispanicos: la marina de la edad media*, Madrid, Editorial San Martin, 1992, pp. 219–23.

11 Lady Goodenough, *The Chronicle of Ramon Muntaner*, Vol. I, London, Hakluyt Society, 1920–1 pp. 89–90.

12 Lady Goodenough, *op. cit.*, p. 330.

13 Lady Goodenough, *op. cit.*, pp. 653–5.

14 See above pp. 46–7.

15 See above p. 62.

16 See above pp. 64–5.

17 Le Citoyen Legrand d'Aussy, *Notice sur l'état de la marine en France au commencement du quatrième siècle: et sur la tactique navale usitée alors dans les combats de mer*, Paris, year VI, pp. 30–1.

18 F. Longo (ed.), *Dannali veneti dal anno 1457 al 1500 del Senatore Domenico Malipiero*, Florence, Archivio Storico Italiano, 1843, t. VII, part I, pp. 174–5.

19 On 16 July 1377, it was noted in the register of the Council of Rogati in relation to galley traffic that, 'in hoc pendet salus et vita nostra'. ASV Register of the Council of Rogati, 1377–81, Copie, book 36, f41v.

20 See above pp. 107–8.

21 ASV, *loc. cit.*, ff185v–188r.

22 ASV Senato Mar, Registro 1469–73, f69v.

23 The word used by Mocenigo here is *investir*. This has varied meanings including 'collide with' or 'crash into' as well as attack.

24 L. Greco (ed.) *Quaderno di Bordo di Giovanni Manzini, Prete-Notaio e Cancelliere 1471–1484*, Venezia, Fonti per la Storia de Venezia, sez. III Archivi Notarili, Il Comitato Editore, 1997, pp. 85–96.

25 Over 19 MSS of the poem exist. C.M. Meale, 'The *Libelle of Englyshe Polycye* and mercantile literary culture in late medieval England', in J. Boffrey and P. King (eds), *London and Europe in the Later Middle Ages*, London, Centre for Medieval and Renaissance Studies, Queen Mary and Westfield College, 1995, p. 209.

26 Sir G. Warner (ed.), *The Libelle of Englyshe Polycye*, Oxford, Oxford University Press, 1926, pp. 51, 55.

27 Sir J. Fortescue, *The Governance of England* (ed. C. Plummer), Oxford, Oxford University Press, 1885, p. 123.

28 The date of 1405 has been suggested but this raises some problems as both Bordeaux and Bayonne are said to be French ports in the text. They did not come into French hands until 1453. The debate was published in H. Pyne (ed.), *England and France in the Fifteenth Century*, London, 1870. It first appeared as *Le debat des Heraulx darmes de France et d'Engleterre*, Rouen, 1500.

29 H. Pyne, *op. cit.*, pp. 49–50, 57–8.
30 J. Paviot (ed.), *L'Instruction de toutes manierès de guerroyer sur mer*, Paris, Libraries Honoré Champion, 1997. The treatise was not published until 1558 but was written earlier being intended for the Emperor Charles V.
31 J. Paviot, *op. cit.*, pp. 49–50.
32 J. Paviot, *op. cit.*, p. 52.
33 J. Paviot, *op. cit.*, pp. 53–5.

Conclusion

Naval warfare clearly changed a great deal between our starting date of c.1000 and our finishing date of c.1500. In the eleventh century, the most successful fleets were all powered during a battle, if not always on the way to a battle, by oars. Once the opponents were in range of each other (a matter of a few 100 yards at the most in some cases) a furious exchange of missiles would be followed by attempts to board the enemy and clear his ship. There are differences between northern and southern waters. Greek fire was unknown in the north, nor are there references to the other possible uses of fire as a weapon at sea in, for example, the *Heimskringla*. It also seems fairly clear that rams, like those used in Greek and Roman galleys were no longer in use in the Mediterranean and had never been used by Norse seamen. Galleys, however, did have beaks at the prow and this feature would clearly have been of great importance when boarding. It would provide, in effect, a kind of bridge over which the attackers could pour undoubtedly hoping that the defenders had been already largely disabled and certainly thrown into disarray by the showers of crossbow bolts, arrows and other missiles. The ships of the Vikings did not have this feature but there are references which seem to point to ships coming up on each other with prow to stern.[1]

The issue of whether galleys, or indeed other types of vessel, were tied together before battle commenced has already been discussed and remains problematic. It does illustrate another difficulty in trying to elucidate the details of medieval sea battles, the nature of the evidence. When so few of the chroniclers had ever been to sea, let alone ever taken part in a naval battle, the suspicion that they are following a model of naval warfare derived to some extent from classical authors cannot be entirely discounted. Pictorial evidence is perhaps even less reliable, largely consisting of conventional images. Unger has attributed 'the pattern of development in naval administration' to 'advances in ship design'.[2] Can the same be said of the tactics and strategy employed in war at sea?

By the end of the fifteenth century vessels using oars as a major form of propulsion are becoming rare in northern fleets. The largest and most successful ships in these waters normally went into battle under sail and the ship handling skills of sailing masters were often of a high order. The balingers with both oars and sails, which were such a feature of Henry V's fleet and which were highly useful in coastal waters, are not found among the ships owned by Henry VII.[3] The increasing use of cannon in sea fights and as part of the expected armament of any ship of war is of importance here. In southern waters cannon were placed forward on the prow of vessels like the great galleys of Venice and were aimed not by manoeuvering the gun but by manoeuvering the ship. Sea conditions made the operation of galleys difficult in the north and therefore other means of deploying artillery as an effective 'ship-killing' weapon at sea were needed. The answer was, of course, eventually found in the placing of cannon on the decks of sailing vessels firing through gunports cut in the hull.[4] This would seem to imply that the impetus for changing tactics in naval warfare came not from changes in ship design but from changes in weapons. Our period ends when this process is still underway with the 'old' tactics of a shower of missiles followed by boarding co-existing with the 'new' use of cannon as more than just a means of frightening the enemy.

The understanding of the possible strategic use of sea power perhaps owes most both to changes in ship design and in the related skills of the sailing master and the navigator. The best ships of the late fifteenth century were able to sail closer to the wind than their predecessors and were thus less often confined to port by adverse winds. Although the sailing qualities of Viking ships were remarkable, the crews of the galleons and barks of, for example the Spanish and Portuguese, could face long sea passages with equanimity. Their vessels were seaworthy and their masters' understanding of navigation was greatly increased. We must not forget that the fifteenth century saw a great expansion in maritime enterprise for other than warlike purposes. At the same time as ports like Valencia were preoccupied by the problem of piracy in the western Mediterranean, Henry the Navigator and his collaborators were promoting voyages south along the north African litoral. Columbus reached the Bahamas seven years before the battle of Zonchio in 1499, while da Gama had sailed into the port of Calicut the previous year. In northern waters, there is less evidence of widespread interest in more distant landfalls, but even so the Iceland route, well known to Scandinavians, was explored mainly by mariners from English east coast ports. There are tantalising speculations concerning voyages to the west from Bristol.[5] Naval warfare could begin to encompass the idea of a blockade and certainly battles could be fought out on the high seas not only in the shelter of a bay or an estuary. Increasingly warships would be differentiated from merchant ships and the term, 'navy' would come to have its modern meaning of 'a regularly organised and maintained naval force', the first appearance of which apparently dates from 1540.[6]

Notes

1 Snorre Sturlason, *Heimskringla or the Lives of the Norse Kings* (ed. E. Mousen), Cambridge, W. Heffer and Sons, n.d. p. 496.

2 R. Unger, 'Admiralties and Warships of Europe and the Mediterranean, 1000–1500', *Ships and Shipping in the North Sea and Atlantic, 1400–1800*, Aldershot, Ashgate-Variorum Press; reprinted from *Technology and Culture*, 22, 1997, p. 36.

3 Oared vessels were found in considerable numbers among those owned by Henry VIII but these were provided to deal with a particular threat, that posed by French oared warships in the 1540s. J. Bennell, 'The Oared Vessels' in C.S. Knighton and D.M. Loades (eds), *The Anthony Roll of Henry VIII's Navy*, Aldershot, Ashgate for the Navy Records Society, 2000, p. 37.

4 An early representation of cannon onboard an English fighting ship can be found in the Warwick Roll of c.1485. It is reproduced as figure 8.7, p. 155 in I. Friel, *The Good Ship: Ships, Shipbuilding and Technology in England 1200–1520*, London, British Museum Press, 1995, and as Plate 3 here.

5 J.R.S. Phillips, *The Medieval Expansion of Europe*, second edition, Oxford, Clarendon Press, 1998, pp. 228–9.

6 OED sub 'navy'.

Glossary

after castle A built up structure at the stern of a vessel originally temporary for use in battle but soon incorporated into the vessel's structure. Cabins for officers or elite passengers would also be situated here.

balinger A type of vessel using both oars and sails which may have been developed near Bayonne; its name links it with whaling but it was the preferred craft for pirates in the fourteenth and fifteenth centuries and also for coastal raids, cutting out expeditions and the like.

barge A) A ceremonial craft used on a river. B) A vessel found in northern waters with both oars and sails often used for trade or for carrying supplies.

besants A gold coin first struck at Byzantium or Constantinople.

carrack A vessel developed in the Mediterranean in the late fourteenth or early fifteenth centuries; usually larger than a cog with high fore and aft castles and more than one mast and sails. Capable of being an effective warship although originally intended as a merchant ship.

caulker A craftsman whose task was to prevent a vessel leaking by ramming oakum or some similar material into the seams between the planking on a vessel's side.

chandlery A general term for all the requirements of a vessel, such as ropes, ironwork and other ships' stores.

cogship The 'work horse' of northern waters from the early fourteenth century; usually with a high freeboard and a single mast and sail; developed as a merchant ship but also found in war fleets.

fore castle A built up structure on the prow of a vessel; originally temporary for use in battle, but by the end of the fourteenth century usually an integral part of the ship's structure.

galie grosse The large merchant galley of Venice which were sailed more frequently than they were rowed.

galie sottil The term used to describe the swift fighting galleys of Venice and other Mediterranean nations.

galiot A small vessel of the galley type.

galley A vessel propelled mainly by oars though usually also possessing a mast or masts and sails.

galley patron The officer in charge of a voyage by a galley; his responsibilities were not so much to sail the vessel as to set out the policy to be followed whether on a trading voyage or one with a warlike purpose.

halyard A rope used to raise or lower a sail or a sailyard.

huissier A vessel specially adapted for the transport of horses, probably with some sort of opening in the hull not unlike that of a modern ferry.

knee A specially shaped beam used to connect two timbers at right angles for example to support the deck timbers.

long ship A vessel whose length greatly exceeds its beam.

mangonel A machine used in warfare to project missiles, usually stones.

mark Money of account used in England in the later middle ages; one mark equalled 13 shillings and fourpence or two thirds of a pound sterling.

nef A term for a large round ship often used in France.

pavisade A protective barrier made up of shields bearing the arms of those on board placed along a vessel's sides.

pavise A shield used in the making of a pavisade.

pinnace A small swift sailing vessel very often used for scouting or similar tasks.

purser An officer in charge of a ship's papers, the payment of the crew, the provision of stores etc.

round ship A vessel the hull of which generally has a high freeboard and which has a relatively low ratio between its length and its beam.

serenissima An abbreviation often used for the Venetian Republic, the reppublica serenissima.

signoria A general term for the government of Venice.

springal A machine used in warfare like a large catapult.

topcastle The fighting platform from which missiles could be thrown at the top of a mast.

weather gauge A vessel is said to have the weather gauge when it is to the windward of another one.

Bibliography

Primary sources

Bibliothèque Nationale, Paris
MSS Latin 7239. *De Machinis Bellicis*

Archivio di Stato di Venezia (ASV)

Regeste di Rogati 1377–81
Senato Misti 1349–1354
Senato Mar Registro 9 1469–73
Senato Mar Registro 14 1493–9

Public Record Office, Kew (P.R.O.)

Exchequer: Accounts Various: Army, Navy and Ordnance
Lord Treasurer's Remembrancer: Foreign Accounts
Pipe Rolls

British Library, London

Cotton Nero C VIII Wardrobe Book for 8 and 9 Edward II
Additional MSS 17364

Unpublished theses

Foster, S.M. *Some Aspects of Maritime Activity and the Use of Sea Power in Relation to the Crusading States, 1096–1169*, D.Phil. Oxford, 1978.

Printed primary sources

Anna Comnena, *Alexiad of Anna Comnena, The* (trans. E.R.A. Sewter, Harmondsworth, Penguin, 1969.
Balletto, M.L., *Navi e Navegazione a Genova nel Quattrocento: la Cabella Marinariorum, 1482–1491*, Collana Storica di Fonti e Studi, Genoa University, Istituto di Paleografia e Storia Medievale, 1973.

Belgrano, Luigi Tommaso and Cesare Imperiale di Sant'Angelo, *Annali Genovesi di Caffaro e suoi contiuatori dal MXCIX al MCCXCIII*, Genova, Tipografia del R. Istituto Sordo-Muti, 1890–1926.

Bréard, Charles, 'Le compte du Clos des Galées de Rouen au XIV siècle 1382–1384' in Blanquart, Bouquet, Bréard, de Circourt, Regnier, Sauvage (eds), *Documents, Deuxième Serie*, Rouen, Société de la Histoire de Normandie, 1893.

Burgess, L.A., *The Southampton Terrier of 1454*, Historical Manuscripts Commission, JP 21, London, Her Majesty's Stationery Office, 1976.

(Merlin)-Chazelas, Anne, *Documents rélatifs au clos des galées de Rouen et aux armées de mer du roi de France de 1293 à 1418*, Collection de documents inédits sur l'histoire de France, serie in. 8, vols 11 and 12, section de philologie et d'histoire jusqu'a 1610. Paris, Bibliothèque Nationale, 1977–8.

Cessi, R. and P. Sambin (eds), *Le Deliberazioni del consiglio dei Rogati (Senato), serie Mixtorum*, Venezia, Deputazione di Storia Patria per la Venezia, 1960–61.

Champollion-Figéac, A., *Lettres des Rois, Reines et autres personages des Cours de France et de l'Angleterre, 1162–1515*, vol. I Paris, no publ., 1839.

Conlon, D.J., *Li romans de Witasse le Moine, roman du treizième siècle*, Chapel Hill, University of North Carolina Press, 1972.

De Bofarull y Mascaró, P., *Coleccion de documentos inéditos del archivo general de la Corona de Aragon*, Barcelona, no publ., 1847.

Delaborde, H.F., *Oeuvres de Rigord et de Guillaume le Breton, historiens de Philippe Auguste*, Paris, Nogent le Retrou, 1882–85.

di Chinazzo, Daniel, *Chronica de la Guerra da Veniciani a Zenovesi* (ed. Vittoreo Lazzarini), Venice, A spese della Deputazione di storia patria per le Venezie, 1958.

Diez de Gamez, Gutierre, *The Unconquered Knight: A Chronicle of the Deeds of Don Pero Niño, Count of Buelna, by his Standard Bearer Gutierre Diez de Gamez, 1431–1449* (ed. and trans. Joan Evans), London, George Routledge and Sons, 1928. The Spanish edition is *El Victorial*, (ed. Juan de Mata Carriaga), Madird, Espasa-Calpe, 1940.

Fermoy, B.E.R., 'A maritime indenture of 1212', *English Historical Review*, 41, 1926.

Finke, H., *Acta Aragonensa: Quellen zur deutschen, italienischen, französischen, spanischen, zur Kirchen und Kulturgeschichte aus der diplomatischen Korrespondenz Jaymes II (1291–1327)*, Berlin, Rothschild, 1908.

Flavius Vegetius Renatus, *Eptitoma Rei Militari* (ed. and trans. L.F. Stelten), New York, Peter Lang, 1990.

Forchieri, G., *Nave e navigazione a Genova nel trecento: il Libro Gazzarie*, Collana Storica di Finti e Studi, Collana Storica dell'oltremare Ligure IV, Bordighera, Istituto Internazionale di Studi Ligure, 1974.

Fourquin, N., 'A medieval shipbuilding estimate (c.1273)', *The Mariner's Mirror*, 85, 1999.

Fortescue, Sir John, *The Governance of England* (ed. C. Plummer), Oxford, Clarendon Press, 1885.

Froissart, J., *Chronicles*, (ed. and trans. G. Brereton), Harmondsworth, Penguin, 1968.

Fulcher of Chartres, *A History of the Expedition to Jerusalem*, (trans. F.R. Ryan), Knoxville, University of Tennesee Press, 1969.

Gabrieli, F., *Arab Historians of the Crusades*, London, Routledge and Kegan Paul, 1969.

Garmonsway, G.N. (trans. and ed.), *The Anglo-Saxon Chronicle*, London, Dent, 1972.

Goodenough, Lady (ed.), *The Chronicle of Muntaner*, 2 vols, London, Hakluyt Society, 1920–1.

Greco, Lucia, (ed.), *Quaderno di bordo di Giovanni Manzini prete-notaio e cancelliere 1471–1484*, Fonti per la storia di Venezia, sez. III Archivi Notatili, Venezia, Il Comitato editore, 1997.

Guillaume de Tyr, *Chronique*, (ed. R.B.C. Huygens), Corpus Christianorum Medievalis LXIII, Turnhout, Brepols, 1986.

Hattendorf, J.B., R.J.B. Knight, A.H.W. Pearsall, N.A.M. Rodger and G. Till, *British Naval Documents 1204–1960*, London, Scolar Press for the Navy Records Society, 1993.

James, T.B. and J. Simons (eds), *The Poems of Laurence Minot, 1333–1352*, Exeter, University of Exeter Press, 1989.

Jones, M., 'Two Exeter ship agreements of 1303 and 1310', *The Mariner's Mirror*, 53, 1967.

Knighton, C.S. and D.M. Loades, *The Anthony Roll of Henry VIII's Navy*, Occasional Publications of the Navy Records Society, Aldershot, Ashgate for the Navy Records Society and the British Library and Magdalene College Cambridge, Vol. 2, 2000.

Lane-Poole, R., 'A medieval cordage account', *The Mariner's Mirror*, 42, 1956.

Livy, *The War with Hannibal, Books XXI–XXX of the History of Rome from its Foundation*, (trans. A. de Selincourt, ed. B. Radice), Harmondsworth, Penguin, 1965.

Longo, F. (ed.), *Dannali veneti dal anno 1457 al 1500 del senatore Domenico Malipiero*, Archivio Storico Italiano, t. VII, part I, Florence, Vieusseux, 1843–44.

Luard, H.R. (ed.), *Matthei Parisiensis, Monachi Sancti Albani, Chronica Majora*, London, Her Majesty's Stationery Office, 1964.

Luce, S. (ed.), *Chronique des Quatre Premiers Valois*, Paris, Société de l'Histoire de France, 1862.

Luce, S. (ed.), *Froissart: Chroniques*, Paris, Société de l'Histoire de France, 1888.

Lumby, J.R. (ed.), *The Chronicle of Henry Knighton*, London, Rolls Series, 1889.

Lunig, J.C. *Codex Italiae diplomaticus*, Frankfurt, no publ., 1725–35.

Lyon, B., M. Lyon and H.S. Lucas (eds), *The Wardrobe Book of William de Norwell, 12 July 1338–27 May 1340*, Brussels, Palais des Académies, 1983.

Madden, F. (ed.), *Matthei Parisiensis, monachi Sancti Albani, Historia Anglorum sive ut vulgo dicitur Historia Minor, item ejusdem Abbrevatio chronicorum Angliae*, London, Longmans, 1869.

Meyer, P., *L'Histoire de Guillaume le Maréchal, comte de Striguil et de Pembroke regent d' Angleterre de 1216 à 1219*, Paris, Société de l'Histoire de France, 1891–1901.

Mitchell, J. (trans.), *The History of the Maritime Wars of the Turks translated from the Turkish of Haji Khalifeh*, London, 1831.

Monleone, Giovanni (ed.), *Iacopo da Varagine e la sua cronica di Genova dalle origine al MCCXCVII*, Rome, Tipografia del Senato, 3 vols, 1941.

Myers, A.R., *English Historical Documents, 1327–1485*, Vol. IV, London, Eyre and Spottiswoode, 1969.

Oppenheim, M., *Naval Accounts and Inventories of the Reign of Henry VII 1485–8 and 1495–7*, London, Navy Records Society, 1896.

Paviot, Jacques (ed.), *Portugal et Bourgogne au XV siècle (1384–1492): recueil de documents extraits des archives bourguignonnes*, Paris, Centre Culturel Calouste Gulbenkian, 1995.

Petti Balbi, Giovanna (ed.), *Girogio Stella, Annales Genuenses*, Rerum Italicarum Scriptores, nuova edizione t. XVII, pt. II, Bologna, Zanichelli, 1975.

Philippe de Cleves, seigneur de Ravestein, *L' Instruction de toutes manières de guerroyer sur mer*, (ed. J. Paviot), Bibliothèque de l'école des hautes études, IV section, sciences historiques et philologiques, fasc. 333, Paris, Librarie Honoré Champion, 1997.

Pyne, H. (ed.), *England and France in the Fifteenth Century*, London, Oriental translation Fund of Great Britain and Ireland, 1870.

Rose, S. (ed.), *The Navy of the Lancastrian Kings: Accounts and Inventories of William Soper, Keeper of the King's Ships, 1422–1427*, London, Allen and Unwin for the Navy Records Society, 1982.

Sanudo, M., *I diarii di Marino Sanuto*, Bologna, Forni Editore, 1969–70.

Scriba, G., *Il cartolare di Giovanni Scriba*, (ed. M. Chiaudano and M. Moresco), Rome, Nelle sede del'Istituto, 1935.

Specialis, Nicolaus, *Libri VIII rerum Sicularum*, Rerum Italicarum Scriptores, 10, Milan, 1727.

Stevenson, J., *Letters and Papers Illustrative of the Wars of the English in France during the Reign of Henry VI*, London, Longman, Green and Co., 1864.

Sturlason, Snorre, *Heimskringla or the Lives of the Norse Kings*, (ed. E. Monsen, trans. A.H. Smith), Cambridge, W. Heffer and Sons, 1932.

Taylor, F. and J.S. Roskell, (ed. and trans.), *Gesta Henrici Quinti, or the Deeds of Henry V*, Oxford, Clarendon Press, 1975.

Vegetius, Liber IV, XLII–XLVI, http://www.gmu.edu/departments/fld/CLASSICS/vegetius4.html

Villani, G., *Cronice di Giovanni, Matteo e Filippo Villani*, (ed. A. Racheli), Trieste, Sezione letterario-artistica del Lloyd austriaco, 1857.

Warner, Sir G. (ed.), *The Libelle of Englyshe Polycye*, Oxford, Clarendon Press, 1926.

William, Archbishop of Tyre, *A History of Deeds Done Beyond the Sea*, (trans. and ed. E.A. Babcock and A.C. Krey), New York, Columbia University Press, 1943.

Wrottesley, G., *Crécy and Calais from the Public Records*, London, William Salt Archaeological Society, 1898.

Chronicon Siciliae auctore anonymo conscripta ab anno circa DCCCXX ubsque ad annum MCCCXXVIII, (ed. E. Martene and U. Durand), Farnborough, Gregg, 1968.

Pageants of Richard Beauchamp, Earl of Warwick, reproduced in facsimile from the Cottonian MS Julius E IV in the British Museum, The, Introduction by William, Earl of Carysfort, Oxford, Roxburghe Club London, 1908.

Rotuli Parliamentorum, London, 1783.

Secondary sources

Abulafia, D., *The Western Mediterranean Kingdoms 1200–1500: The Struggle for Dominion*, London and New York, Longman, 1997.

Ahrweiler, H., *Byzance et la Mer*, Paris, Presses Universitaires de France, 1966.

Ahrweiler, H., 'Course et Piraterie dans le Mediterranée Orientale aux IVième–XVième siècles (Empire Byzantin)', in *Course et Piraterie*, Paris, Institut de Recherche et d'Histoire des Textes, 1975.

Airaldi, Gabriella, 'Roger of Lauria's expedition to the Peloponnese', *Mediterranean Historical Review*, 10, 1995.

Alban, J.R., 'English coastal defence: some fourteenth century modifications within the system', in R.A. Griffiths, *Patronage the Crown and the Provinces*, Gloucester, Alan Sutton, 1981.

Allmand, C., *The Hundred Years War: England and France at War c.1300–c.1450*, Cambridge, Cambridge University Press, 1989.

Anderson, R.C., 'The Bursledon Ship', *The Mariner's Mirror*, 20, 1934.

Anderson, R.C., *Oared Fighting Ships: From Classical Times to the Coming of Steam*, London, Percival Marshall, 1962.

'Las Costas de los galeros en el siglo XV: la galera *Sant Narcis* destinada a las comunicaciones con Italia', *Anuario de estudios medievales*, 10, 1980.

Arenson, Sarah, 'Food for a maritime empire: Venice and its bases in the Middle Ages', in K. Friedland (ed.), *Maritime Food Transport*, Quellen und darstellen zur Hansichen Geschichte, XL, Cologne, Bohlau, 1994.

Arnaldi, Girolamo, Giorgio Greco and Alberto Tenenti, *Storia di Venezia dalle Origine alla caduta della Serenissima: Vol. II, La Formazione dell Stato Patrizio*, Roma, Istituto della Enciclopedia Italiana, 1995.

Ashtor, E., *Levant Trade in the Later Middle Ages*, Princeton, Princeton University Press, 1983.

Ayalon, D., 'The Mamluks and naval power', *Proceedings of the Israel Academy of Sciences and Humanities*, I(8), 1965.

Barnie, J., *War in Medieval Society: Social Values and the Hundred Years War 1337–99*, London, Weidenfeld and Nicolson, 1974.

Bernard, J., *Navires et gens du mer à Bordeaux vers 1400–vers 1550*, Paris, no publ., 1968.

'La marine au siège de Calais', *Bibliothèque des écoles de Chartes*, 58, 1897; 80, 1994.

Bourel de la Roncière, Charles, *Histoire de la Marine Française*, Paris, Librarie Plon, 1899–1900.

Bréard, C., *Le Crotoy et les armements maritimes des XIVe et XVe siècles*, Amiens, no publ.,, 1902.

Brooks, F.W., 'The Cinque Ports', *The Mariner's Mirror*, 15, 1929.

Brooks, F.W., 'Naval administration and the raising of fleets under John and Henry III', *The Mariner's Mirror*, 15, 1929.

Brooks, F.W., 'The King's Ships and Galleys mainly under John and Henry III', *The Mariner's Mirror*, 15, 1929.

Brooks, F.W., 'The Battle of Damme 1213', *The Mariner's Mirror*, 16, 1930.

Brooks, F.W., 'The Cinque Ports feud with Yarmouth in the thirteenth century', *The Mariner's Mirror*, 19, 1933.

Brooks, F.W., *The English Naval Forces 1199–1272*, London, A. Brown and Sons, n.d.

Burgess, G.S. and D.S. Brewer, *Two Medieval Outlaws: Eustace the Monk and Fouke Fitzwarren*, Woodbridge, Boydell and Brewer, 1997.

Burley, S.J., 'The victualling of Calais, 1347–1365', *Bulletin of the Institute of Historical Research*, 31, 1958.

Burns, R.I., 'Piracy as an Islamic–Christian interface in the thirteenth century', *Viator*, 11, 1980.

Burwash, D., *English Merchant Shipping 1460–1540*, Newton Abbot, David and Charles, 1969.

Byrne, E.H., *Genoese Shipping in the Twelfth and Thirteenth Centuries*, Cambridge, MA, Harvard University Press, 1930.

Cannon, H.S., 'The Battle of Sandwich and Eustace the Monk', *English Historical Review*, 27, 1912.

Carpenter Turner, B., 'Southampton as a naval centre, 1414–1458', in J.B. Morgan and P. Peberdy (eds), *Collected Essays on Southampton*, Southampton County Borough Council, 1961.

Carpenter Turner, J.W., 'The building of the *Gracedieu*, *Valentine* and *Falconer* at Southampton, 1416–1420', *The Mariner's Mirror*, 40, 1954.

Carpenter Turner, J.W., 'The building of the *Holy Ghost of the Tower*, 1414–1416, and her subsequent history', *The Mariner's Mirror*, 40, 1954.

Carr Laughton, L.G., 'The Great Ship of 1419', *The Mariner's Mirror*, 9, 1923.

Carr Laughton, L.G., 'The *Roccafortis* of Venice, 1268', *The Mariner's Mirror*, 42, 1956.

Carr Laughton, L.G., 'Early Tudor ship guns', *The Mariner's Mirror*, 46, 1960.

Childs, W., 'The commercial shipping of South Western England in the later fifteenth century', *The Mariner's Mirror*, 83, 1997.

Ciano, Cesare, 'Le navi della Meloria carattistiche costrutitive e di impiego' in *Genova, Pisa e il mediterraneo tra due e trecento per il vii centenaurio della battaglia della Meloria*, XXIV Fasc. II, Genova, Atti della Societa Ligure di Storia Patria N.S., 1984.

Cipolla, Carlo, *Guns and Sails in the Early Phase of European Expansion*, London, Collins, 1965.

Clarke, R., M. Dean, G. Hutchinson and J. Squirrell, 'Recent work on the R. Hamble wreck near Bursledon, Hampshire', *The International Journal of Nautical Archaeology*, 22, 1993.

Cogar, W.B., *New Interpretations in Naval History: Selected Papers from the 8th Naval History Symposium*, Annapolis, Naval Institute Press, 1989.

Cogo, G., 'La Guerra di Venezia contro I Turchi', *Nuovo Archivio Veneto* 18, 1899.

Course et Piraterie, Paris, Institut de Recherche et d'Histoire des Textes, 1975.

Cracco, Giorgio and Gherendo Ortalli, *Storia di Venezia dalle Origine alla caduta della Serenissima: Vol. I, L'Eta del Comune*, Roma, Istituto della Enciclopedia Italiana, 1995.

Curry, A. and M. Hughes, *Arms, Armies and Fortifications in the Hundred Years War*, Woodbridge, Boydell Press, 1994.

Davies, C.S.L., 'The alleged sack of Bristol: international ramifications of Breton privateering, 1484–5', *Historical Research*, 67, 1994.

Davis, J.C., 'Shipping and spying in the early career of a Venetian Doge, 1496–1502', *Studi Veneziani*, 16, 1974.

Davis, R.C., *Shipbuilders of the Venetian Arsenal*, Baltimore, Johns Hopkins University Press, 1991.

De Lafaye, Monsieur, 'Les premiers arsenaux de la marine: le clos des galées de Rouen sous Charles V (1364–1380)', *Revue Maritime et Coloniale*, 54, 1877.

De Rostaing, Baron, 'La marine militaire de la France sous Philippe le Bel, 1294–1304', *Revue Maritime et Coloniale*, 62, 1879.

DeVries, K., 'God, leadership, Flemings and archery: contemporary perceptions of victory and defeat at the Battle of Sluys, 1340', *American Neptune*, 55, 1995.

DeVries, K., 'The effectiveness of fifteenth century shipboard artillery', *The Mariner's Mirror*, 84, 1998.

d'Haenens, A., *Europe of the North Sea and the Baltic: The World of the Hanse*, Antwerp, Fonds Mercator, 1984.

Doehaerd, R., 'Les galères génoises dans la Manche et la mer du Nord à la fin du XIIs et au début du XIVs', *Bulletin de l'Institut Historique Belge de Rome*, 18, 1937.

Dollinger, Philippe, *The German Hanse*, (trans D.S. Ault and S.H. Steinberg), Basingstoke, Macmillan, 1964.

Dotson, J.E., 'Merchant and naval influences on galley design at Venice and Genoa in the fourteenth century', in C.L. Symonds (ed.), *New Aspects of Naval History: Selected Papers Presented at the Fourth Naval History Symposium*, Annapolis, Maryland, Naval Institute Press, 1981.

Dotson, J.E., 'Naval strategy in the first Genoese-Venetian War 1257–1270', *American Neptune*, 46, 1986.

Dotson, J.E., 'Fleet operations in the first Genoese-Venetian War, 1264–66', *Viator*, 30, 1999.

Doumerc, B., 'La crise structurelle de la marine Vénitienne au xv siècle: le problème du retard des *mudes*', *Annales: E.S.C.*, 40, 1985.

Ducéré, E., *Histoire de la Marine Militaire de Bayonne*, (no publication details available).

Duffy, S., *Ireland in the Middle Ages*, Basingstoke, Macmillan, 1997.

Dufourq, C.-E., 'Les relations de la péninsule ibérique et de l'Afrique du Nord au XIV siècle', *Anuario de estudios medievales*, 7, 1970.

Dufourq, C.-E., 'Chrétiens et Musulmans durant les derniers siècles du Moyen Age', *Anuario de estudios medievales*, 10, 1980.

Ehrenkreutz, A.S., 'The place of Saladin in the naval history of the Mediterranean Sea in the Middle Ages', *Journal of the American Oriental Society*, 75, 1955.

Fahmy, A.M., *Muslim Sea Power in the Eastern Mediterranean from the Seventh to the Tenth Centuries*, London, Tipografia Don Bosco, 1950.

Fernandez Duro, C., *La Marina de Castilla desde su origen y pugna con la de Inglaterra hasta la refundición en la Armada española*, Madrid, 1894.

Fernando de Bordeje Morencos, F., 'La Edad Media: los años obscuros del poder naval', *Revista de Historia Naval*, 11, 1993.

Ferrer I Mallol, M.T., 'Els corsaris Castellans i la campanya de Pero Niño al Mediterrani (1404)', *Anuario de estudios medievales*, 5, 1968.

Ford, C.J., 'Piracy or policy: the crisis in the Channel, 1400–1403', *Transactions of the Royal Historical Society*, 5th series, 29, 1979.

Freeman, A.Z., 'A moat defensive: the coast defence scheme of 1295', *Speculum*, 42, 1967.

Friel, I., 'The documentary evidence for shipbuilding in England, 1294–c.1500', in C. Villain Gandossi, *Medieval Ships and the Birth of Technological Societies*, Vol. I, Malta, Foundation for International Studies, 1989.

Friel, I., 'Henry V's *Gracedieu* and the wreck in the R. Hamble near Bursledon, Hampshire', *The International Journal of Nautical Archaeology*, 22, 1993.

Friel, I., *The Good Ship: Ships, Shipbuilding and Technology in England 1200–1520*, London, British Museum Press, 1995.

Fudge, J.D., *Cargoes, Embargoes and Emissaries: The Commercial and Political Interaction of England and the German Hanse, 1450–1510*, Toronto, University of Toronto Press, 1995.

Gairdner, J. (ed.), *The Paston Letters*, 3 vols, Edinburgh, John Grant, 1910.

Gatti, L., *L'Arsenale e le galee: pratiche di costruzione e linguaggio tecnico a Genova tra medievo ed eta moderna*, Genova, Centro di Studio sulla Storia della Technica, 1990.

Genova, La Liguria, Il Mediterraneo, Catologue of an exhibition in Genoa in September 1985, Genoa, Fabbri Editori and Comune di Genoa.

Gertwagen, Ruthi, 'The Venetian port of Candia, Crete 1299–1363: construction and maintenance', *Mediterranean History Review*, 3, 1988.

Gillingham J., 'Richard I, galley warfare and Portsmouth: the beginnings of a royal navy', in M. Prestwich, R.H. Britnell and R. Frame (eds), *Thirteenth Century England*, VI, Woodbridge, Boydell Press, 1997.

Gillingham, J., *Richard I*, New Haven and London, Yale University Press, 1999.

Gillmor, C.M., 'Naval logistics of the cross-Channel operation, 1066', *Anglo-Norman Studies*, 7, 1984.

Goimard, J. (ed.), *Venise au temps de galères*, Paris, Hachette, 1968.

Goitein, S., *A Mediterranean Society: The Jewish Communities of the Arab World as Portrayed in the Documents of the Cairo Geniza*, 2 vols, Berkeley, University of California Press, 1967.

Grainge, C. and G. Grainge, 'The Pevensey expedition: brilliantly executed plan or near disaster?', *The Mariner's Mirror*, 79, 1993.

Grummitt, D., 'The defence of Calais and the development of gunpowder weaponry in England in the late fifteenth century', *War in History*, 7, 2000.

Guilmartin, J.F., *Gunpowder and Galleys: Changing Technology and Mediterranean Warfare at Sea in the Sixteenth Century*, Cambridge, Cambridge University Press, 1974.

Hale, J.R., 'Men and weapons: the fighting potential of sixteenth century Venetian galleys', *Renaissance War Studies*, London, Hambledon Press, 1983.

Hall, A.T., 'A medieval *Victory*', *The Mariner's Mirror*, 47, 1961.

Hamblin, W., 'The Fatimid navy during the early Crusades 1099–1124', *American Neptune*, 46, 1986.

Haywood, J., *Dark Age Naval Power: A Reassessment of Frankish and Anglo-Saxon Seafaring Activity*, London, Routledge, 1991.

Hewitt, H.J., *The Organisation of War under Edward III*, Manchester, Manchester University Press, 1966.

Hillenbrand, C., *The Crusades: Islamic Perspectives*, Edinburgh, Edinburgh University Press, 1999.

Hillgarth, J.N., 'El Problemo del Imperio Catalano-Aragonese (1229–1327)', *Anuario de estudios medievales*, 10, 1980.

Holmes, G., *Europe Hierarchy and Revolt, 1320–1450*, London, Fontana Press, 1975.

Hooper, N., 'Some observations on the navy in late Anglo-Saxon England', in C. Harper-Bill, C.J. Holdsworth and J. Nelson (eds), *Studies in Medieval History presented by R. Allen Brown*, Woodbridge, Boydell Press, 1992.

Howard, G.F., 'The date of the Hastings Manuscript ships', *The Mariner's Mirror*, 63, 1977.

Hutchinson, G., *Medieval Ships and Shipping*, London, Leicester University Press, 1994.

Jacoby, D., 'Les gens de mer dans la marine de guerre vénitienne de la mer Egée aux XIVe et XVe siècles', XI, in *Studies on the Crusader States and on Venetian Expansion*, Northampton, Variorum, 1989.

Jal. A., *Archéologie navale*, Paris, Arthur Berthaud, 1840.

Jenks, S., *England, Die Hanse und Preussen: Handel und Diplomatie 1377–1471*, Cologne and Vienna, Bohlau Verlag, 1992.

Jourdain, C., 'Les commencements de la Marine Militaire sous Phillips le Bel', *Revus des Questions Historiques*, 28, 1880.

Kagay, D.J. and L.J.A. Villalon (eds), *The Circle of War in the Middle Ages*, Woodbridge, The Boydell Press, 1999.

Kingsford, C.L., *Prejudice and Promise in XVth Century England*, Oxford, Clarendon Press, 1925.

Kleineke, H., 'English shipping to Guyenne in the mid-fifteenth century: Edward Hull's Gascon voyage of 1441', *The Mariner's Mirror*, 85, 1999.

Knobloch, Eberhard (ed.), *De Rebus Militaribus: (de machinis 1449)*, Baden Baden, V. Koener, 1984.

Kreutz, B., 'Ships, shipping and the implications of change in the early medieval Mediterranean', *Viator*, 7, 1976.

Krueger, H.C., 'Genoese shipowners and their ships', *American Neptune*, 47, 1987.

Labrousse, H., 'La guerre de course en Mer Rouge pendant les Croisades: Renaud de Chatillon (1182-3), in *Course et Piraterie*, Paris, Institut de Recherche et d'Histoire des Textes, 1975.

Lane, F.C., *Venice: A Maritime Republic*, Baltimore, Johns Hopkins University Press, 1973.

Lane, F.C., *Studies in Venetian Social and Economic History* (ed. B.G. Kohl and R.C. Mueller), London, Variorum, 1987.

Laporte, J., 'Les opérations navales en Manche et Mer du Nord pendant l'année 1066', *Annales de Normandie*, 17, 1967–8.

Laures, F.F., 'The warships of the Kings of Aragon and their fighting tactics during the 13th and 14th centuries AD, '*The International Journal of Nautical Archeaology and Underwater Exploration*, 16, 1987.

Laures, F.F., 'La Tactica de Combata de los Flotas Catalano-Aragoneses del siglo XIII segun la describe Ramon Muntaner 1265–1315', *Revista de Historia Naval*, 5 1987.

Lazzarini, V., 'La Battaglia di Porto Longo nell isola di Sapienza', *Nuovo Archivio Veneto*, 8 (1), 1894.

Lee C.D., 'England's naval trauma: 1066', *The Mariner's Mirror*, 80, 1994.

Legrand d'Aussy, le citoyen, 'Notice sur l'état de la marine en France au commencement du quatorzième siècle: et sur la tactique navale usitée alors dans les combats de mer, lu a l'Institut National le 17 Thermidor an 6'. Mémoires de l'Institut de France, Classe de Sciences morales et politiques, vol. II, year VII.

Lev, Y., 'The Fatimid navy: Byzantium and the Mediterranean Sea 909–1036CE, 297–427AH', *Byzantion*, 54, 1984.

Lewis, A.R., *Naval Power and Trade in the Mediterranean AD 500–1100*, Princeton, Princeton University Press, 1951.

Lewis, A.R., 'Northern European sea power and the Straits of Gibraltar, 1031–1350 AD', in W.C. Jordan, B. McNab and T.F. Ruiz (eds), *Order and Innovation in the Middle Ages*, Princeton, Princeton University Press, 1976.

Lewis, A.R., 'Byzantine and Moslem shipping in the Mediterranean, 500–1250', *American Neptune*, 47, 1987.

Lewis, A.R. and T.J. Runyan, *European Naval and Maritime History, 300–1500*, Bloomington, Indiana University Press, 1985.

Lloyd Gruffydd, K., 'Sea power and the Anglo-Welsh wars, 1210–1410', *Maritime Wales*, 11(xi), 1987.

Lloyd, T.H., 'A reconsideration of two Anglo-Hanseatic Treaties of the fifteenth century', *English Historical Review*, 102, 1987.

Lloyd, T.H., *England and the German Hanse 1157–1611: A Study of Their Trade and Commercial Diplomacy*, Cambridge, Cambridge University Press, 1991.

Lopez, R., *Genova marinara nel duecento: Benedetto Zaccaria ammiraglio e mercante*, Milan, Messina, 1933.

Lucas, H.S., 'John Crabbe: Flemish pirate, merchant and adventurer', *Speculum*, 20, 1945.

Lucchetta, G., 'L'oriente Mediterraneo nella cultura di Venezia tra quattro e cinquecento', in *Storia della cultura Veneta dal primo quattrocento al consiglio di Trento*, vol, II, Vicenza, Neri Pozza, 1980.

Luce, S., *La France pendant la guerre de Cent Ans*, Paris, Hachette, 1870.

Mackay, A., *Spain in the Middle Ages*, London, Macmillan, 1977.

Manfroni, C., *Storia della marina italiana*, vols I and II, Livorno, no publ., 1897–1902.

Martinez-Valverde, Carlos, 'La nota marinera en la chronica de Don Pero Niño', *Revista de Historia Naval*, 8, 1985.

Mayer, H.E., *The Crusades*, (trans. J. Gillingham), Oxford, Oxford University Press, 2nd edition, 1988.

McGrail, S., 'The future of the designated wreck site in the R. Hamble', *The International Journal of Nautical Archaeology*, 22, 1993.

McGrail, S., *Ancient Boats in North-West Europe: the Archaeology of Water Transport to AD 1500*, London and New York, Longman, 2nd edition, 1998.

Meale, C.M., 'The *Libelle of Englyshe Polycye* and mercantile literary culture in late medieval London', in J. Boffey and P. King (eds), *London and Europe in the Later Middle Ages*, London, Centre for Medieval and Renaissance Studies, Queen Mary and Westfield College, 1995.

Meloni, G., *Genova e Aragona all epoca di Pietro il Ceremonioso*, 3 vols, Padova, CEDAM, 1971.

Mollat du Jourdan, Michel, *Les sources de l'histoire maritime*, Paris, SEVPEN, 1962.

Mollat du Jourdan, Michel, 'Problèmes navales de l'histoire des Croisades', *Cahiers de Civilisation medievale*, 10, 1967.

Mollat du Jourdan, Michel, *Europe and the Sea*, Oxford, Blackwell, 1993.

Moore. A., 'Accounts and inventories of John Starlyng, Clerk of the King's Ships to Henry IV', *The Mariner's Mirror*, 4, 1914.

Moore. A., 'A barge of Edward III', *The Mariner's Mirror*, 6, 1920.

Morgan, J.B. and P. Peberdy, *Collected Essays on Southampton*, Southampton, Southampton County Borough Council, 1961.

Mott, L.V., 'The Battle of Malta, 1283: prelude to disaster', in D.J. Kagay and L.J.A. Villalon (eds), *The Circle of War in the Middle Ages*, Woodbridge, The Boydell Press, 1999.

Nicholas, D., *Medieval Flanders*, London, Longman, 1992.

Nicholas, D., *The Transformation of Europe 1300–1600*, London, Arnold, 1999.

Nicolas, Sir N.H., *A History of the Royal Navy from the Earliest Times to the Wars of the French Revolution*, London, R. Bentley, 1847.

Oppenheim, M., *A History of the Administration of the Royal Navy and of Merchant Shipping in Relation to the Navy: from MDIX to MDCLX with an Introduction Treating of the preceding Period* (orig. publ. London, Lane, 1896), The Shoe String Press, 1961.

Paviot, Jacques, *La politique navale des ducs de Bourgogne, 1384–1482*, Lille, Presses Universitaire de Lille, 1995.

Pepper, S., 'Fortress and Fleet: the defence of Venice's mainland Greek colonies in the late fifteenth century', in D.S. Chambers, C.H. Clough and M.E. Mallett (eds), *War, Culture and Society in Renaissance Venice: Essays in Honour of John Hale*, London, Hambledon Press, 1993.

Perez-Embid, F., 'La marina real Castellana en el siglo XIII', *Anuario de Estudios medievales*, 10, 1969.

Pery, Jose Cervera, *El Poder naval en los reinos hispanicos: la marina de la edad media*, Madrid, Editorial San Martin, 1992.

Phillips, J.R.S., *The Medieval Expansion of Europe*, Oxford, Clarendon Press, 2nd edition, 1998.

Picard, Christophe, *La Mer et les Musulmans d'Occident au Moyen Age, VIII–XIII siècles*, Paris, Presses Universitaires de France, 1997.

Pistono, S.J., 'Henry IV and John Hawley, Privateer, 1399–1408', *Devonshire Association for the Advancement of Science, Literature and Art Report and Transactions*, 3, 1979.

Prestwich, M., *War Politics and Finance Under Edward I*, London, Faber, 1972.

Prestwich, M., *Armies and Warfare in the Middle Ages: the English Experience*, New Haven and London, Yale University Press, 1996.

Pryor, J.H., 'Transportation of horses by sea during the era of the Crusades: eighth century to 1285 AD', *The Mariner's Mirror*, 68, 1982.

Pryor, J.H., 'The naval battles of Roger of Lauria', *Journal of Medieval History*, vol. 9, 1983.

Pryor, J.H., *Commerce, Shipping and Naval Warfare in the Medieval Mediterranean*, London, Variorum Reprints, 1987.

Pryor, J.H., *Geography, Technology and War: Studies in the Maritime History of the Mediterranean 649–1571*, Cambridge, Cambridge University Press, 1988.

Pryor, J.H., 'The crusade of Emperor Frederick II 1220–9: the implications of the maritime evidence', *American Neptune*, 52, 1992.

Quand voguaient les galères (exhibition catalogue), Rennes, Editions Ouest-France, 1990.

Reid, W. Stanford, 'Sea-power in the Anglo-Scottish War, 1296–1328', *The Mariner's Mirror*, 46, 1960.

Reith, E., 'Le clos des galées de Rouen: lieu de construction navale à clin et à carvel' in C. Villain Gandossi, *Medieval Ships and the Birth of Technological Societies*, Vol. I, Malta, Foundation for International Studies, 1989.

Richmond, C.F., 'The keeping of the seas during the Hundred Years War: 1422–1440', *History*, 49, 1964.

Richmond, C.F., 'English naval power in the fifteenth century', *History*, 52, 1967.

Richmond, C.F., 'The war at sea', in K. Fowler (ed.), *The Hundred Years War*, Basingstoke, Macmillan, 1971.

Richmond, C.F., 'The Earl of Warwick's domination of the Channel and the naval dimension to the Wars of the Roses, 1456–1460', *Southern History*, 20/21, 1998–9.

Riley Smith, J., *The Crusades: A Short History*, London, Athlone Press. 1987.

Rodger, N.A.M., 'The Norman invasion of 1066', *The Mariner's Mirror*, 80, 1994.

Rodger, N.A.M., 'The naval service of the Cinque Ports', *English Historical Review*, CXI, 1996.

Rodger, N.A.M., *The Safeguard of the Sea: A Naval History of Great Britain, Vol. 1, 660–1649*, London, HarperCollins, 1997.

Rodgers, W.L., *Naval Warfare under Oars, 4th to 16th Centuries*, Annapolis, Naval Institute Press, 1967.

Rosalba, R., *Le genti del Mediterraneo*, Naples, Lucio Pironti, 1981.

Rose, S., 'Henry V's *Gracedieu* and mutiny at sea: some new evidence', *The Mariner's Mirror*, 63, 1977.

Rose, S., 'Edward III: Sluys, 1340', in E. Grove (ed.), *Great Battles of the Royal Navy as Commemorated in the Gunroom, Britannia Royal Naval College, Dartmouth*, London, Arms and Armour Press, 1994.

Rose, S., 'The wall of England, to 1500', in J.R. Hill (ed.), *The Oxford Illustrated History of the Royal Navy*, Oxford, Oxford University Press, 1995.

Rose, S., *Southampton and the Navy of Henry V*, Hampshire Papers 14, Winchester, Hampshire County Council, 1998.

Rose, S., 'Bayonne and the King's Ships, 1204–1420', *The Mariner's Mirror*, 86, 2000.

Runyan, T.J., 'Ships and mariners in later medieval England', *Journal of British Studies*, 16, 1977.

Runyan, T.J., 'Ships and fleets in Anglo-French warfare, 1337–1360', *American Neptune*, 46, 1986.

Runyan, T.J., 'Naval logistics in the late Middle Ages: the example of the Hundred Years War', in J.A. Lynn (ed.), *Feeding Mars: Logistics in Western Warfare from the Middle Ages to the Present*, Boulder, CO, Westview Press, 1993.

Russell, P.E., *The English Intervention in Spain and Portugal in the Time of Edward III and Richard II*, Oxford, Clarendon Press, 1955.

Santamaria Arandez, A., 'La Reconquista de las Vias Maritimas', *Anuario de Estudios Medievales*, 10, 1980.

Santi-Mazzini, G., 'A sea fight 500 years ago', *The Mariner's Mirror*, 85, 1999.

Sanz, A.G., *Historia de la Marina Catalana*, Barcelona, Aedos, 1977.

Sherborne, J.W., 'The Hundred Years War: The English navy: shipping and manpower, 1369–89', *Past and Present*, 37, 1967.

Sherborne, J.W., 'The battle of La Rochelle and the war at sea', *Bulletin of the Institute of Historical Research*, 42, 1969.

Sherborne, J.W., 'English ships and balingers of the late fourteenth century', *The Mariner's Mirror*, 63, 1977.

Smout, T.C., *Scotland and the Sea*, Edinburgh, John Donald, 1992.

Sottas, J., *Les messageries maritimes de Venise aux XIVe et XVe siècles*, Paris, Société d'Editions Géographiques, Maritimes et Coloniales, 1938.

Stockly, D., *Le système de l'incanto des galées du marché à Venise (fin XIIIe siècle – milieu XVe siècle)*, Leiden, E.J. Brill, 1995.

Suarez Fernandez, L., *Navegacion y Comercio en el golfo de Vizcaya: un estudio sobre la politica marinera de la casa de Trastamara*, Madrid, Escuela de Estudios Medievales, 1959.

Surdich, F., *Genova e Venezia fra tre e quatrocento*, Collana storici di fonti e studi, Genova, Fratelli Bozzi, 1970.

Tenenti, Alberto and Corrado Vivanti, 'Le film d'un grand système de navigation: les galères marchandes vénitiennes XIV–XV siècles', *Annales E.S.C.*, 16, 1961.

Terrier de Loray, Henri, *Jean de Vienne, Amiral de France*, Paris, Librarie de la Société Bibliographique, 1877.

Tinniswood, J.T., 'English galleys, 1272–1377', *The Mariner's Mirror*, 35, 1949.

Tipping, C., 'Cargo handling and the medieval cog', *The Mariner's Mirror*, 1994.

Unger, Richard W., 'Admiralties and warships of Europe and the Mediterranean, 1000–1500' in *Ships and Shipping in the North Sea and Atlantic, 1400–1800*, Aldershot, Ashgate-Variorum Press, 1997.

Unger, Richard W., 'Warships and cargo ships in medieval Europe', in *Ships and Shipping in the North Sea and Atlantic, 1400–1800*, Aldershot, Ashgate-Variorum Press, 1997.

Vale, M., *The Angevin legacy and the Hundred Years War*, Oxford, Basil Blackwell, 1990.

Waites, B., 'The Medieval Ports and Trade of North-East Yorkshire', *The Mariner's Mirror*, 63, 1977.

Ward, R., 'Cargo handling and the medieval cog', *The Mariner's Mirror*, 80, 1994.

Warren Hollister, C., *Anglo-Saxon Military Institutions on the Eve of the Norman Conquest*, Oxford, Clarendon Press, 1962.

Warren Hollister, C., *The Military organisation of Norman England*, Oxford, Clarendon Press, 1965.

Weir, M., 'English naval activities, 1242–1243', *The Mariner's Mirror*, 58, 1972.

Wiel, A., *The Navy of Venice*, London, John Murray, 1910.

Willard, J.F. and W.A. Morris, *The English Government at Work 1327–1336*, Cambridge, MA, Medieval Academy of America, 1940.

Wood, A.B., 'The Mediterranean galley and her rig', *The Mariner's Mirror*, 6, 1920.

Xavier de Salas, F., *Marina Española de la edad media*, Madrid, no publ., 1864.

Index

CPSIA information can be obtained at www.ICGtesting.com
Printed in the USA
BVOW06s0141020816

457563BV00020B/35/P